Gold Mountain Turned to Dust

Frontispiece. Mohave Indians in front of Sam Kee Laundry, Yuma, Arizona Territory, ca. 1890. Reynolds Collection, Arizona Historical Society Library, Tucson.

Gold Mountain Turned to Dust

ESSAYS ON THE LEGAL HISTORY OF THE CHINESE
IN THE NINETEENTH-CENTURY AMERICAN WEST

John R. Wunder

FOREWORD BY Liping Zhu

University of New Mexico Press   Albuquerque

© 2018 by the University of New Mexico Press
All rights reserved. Published 2018
Printed in the United States of America

Library of Congress Cataloging-in-Publication Data
Names: Wunder, John R., author. | Zhu, Liping, writer of foreword.
Title: Gold mountain turned to dust: essays on the legal history of the Chinese in the nineteenth-century American West / John R. Wunder; foreword by Liping Zhu.
Description: Albuquerque: University of New Mexico Press, [2018] | Includes bibliographical references and index. |
Identifiers: LCCN 2018016226 (print) | LCCN 2018017102 (e-book) | ISBN 9780826359391 (e-book) | ISBN 9780826359384 (pbk.: alk. paper)
Subjects: LCSH: Chinese Americans—Legal status, laws, etc.—West (US)—History—19th century. | Law—West (US)—History.
Classification: LCC KF4757.5.C47 (e-book) | LCC KF4757.5.C47 W86 2018 (print) | DDC 342.7308/73—dc23
LC record available at https://lccn.loc.gov/2018016226

Cover illustration courtesy of the Library of Congress Prints and Photographs Division, LC-USZ62-27755
Designed by Felicia Cedillos
Composed in Minion Pro 10.25/14.25

Original publication information is provided for the essays in this collection at the beginning of each essay's Notes section.

For Susan

CONTENTS

FOREWORD
No Equal Justice for Chinese   ix
Liping Zhu

PREFACE
A Personal Commentary   xv

ACKNOWLEDGMENTS   xix

Reception

CHAPTER 1
Anti-Chinese Violence in the American West, 1850–1910   3

CHAPTER 2
Chinese in Trouble
Criminal Law and Race on the Trans-Mississippi West Frontier   35

California

CHAPTER 3
People v. Hall **(Cal, 1854) Revisited**   59

CHAPTER 4
The Chinese and California
A Torturous Legal Relationship   93

CHAPTER 5
Chinese Laundries and the Fourteenth Amendment   111

Pacific Northwest

CHAPTER 6
The Chinese and the Courts in the Pacific Northwest
Justice Denied? 121

CHAPTER 7
The Courts and the Chinese in Frontier Idaho 143

CHAPTER 8
Law and Chinese in Frontier Montana 159

Southwest

CHAPTER 9
Law and the Chinese on the Southwest Frontier, 1850s–1902 179

CHAPTER 10
Territory of New Mexico v. Yee Shun
*A Turning Point in Chinese Legal Relationships
in the Trans-Mississippi West* 199

INDEX 215

FOREWORD

No Equal Justice for Chinese

Since the founding of the republic, Americans have been fiercely engaged in a political and ideological debate over the idea of equal rights. This continuous discourse, sometimes manifested in very violent ways, helps to define our nation. To fight for every person and group in search of equality is a never-ending task as well as a paramount mission of the country. In its long, difficult journey of making a more tolerant and inclusive society, however, the United States has suffered many setbacks and overcome many obstacles. In the second half of the nineteenth century, the Chinese, then a group of new Asian immigrants, suddenly took center stage in this fundamental American struggle. Numerous occurrences of unfair treatment of these immigrants and their resistance to injustice were an inseparable part of the larger national experience.

In the final conquest of the nineteenth-century trans-Mississippi West, the Chinese played a dual role of victor and victim. During that period about half a million Chinese arrived in the United States, most of them residing in the West. Their exceptional contributions to major economic spheres, such as gold mining, railroad construction, and land reclamation, were crucial to the speedy settlement of the region. The Chinese, like many other unwelcome groups, also became a target of systematic political discrimination and widespread racial violence. In any ethnic subjugation throughout history, legal mistreatment and physical attack have often gone hand in hand. In learning about the sorrowful experience of early Chinese immigrants, however, more research has been done on ethnic violence than on biased jurisprudence. John Wunder belongs to a very elite circle of scholars who have proper training in both history and law. Such a special educational background allows him to pursue his interest in the legal history of the Chinese in the nineteenth-century American West. He has devoted much of his academic life to this field and become a revered expert. This book properly caps his successful scholarly career.

In addition to such notability, John Wunder's work also demonstrates a lifelong journey of intellectual inquiry into the relationship between American laws and Chinese immigrants. In the mid-1970s, Wunder, an ambitious young historian, was contemplating producing, in timely fashion, a comprehensive legal history of Chinese immigrants in the nineteenth-century American West. He soon realized that producing such a monograph was not feasible because of the enormous number of trial-case files scattered across the West. It might take many years to amass all the necessary materials. However, this logistical hurdle didn't diminish his enthusiasm for the study. Taking a more manageable case-study approach, he decided to write a single essay at a time, focusing on a small area or region. In the following forty-plus years, Wunder published, in addition to many other works, eight single-authored articles and one coauthored article on the subject. To cap his extraordinary scholarship in the study of western legal history, Wunder has now gathered all nine articles, plus a new piece, into this single volume. Amazingly, these ten separately written essays cover almost the entire American West, from California to Montana and Washington to New Mexico. The broad geographical scope of these studies indicates that Wunder, despite at first doubting the feasibility, eventually visited all the archives necessary to complete his grand project. This four-decade-long circuit ride also helped Wunder to find many unrelated local cases that shared either common political themes or legal doctrines.

Although *Gold Mountain Turned to Dust* is not exactly the kind of book Wunder envisioned forty years ago, this collection of conceivably connected and mutually supportive articles does meet the original goal of furnishing a basic text on the legal treatment of Chinese immigrants in the West. As in most anthologies, the essay-chapters are arranged according to their scope and focus, moving from general to specific. The first two essays deal with a pair of intertwined themes regarding the mistreatment of

Chinese immigrants: racial violence and judicial discrimination, serving as a broad introduction to the book. Especially the leading chapter, "Anti-Chinese Violence in the American West, 1850–1910," a quarter-century-old classic, remains as the first source to be consulted by anyone who wants to learn about anti-Chinese violence. The following eight pieces each examine legal precedents or judicial doctrines derived from these Chinese cases, which greatly complicated the western legal system.

No case involving Chinese immigrants is more discussed than *People v. Hall* (1854). What it did to the Chinese is equivalent to what the *Dred Scott* decision (1857) did to African Americans. In 1853, three white miners, including George Hall, robbed and murdered a Chinese miner in Nevada County, California. At the trial, both Chinese and white witnesses were called. The jury quickly convicted Hall and sentenced him to death. The defendant then appealed to the California Supreme Court on the grounds that he was convicted of murder upon the testimony of Chinese witnesses. At that time, California statutes prohibited only Indians and blacks from testifying against a "white man." Introducing ingenious concepts of racial categorizing, the justices argued that since Chinese immigrants and Native Americans had the same Asian ancestors, the Chinese, of course, should not be allowed to possess the legal privilege to testify against whites. Therefore, the state supreme court reversed the lower court's verdict and set Hall free. By crafting such a precedent, denying Chinese the right to testify in both civil and criminal proceedings, the ruling had an extremely deleterious impact on the life of Chinese immigrants in California—it made it more difficult to bring white perpetrators to justice. This case was directly responsible for many subsequent anti-Chinese violent acts. Despite the modest title, "*People v. Hall* (Cal, 1854) Revisited" is the first complete study of this landmark case. While providing a historical narrative, the essay dissects a number of intricate issues, such as racial classification, judicial activism, and legislative intrusion. With this, Wunder has moved up to a new level of the understanding of biased western legal tradition.

Less known, but no less significant, is *Yick Wo v. Hopkins* (1886), a US Supreme Court case that also receives a thorough examination here. Aimed at Chinese residents, San Francisco city and county ordinances in 1880 placed strict restrictions on laundry operations. By 1885 the Board of Supervisors had denied 200 of the 240 Chinese-owned laundries a license to operate because of alleged health and safety violations. Following the action of many rejected applicants, Yick Wo maintained his business without a license. Consequently, he was arrested by Sheriff Hopkins and found guilty in the police court. His refusal to pay a ten-dollar fine resulted in him spending ten days in jail. To carry on his fight against such injustice, Yick Wo hired a team of powerful white lawyers and made an appeal to the state supreme court. After having his appeal denied, Yick Wo took his case to the US Supreme Court, arguing that this state "police action" violated the recent US-China treaty and the Fourteenth Amendment. To the surprise of many, the justices agreed that the racially motivated ordinances targeted a particular group and declared them unconstitutional. A decade before *Plessy v. Ferguson*, the Chinese bravely challenged local discriminatory laws in the nation's highest court and achieved a rare victory of its kind.

Aside from such high-profile legal battles, Wunder has discovered a great number of forgotten cases that clearly show the complexity of Chinese experiences in the western justice system. Chinese legal privileges in American courts differed from place to place, depending on local political atmospheres and individual dispositions. Compared to California and the Southwest, the Pacific Northwest gave the Chinese fairer legal treatment. Idaho's courts, in particular, were most friendly to them and guaranteed several legal privileges. Taking credit, the Idaho Supreme Court played a crucial role in assuring such fairness for everyone, regardless of race or ethnicity. Not entirely dependent on the goodwill of a particular individual or court, the Chinese throughout the West fought aggressively against discrimination and injustice. They knew how to use effectively the American legal system to maximize their protection. In another distinctive aspect, these "Chinese cases" in the Pacific Northwest covered a variety of categories and tested a score of key legal doctrines, regarding taxation, assault, larceny, murder, lynching, prostitution, human trafficking, the drug trade, property ownership, business regulation, and employment opportunity. Despite handling evident disputes, many small cases forced the courts to make sophisticated arguments and complicated rulings. On many occasions, judges were forced to deal with such deep-seated concepts as natural rights, state sovereignty, due process, equal protection, legal representation, and dying declarations. After reading this volume, there should be no doubt about the rich contributions made by Chinese immigrants to western legal history.

In light of these profound revelations, the central theme of this book is that the passage of the Chinese Exclusion Act in 1882 marked a turning point for Chinese in the American legal system. Reflecting national political developments, anti-Chinese juridical sentiment steadily intensified in the late nineteenth century. The collapse of the Republican Reconstruction experiment gave a green light to Jim Crow and racial oppression. The Chinese had been blamed for an economic depression and white unemployment in the West. Under tremendous pressure from the region, Congress eventually passed the Chinese Exclusion Act to restrict Chinese immigration. Emboldened by this federal action, westerners also stepped up their own tempo of hostility toward Chinese. Consequentially, the 1880s witnessed a sharp increase in anti-Chinese violence. Nevertheless, Wunder is the first scholar to thoroughly examine the direct impact of this legislation on the western judicial system. As western legislators, judges, and jurists watched the enactment of discriminatory federal policies, local courts across the region became less sympathetic to the idea of equal protection and treated the Chinese less equitably. Statistical data show a clear trend of the precipitous decline of winning rates for Chinese parties in both criminal and civil courts. By the turn of the twentieth century, the doors to equal justice for the Chinese had been closed.

Wunder has given us an intelligible book with implications far beyond circumscribed legal history. As we all know, many important battles over racial conflicts are fought in courtrooms. Thus *Gold Mountain Turned to Dust* provides another angle to view how the Chinese fared on the nineteenth-century American frontier. Yet the study is about more than just Chinese-white relationships. Since "Chinese litigations" often involved multiethnic groups and engaged in major political debates, the historical impact of these legal cases was enormous. Wunder also pays special attention to the top-down process of judicial discrimination by showing how national politics fueled anti-Chinese sentiment at the local level. What happened to the Chinese in the West fits squarely into a general pattern of Gilded Age race relations as the nation was retreating from the principle of equal rights. This legal history of Chinese immigrants, which Wunder successfully presents, is an inseparable part of the larger national experience of American race relations.

LIPING ZHU

PREFACE

A Personal Commentary

It all began in 1974. It involved three places, unlikely places to pursue a project on the legal history of the Chinese in the American West. It started with my trip from Cleveland, Ohio, where I was a first-year assistant professor of history at Case Western Reserve University, to my first meeting of the American Society for Legal History (ASLH) in Philadelphia. There I met similar young scholars who were excited about American legal history. I even found two scholars at the forefront of the legal history of the American West: Kermit Hall and Gordon Bakken. Sadly, both of these pioneers are no longer with us.

Together we attended many sessions in Philadelphia. In particular, the ASLH often held informal seminars on the teaching of American legal history, something all three of us needed; we gobbled up sample syllabi and the titles of monographs and articles with potential for assignments and lecture research. One of the more formal sessions I attended in Philadelphia featured several scholars who presented their research on how supreme courts in both slave and free states and territories handled legal disputes over slavery in the decades prior to the American Civil War. They uncovered a number of legal anomalies as well as hidden heroes of the law, men who sought to find ways to lessen the brutality of slavery as well as to end the barbarous treatment of African American men, women, and children.

It was in this session that I began to think about a potential comparative project featuring the legal history of African Americans and Chinese, in other words, the South and the West. I knew at this point that Chinese sometimes were not willingly traveling to the United States, and their journeys matched some of those experiences of the African passage to America. As I heard about the legal rights of African American slaves and free men and women, I wondered about whether these rights had been extended to Chinese immigrants and how that process worked.

The trip back to Cleveland found me sitting by Kermit and Gordon on the plane, and we had an intense talk about all that we had witnessed. I shared with them the beginnings of my thoughts on a project that would examine the legal rights of the Chinese in the American West. They were both encouraging. Little did I know then how long and complicated such a research project might become.

My thinking about the history of western law and the Chinese began actually before 1974, when I was strongly encouraged by my graduate school mentor at the University of Washington, Professor Vernon Carstensen, to write about Pacific Northwest legal history and justices of the peace in particular. With my JD and history MA from the University of Iowa, he believed I was uniquely positioned to study western legal history, and he was most encouraging. I arrived in Seattle in January 1971, and in 1974 I received my PhD from Washington and a one-year visiting position at Case Western that would turn into an assistant professorship.

Choosing to do a dissertation on Pacific Northwest justices of the peace was a challenge in that during the late nineteenth century, many of the wooden county courthouses that held justice of the peace original records had burned down, so much so that justice of the peace court records were in scarce supply. I diligently tracked down all that were available for Washington Territory. The largest trove, a complete run of records from 1854 to 1889, was located on Whidbey Island, a picturesque Pacific peninsula north of Seattle, in Island County's county seat, Coupeville. There I spent the summer of 1975 copying and reading hundreds of justice of the peace case decisions and finding as much local history as I could discover. Island County's auditor, Jimmie Jean Cook, made all of the records easily accessible. At the same time, my graduate school contemporary and good friend Richard White was researching his environmental history dissertation on Island County, and we collaborated frequently about these sources.

One of the justice of the peace cases I found surprisingly resulted in the conviction of Ah Loy for violating Washington Territory game laws when he killed six quail. I noted that this was the only prosecution of game law violations by justices of the peace in the thirty-five years of the territorial period. Three Chinese—Ah Tune, Ah Torn, and Ah Goon (Chinese names in court documents are most often recorded phonetically and do not represent accurate naming)—were found guilty of opium smoking during that same time. These are documented in my book *Inferior Courts, Superior Justice: A History of the Justices of the Peace on the Northwest Frontier, 1853–1889* (Westport, CT: Greenwood Press, 1979). I wondered, Why were these Chinese singled out by the legal system?

The third place I would learn about is Nevada City, California, where in 1853 a jury found young gold miner George Hall guilty of murdering another young gold miner, Ling Sing. This controversial case went all the way to the California Supreme Court, whose justices in essence ruled that the Chinese were from Asia and American Indians came from Asia, and therefore a Chinese person could not testify against a white person in California's courts because American Indians were banned from testifying against whites. Early in California history a racialization of the law took hold. Not long ago I visited Nevada City and found extensive records of the people involved in this seminal case. Thus, Philadelphia, Coupeville, and Nevada City introduced me to the legal history of the Chinese in the American West.

Hall and Bakken thought I should create a prospectus on this project to do a legal history of the Chinese in the American West and submit it for the western series at the University of Nebraska Press. Hall had published one of his first books with the press and had been treated well. I did just that, submitted it to the University of Nebraska Press, and received a preliminary contract. Shortly thereafter, when I began to work on this project in earnest, I discovered a major impediment to the speedy completion of a monograph: disparate source locations. Documents tracing the legal history of the Chinese are not located in one or a few repositories. They are confined to multiple individual state and territorial locations. This impediment caused my preliminary contract with the University of Nebraska Press to expire.

Moreover, Chinese documents in the West were too often hidden away and not obvious. One example will suffice. From federal records, I found that there were two anti-Chinese movements in New Mexico—one supposedly in Taos, and one in Silver City and southwestern New Mexico. Each community had requested federal troops and the infusion of federal funds for their towns. Silver City, I discovered by going there, had a significant history of Chinese settlement because of mining, and it even had a secret underground location below the Main Street stores where Chinese went for security. But Taos was another matter. I spent several days in Taos trying to find a Chinese presence; no newspapers had Chinese stories, no local hospitals or funeral homes had records of Chinese. I began to doubt the Chinese were there. As I was driving out of town, hopelessly frustrated, I drove by a privately owned museum that looked like simply a collection of junk. Even so, I decided to go inside, and there I found the proprietor and asked him about any records or evidence of Chinese in Taos that he had. He said to wait a minute, and he went into his back room. After much banging and moving of furniture around, he came out and presented me with an 1880s quilt done by a Presbyterian women's group. It was a city directory, and on the quilt were three Chinese business establishments—two laundries and a restaurant—with their business names and addresses. This little story tells how searching for sources on this topic can be a complicated and yet rewarding historical task.

Rather than attempt the monograph, over the years I have written and published a number of essays on this topic. They have been printed in different journals and collections. Each essay required a visit to local archives. Each required reconstructing the Chinese presence. And each necessitated exploring local as well as state and territorial legal records. It has been a tremendously engaging experience, but it has taken significant time to digest and synthesize. One must be very careful to ask the tough questions of one's sources, and this challenge is magnified by the fact that individual Chinese, with the exception of some in San Francisco and some other California areas, did not leave written diaries, accounts, or journals. Many Chinese were nonliterate. That means one must rely all too often on secondary sources of the times and places, and they must be carefully weighed.

Thus, before you lies a collection of ten essays that represents over forty-plus years of painstaking research from throughout the American West. I am the sole author of most of them (one was coauthored with a now-late PhD student of mine, Clare [Bud] McKanna Jr.), and all but one ("*People v. Hall* [Cal, 1854] Revisited") has been previously published. The actual seven-page California Supreme Court case is included at the end of the *People v. Hall* essay.

I wish you good reading.

JOHN R. WUNDER
Professor Emeritus of History
University of Nebraska–Lincoln

ACKNOWLEDGMENTS

I wish to thank the numerous persons who assisted in the original collection of evidence and the publication of these essays. Some essays do note specifically these persons, but there are many archivists and assistants who must be thanked. This research ranged throughout the American West, and it involved numerous repositories of original sources and legal documents in New Mexico, Arizona, Colorado, Utah, California, Nevada, Oregon, Washington, Idaho, Montana, Wyoming, and South Dakota. These are the primary locations where Chinese immigrants concentrated in the nineteenth century.

I also wish to recognize the strength and commitment to American law that the hundreds of Chinese exhibited in their efforts to make a decent living on the frontier of the American West.

Special recognition is accorded to Clark Whitehorn and Sonia Dickey and everyone at the University of New Mexico Press, who made this project work; to Liping Zhu of Eastern Washington University for his fine and thoughtful introduction; and to Siu G. Wong and her Albuquerque network, who have taken to heart the message found in the experiences of Yee Shun.

This book would not have happened without the strong support and help of Susan Wunder.

JOHN R. WUNDER
Lincoln, Nebraska

Reception

CHAPTER 1

Anti-Chinese Violence in the American West, 1850–1910

> American Laws, more ferocious than tigers:
> Many are the people jailed inside wooden walls,
> Detained, interrogated, tortured,
> Like birds plunged into an open trap—
> What suffering!
> To whom can I complain of the tragedy?
> I shout to Heaven, but there is no way out!
> Had I only known such difficulty in passing the Golden Gate...
> Fed up with this treatment, I regret my journey here.[1]

THIS POEM WAS written by an unknown Chinese resident of San Francisco's Chinatown around 1910. It contains telling words, words of frustration, resignation, and regret, but also words describing the brutality of the failure of American law to stem the wrath of the crowd toward America's newest immigrants of the late nineteenth century.

Almost from the first moment Chinese came ashore at San Francisco, anti-Chinese violence occurred. This violence took a variety of forms.[2] Foremost in the public eye was the anti-Chinese riot or movement. It consisted of groups of armed non-Chinese, usually whites, who wantonly attacked Chinese individuals or groups. Crimes of arson, assault, robbery, burglary, kidnapping, and murder were frequent byproducts of this action.

Very little attention has been drawn to this particular aspect of American history. A number of scholars have written brief essays about the anti-Chinese movement in specific places and times, but minimal analysis of it has occurred. Recent texts have also included sections about anti-Chinese riots. No summary of existing secondary sources exists, and some riots that cry out for original source documentation have never been perused by historians.[3]

Moreover, basic questions have not been investigated. How many anti-Chinese movements were there? Where did they occur? When did they occur? Are there trends that can be identified that flow from the geographical and temporal demarcation of anti-Chinese riots? The specific victims of the violence need to be identified and personalized. Who were they? What was done to the victims? What was the nature of the violence? How many Chinese were murdered and displaced? What was the Chinese reaction to the violence? These questions require answers, as do many others about anti-Chinese violence.

Anti-Chinese Violence: Place and Time

There has been no systematic cataloging of anti-Chinese violence in the American West. In part this is due to the only recent discovery of this phenomenon by historians of American law and historians of the American West. Two recent works have attempted a limited survey of major anti-Chinese riot locations. In 1987, Sucheng Chan, in her introduction to *Bitter Melon: Stories from the Last Rural Chinese Town in America*, recorded seventy-one outbreaks of violence in nine states (Arizona, California, Washington, Idaho, Montana, Oregon, Wyoming, Utah, and Nevada).[4] One year earlier Shih-Shan Henry Tsai, in *The Chinese Experience in America*, identified fifty-five anti-Chinese riots in nine states (Alaska, California, Colorado, Hawaii, Nevada, Oregon, South Dakota, Washington, and Wyoming).[5]

Research in the secondary literature and several primary sources has yielded 153 examples of anti-Chinese violence in the American West ranging through fourteen states (including those five states held in common by Shih-Shan Henry Tsai and Sucheng Chan—California, Nevada, Oregon, Washington, and Wyoming; the four states examined by Shih-Shan Henry Tsai—Arizona, Idaho, Montana, and Utah; the four states discussed by Sucheng Chan—Alaska, Hawaii, South Dakota, and Colorado; and the additional state of New Mexico, not previously observed). The time frame covers from 1852 and the first outbreak of anti-Chinese violence in San Francisco to the last major acts of violence, in 1903 in Tonopah, Nevada, and the destruction of a Chinatown in Reno in 1908.[6] This compilation lends itself to examining and identifying several new generalizations about anti-Chinese movements in the nineteenth-century American West.

The Geography of Anti-Chinese Violence

Much can be gained from asking basic questions about the distribution of anti-Chinese violence. Where this violence took place is important in understanding why it happened. In addition, the nature of the violence needs cataloguing. This is not an easy task, as the literature available does not always include this kind of information. Nevertheless, the number of murders per anti-Chinese outbreak and estimates on the dislocation of Chinese can be ascertained from table 1.[7]

Table 1 suggests a variety of surprises. First, it should be noted that these figures are underestimates. Chinese were reluctant to report accurately their numbers, as were African Americans and Native Americans, two other groups subjected to significant racial violence in the United States during the nineteenth century. Indeed, in both primary and secondary sources, writers were oftentimes estimating displacements and deaths of Chinese based on firsthand or second- and thirdhand knowledge.

The greatest number of situations of anti-Chinese violence occurred in California. This is not surprising since the largest migration of whites and Chinese came to California. More unexpected is the fact that the second-highest number of anti-Chinese incidents is a tossup among Nevada, Washington, Arizona, Idaho, and Oregon. Neither Arizona, Idaho, nor Oregon had significant numbers of Chinese, and where the actual violence took place was in isolated rural areas.

Clearly, anti-Chinese outbreaks in specific states do not correlate with the number of recorded murders from the riots. The most killed were in Oregon, not California, with Wyoming a close third. This is because most of the anti-Chinese movements in California were devoted more to the destruction of Chinese property and to forcing Chinese into a refugee status. The high numbers for Oregon and Wyoming come from two particularly violent

TABLE 1. Anti-Chinese Violence in the American West, 1852–1908

State	Number of outbreaks	Number of Chinese murdered	Number of Chinese dislocated
Alaska	1	0	100
Arizona	11	13	100
California	63	29	4,066
Colorado	6	2	631
Hawaii	1	0	400
Idaho	11	25	528
Montana	9	4	250
Nevada	16	5	1,250
New Mexico	4	0	200
Oregon	11	31	675
South Dakota	1	1	20
Utah	1	0	175
Washington	12	5	1,130
Wyoming	6	28	1,000
Total	153	143	10,525

outbreaks. In Oregon in 1887 seven whites, cowhands on nearby ranches, came upon a group of about forty Chinese miners northeast of Enterprise near the Snake River and the Idaho border. Thirty-one Chinese were murdered, and the murderers took $10,000 in gold dust. Eventually four of the seven were apprehended. The three who were not escaped to Latin America. Of the four arrested, one died in jail, and at the trial a local jury acquitted the others.[8]

Wyoming's anti-Chinese violence has become much more famous. It stems from the Rock Springs Massacre, which many historians incorrectly attribute as the beginning of anti-Chinese sentiment and riots in the American West. In the late 1860s coal mines were opened in western Wyoming by the Union Pacific Railroad. At first the mines were staffed by miners from Ireland, Wales, and Scandinavia. However, a bitter strike in 1875 resulted in Union Pacific hiring Beckwith, Quinn & Company from Evanston, Wyoming Territory, to supply strikebreakers. They did so with Chinese labor.

By 1885, 500 miners resided in Rock Springs: 150 were white and 350 were Chinese. An additional 100 unemployed white miners were living in the town. On September 2 a conflict over work assignments occurred at the No. 6 Mine. This led to the formation of a mob of approximately 150 white miners, who, armed with rifles, opened fire on the Chinese section in Rock Springs. Houses and stores were set aflame. By the next morning 28 Chinese were killed and 15 were wounded, while 500 more Chinese fled for their lives into the hills. Approximately $150,000 worth of damage to Chinese property had occurred; seventy-nine buildings were torched.

The railroad took the refugees to Evanston. There it decided that this form of labor violence had to be resisted at all costs. Thus, on September 9, 1885, seven hundred Chinese boarded the train in Evanston and returned to Rock Springs. They were joined by federal troops, who were based at Rock Springs to maintain order. On September 21, the mines were reopened. Whites were encouraged to leave the area. The railroad replaced Chinese homes, and the troops stayed in Rock Springs for nearly fourteen years. Eventually the United States sent $147,000 to China as payment for the losses sustained in the Rock Springs Massacre. Later that year a grand jury met in the neighboring community of Green River to consider indictments against sixteen whites arrested for the Chinese murders, but it decided that none should be charged. There were no trials and no convictions.[9]

The Rock Springs Massacre and the Snake River Massacre both occurred in rural areas of the West. This highlights another important generalization that can be made from table 1. Massacres of Chinese occurred with equal frequency in rural and urban areas. Ten or more Chinese were murdered in or near Tubac, Arizona Territory (1873), Los Angeles (1871), Loon Creek, Idaho Territory (1872), Enterprise, Oregon (1887), and Rock Springs, Wyoming Territory (1885).

Over 10,500 Chinese were driven from their homes and businesses during the era of anti-Chinese upheavals in the West. The dislocation of Chinese residents was, of course, much greater in urban areas. Most significant among these upheavals were the anti-Chinese outbreaks in Los Angeles (1871), San Francisco (1877), Denver (1880), Tacoma (1885), Seattle (1886), and Portland (1886). Each of these cities participated in a significant attempt to force its Chinese residents to leave. The most common form of criminality used to force out the Chinese was arson. Other, more creative means involved cities declaring Chinatowns unsafe or unsanitary. Robbery, threats, and mass public meetings were also used effectively. Chinese displacements in western cities have been estimated from two hundred Chinese in Los Angeles to over one thousand Chinese in Tacoma and Seattle.

Although Seattle and Tacoma are cities in close proximity and they both participated in the anti-Chinese hysteria of the mid-1880s, they approached the matter differently. In 1884 anti-Chinese agitation began in Tacoma when a water company hired Chinese to lay pipe in the city despite increasing white unemployment from the lumber mills. The local newspaper published rabid editorials condemning the Chinese. The Workingmen's Union was formed by 125 laborers, and it quickly became involved in local politics, eventually electing a Sinophobic mayor, R. Jacob Weisbach. On September 28, 1885, an anti-Chinese congress convened in Seattle, presided over by Mayor Weisbach of Tacoma. The congress included delegates from all over western Washington. Labor organizations were well represented. The delegates declared that the Chinese must leave western Washington by November 1. To accomplish this demand, the congress encouraged communities to set up anti-Chinese cells, or "ouster committees."

On October 3, a mass meeting was held in Tacoma. It selected a Committee of Fifteen and instructed its members to plan the exodus of the Chinese to occur by the November 1 deadline. On November 3, one month later, five hundred whites went to Chinatown and demanded that the Chinese leave Tacoma. The mob began forcibly ejecting the Chinese from their homes and businesses. What few possessions they could retrieve were dumped in wagons. Chinese Tacomans were then forced to walk in the cold and rain to the railroad depot, where they were sent on their way to Portland. Two Chinese died during this ordeal.

Immediately after the Tacoma riot, other communities near the Puget Sound sought to implement the "Chinese Must Go" campaign. Puyallup (Pierce County), Issaquah (King County), Port Townsend (Kitsap County), Everett (Snohomish County), Anacortes (Skagit County), and Bellingham (Whatcom County) accomplished what were called "peaceable expulsions," and Seattle began to consider what it should do. On November 8, US troops were sent to Seattle to protect the Chinese. Unlike the Rock Springs detachment that stayed for over a decade, troops in Seattle remained in place for barely a week. The sheriff of King County, John McGraw, and Seattle businessmen reassured the governor, federal troops, and Seattle's Chinese community that no anti-Chinese riot would occur in Seattle. They were wrong.

In January 1886, the Tacoma Committee of Fifteen was placed on trial in Seattle for conspiring to deny Chinese their civil rights. The committee was acquitted. In February, the committee and its followers decided to inspect Seattle's Chinatown for sanitary law violations, but the primary goal was to force the Chinese onto a steamer set to sail to San Francisco. With the acquiescence of Seattle's police force, four hundred Chinese were forced to the Seattle docks. The captain of the boat demanded fare for the Chinese; the crowd came up with enough money to put about one hundred on board. Finally Sheriff McGraw, the fire department, and a group of University of Washington college students stopped the forced exodus and gained control of the dock. The Chinese were asked if they wished to stay or leave, but by this point most preferred to leave Seattle; all but fifteen left that week, presumably for San Francisco. Thus, by the end of March 1886, most of the Chinese had been forced to leave western Washington, the two largest contingents coming from Seattle and Tacoma.[10]

Rural areas also participated in the removal of the Chinese. Major efforts to force out Chinese residents were made in Chico, California, in 1877; Eureka, California, in 1885; and Bonners Ferry, Idaho, in 1892. Chico, located in the Sacramento Valley of north central California, was an early center of anti-Chinese activities in the 1850s and 1860s and experienced many vicious efforts to remove its Chinese residents. Its newspaper, the *Butte County Free Press*, changed its name to the *Chico Caucasian* to emphasize its opposition to the Chinese. Several attempts were made in the 1870s to burn down Chico's Chinatown, and approximately three hundred Chinese were displaced by 1877. That same year nine Chinese were murdered in attacks on Chinese gardeners, woodchoppers, and miners in or near Chico.[11]

Eight years later, along the northern California coast in Eureka, a city councilman was killed by a stray bullet from the gun of one of two Chinese having a dispute. The *Humboldt Times* editorialized advocating removal, and a citizens' committee organized. On February 8, two days after the councilman's death, a rally was held in Eureka and a riot ensued whereby 480 Chinese were forced to leave Eureka and the surrounding communities. The Chinese in Eureka were not about to leave without compensation. Wing

Hing sued the city of Eureka for restitution of the value of his property. A hearing was held in San Francisco, and federal district court judge Lorenzo Sawyer found in *Wing Hing v. Eureka* that no claims for damage to any property could be claimed, because the Chinese could own no real estate in Eureka.[12]

A similar situation happened to the Chinese in northern Idaho in 1892. Bonners Ferry, on the Kootenai River, was founded by miners and assisted by the Great Northern Railroad, which came to the region in the 1890s. The railroad brought Chinese workers who settled in shacks on the town's outskirts. In June 1892, a mob assembled and issued a declaration that the Chinese were a nuisance. Several hundred whites marched to the laundries and Chinese homes and informed their residents that they had two hours to pack. At least fifty, and as many as two hundred, Chinese left Bonners Ferry crammed into several boxcars. No physical violence occurred.[13]

Thus, the geography of anti-Chinese violence takes on a diverse character. Chinese dislocations, like murders, occurred in urban and rural areas with equal harshness. Large cities of the West were not immune to anti-Chinese riots, nor were small villages. Each state experienced some form of anti-Chinese violence, with California providing the setting for most of the outbreaks.

Temporal Considerations in Anti-Chinese Movements

Anti-Chinese violence began almost at the same time that Chinese migrated to the American West. The first recorded outbreak occurred in San Francisco in 1852. Mass meetings were called to protest increased Chinese immigration, and a Committee of Vigilance was formed. Riots occurred, property was burned, and the city government began a long tradition of legal harassment of the Chinese, passing ordinances designed to encourage Chinese removal.[14]

When anti-Chinese violence spread throughout the West has been the subject of conjecture. Certainly the greatest amount of anti-Chinese violence occurred in the 1880s, but its extent and the evolution of anti-Chinese movements over time have not been examined closely. Tables 2 and 3 help shed some light on the temporal dimension of anti-Chinese violence in the West.

TABLE 2. Timing Frequency of Anti-Chinese Violence in the American West, 1852–1908

State	1850s	1860s	1870s	1880s	1890s	1900s	Total
Alaska	0	0	0	0	1	0	1
Arizona	0	2	2	7	0	0	11
California	4	0	13	39	7	0	63
Colorado	0	0	4	2	0	0	6
Hawaii	0	0	0	0	1	0	1
Idaho	0	4	1	5	1	0	11
Montana	0	0	1	7	1	0	9
Nevada	1	4	9	0	0	2	16
New Mexico	0	0	0	4	0	0	4
Oregon	0	1	2	8	0	0	11
South Dakota	0	0	1	0	0	0	1
Utah	0	0	0	1	0	0	1
Washington	0	0	0	12	0	0	12
Wyoming	0	0	0	6	0	0	6
Total	5	11	33	91	11	2	153

Several observations can be made from tables 2 and 3 that will correct some misunderstandings.[15] Most general American history texts and most texts devoted to the history of the American West or American law that actually discuss anti-Chinese movements—and not all do—begin their discussions with the Rock Springs Massacre of 1885. Yet approximately one-third (54 of 153) of recorded anti-Chinese riots occurred prior to 1885 and the Rock Springs Massacre.

Butte, Montana; Clifton, Arizona; and San Francisco are representative of areas of anti-Chinese activity prior to the Rock Springs Massacre. In Butte in 1881 a "War of the Woods" ensued between whites and Chinese. A contractor had hired ten or twelve Chinese to cut cordwood on contract. According to the employers, whites would not contract for the job at a reasonable price. Nevertheless, Butte residents saw this as further evidence of solidifying a Chinese presence in Montana, and led by attorney Chance L. Harris, a mob of two hundred mounted men went off to force the woodchoppers to leave or to fight them. A confrontation occurred in the woods, but before the

TABLE 3. Timing Frequency of Anti-Chinese Violence in the American West, 1880s

State	1880–1884	1885	1886	1887–1889	Total
Alaska	0	0	0	0	0
Arizona	2	0	0	5	7
California	0	8	31	0	39
Colorado	2	0	0	0	2
Hawaii	0	0	0	0	0
Idaho	1	1	3	0	5
Montana	1	2	0	4	7
New Mexico	0	2	1	1	4
Oregon	0	0	7	1	8
South Dakota	0	0	0	0	0
Utah	0	0	0	1	1
Washington	0	11	1	0	12
Wyoming	0	6	0	0	6
Total	6	30	43	12	91

mob could assert itself the Chinese escaped. It is not known if any Chinese were injured or killed. Back in Butte, the employer was strongly encouraged to hire white labor.[16]

Unlike their counterparts in Butte, the citizens of Clifton, Arizona, did not react violently when Chinese labor entered their community. Chinese helped build a railroad to the copper-smelting works, and they gathered and burned the mesquite used for charcoal in the copper-reduction process. However, in 1879 when the mining company hired Chinese to work in the underground shafts, labor would not stand for it. White miners rebelled and forced the Chinese to withdraw from the mines.[17]

The anti-Chinese violence in Clifton and Butte was not as extensive as that in San Francisco during the 1870s. Previously, the first Chinese residents of the Bay Area had met mob action, but during the 1860s a calmer atmosphere had replaced the earlier hysteria. By 1877, however, agitation to force the Chinese to leave had once again become strong.[18] On the evening of July 23, anti-Chinese politicos began the first of three nights filled with militant speeches. The speakers demanded mass riots against the Chinese in order to force them from

San Francisco. Twenty-five laundries were destroyed after anti-Chinese riots, and an estimated $1 million worth of damage was done to Chinese businesses. The governor called in the US Army and Navy and the California militia to restore order in the city.[19] Thus, San Francisco launderers, along with Idaho woodchoppers, Arizona copper miners, and many others in the American West, were targets of anti-Chinese violence before 1885.

Most texts also portray the anti-Chinese movement as a temporary happening in 1885 with a spillover effect in 1886. It is true that seventy-three riots, or approximately 48 percent of all outbreaks, did occur in these two years, but twenty-five upheavals occurred later, including several with extreme forms of physical violence (such as the Snake River Massacre in Oregon in 1887; in Bonners Ferry, Idaho, in 1892; and in Tonopah, Nevada, in 1903).

The time framework of anti-Chinese riots is also important to understanding these events. Several historians have offered observations about the timing of the anti-Chinese riots that have proved useful. These generalizations are based on very specific considerations. Sucheng Chan, in *This Bittersweet Soil*, delineates three time phases for anti-Chinese activities in rural agricultural California. They occurred in 1876–79, 1886, and 1893–94.[20] Separating the California data from the information for the entire West confirms this. There were twelve outbreaks of anti-Chinese violence in California in 1876–79, thirty-one in 1886, and seven in 1893–94—a total of fifty of the sixty-two outbreaks in California during the entire period.

Roger Daniels, in *Asian America: Chinese and Japanese in the United States since 1850*, surveyed anti-Chinese violence.[21] He confines his specific discussion to the "worst outrages," the urban anti-Chinese riots, while recognizing that there were significant rural movements. Daniels observes that the initial center for anti-Chinese activity was California, but this shifted in the 1880s to the Pacific Northwest.[22] This is for the most part an accurate generalization. Table 2 shows that prior to the 1880s most of the anti-Chinese violence occurred in California (seventeen outbreaks), but Nevada was also a very significant anti-Chinese center (fourteen outbreaks).

In fact Nevada, more than any other state, embraced the anti-Chinese movement throughout the six decades. Anti-Chinese activities in Virginia City are particularly representative. They spread from 1865 to 1877. In 1869, three hundred Chinese were working for the Virginia and Truckee Railroad in its mines near Virginia City. On August 3 a convention was convened at the Storey County Courthouse of the Miner's Unions of Virginia City, Gold Hill, Humboldt, and White Pine. Other labor unions sent sympathetic representatives. They issued a statement decrying Chinese labor and offered a plan to drive the Chinese from Nevada. On September 29 a mob of nearly four hundred miners from Virginia City marched on the Chinese. They overwhelmed the sheriff, who gamely tried to prevent violence, and destroyed all of the Chinese shanties and their property. William Sharon, a railroad official, came to a far-reaching agreement with the mob, promising not to hire any more Chinese miners. They were allowed to work briefly on railroad construction, but they were never again allowed to work in company mines or even to ride on the railroad once it was completed. Their only solace was that no Chinese were injured that fateful day.[23]

Table 3 shows the shift of anti-Chinese activity to the Pacific Northwest in the 1880s. In fact, in 1885 the primary anti-Chinese outbreaks occurred in Wyoming and Washington, anchored by the Rock Springs and Seattle-Tacoma upheavals. Five days after the Rock Springs Massacre anti-Chinese violence came to Washington. In the Squak Valley near Issaquh, a mob of five whites and two Native Americans attacked a camp of Chinese hop pickers as they slept. Three Chinese were murdered and three or four were wounded; twenty-eight others escaped into the woods. The surviving Chinese left the valley the next day.[24] This led to active anti-Chinese movements throughout the Puget Sound region.

In 1886, Oregon and California were very active, with the Willamette Valley area in flames. Leaders of the International Working People's Association arrived in Portland from San Francisco shortly after the Tacoma riots. Portland's business leaders were upset at the prospect of violence and supported the mayor, who increased the police force in anticipation. On February 27 a large anti-Chinese protest march was held in Portland. It ended up in nearby Oregon City where thirty-nine Chinese working at the Jacob Woolen Mills were kidnapped and taken to the center of Portland. The next day a group of masked men drove 180 Chinese woodcutters from rural areas to Portland. Then, on March 4, a similar mob forced 125 Chinese from Mount Tabor. Eight days later whites attacked Chinese vegetable farmers, and a Chinese laundry in downtown Portland was almost blown up. Sporadic violence occurred against the Chinese throughout Portland, with many Chinese leaving.[25]

After 1886, anti-Chinese activities picked up in Montana in the Northwest and Arizona in the Southwest. There were outbreaks of violence in Helena, Butte, and Missoula in Montana and in Flagstaff, Bisbee, Kingman, Nogales, Tombstone, and Yuma in the Arizona Territory. These were on a smaller scale than previous outbreaks, and no murders were recorded.

Thus, certain trends are discernable about anti-Chinese violence by looking at the numbers of anti-Chinese riots over time. Anti-Chinese movements appear to cover the entire six-decade period, but the primary time of violence was the 1880s. Most of the outbreaks were recorded in 1885 and 1886, but they were not isolated incidents in time or geography—anti-Chinese violence proved to be long-standing in the American West.

The Victims

Chong Bing Long, Sing Lee, and Chung Sun never knew each other, but they had a great deal in common. All three came to Gold Mountain, the United States, from China during the 1860s or early 1870s. There were reasons for these migrations, some personal and unrecorded, others economic. Chong Bing Long and Sing Lee most certainly did not have much and came to the United States seeking to improve their station in life. Toward that end both became laundry workers, perhaps having been miners or railroad workers before turning to a traditional occupation among Chinese immigrants. Chung Sun was better off, arriving with $600, an ability to speak English, and a desire to establish a tea plantation in southern California.[26]

All three were victims of anti-Chinese violence. Chung Sun arrived in Los Angeles in 1871 at an unfortunate time. He moved into Chinatown on what whites of Los Angeles called "Nigger Alley." Los Angeles's Chinatown was not very large, holding several hundred Chinese; certainly, it was quite small when compared to that of San Francisco and other northern California cities. Most of the Chinese in Los Angeles held positions as gardeners, laundry operators, or domestic help.

Los Angeles was known as a rowdy town. Law enforcement was relatively undeveloped, and some prostitution and opium dens were located in Chinatown. During the late 1850s gold miners and failed businessmen migrated to Los Angeles from northern California, and the racial climate of the city changed. Anti-Chinese agitation began. In 1857 meetings were held concerning

Chinese "coolieism." Periodic hate gatherings were held throughout the 1860s; those attending expressed concern about increased Chinese immigration and potential American citizenship for the Chinese.

On the evening of October 24, 1871, Chung Sun was in Chinatown. Suddenly he was attacked by some of a huge mob, estimated by those present at over five hundred whites and Hispanics. The riot started ostensibly from a police action. Supposedly a feud had erupted among several Chinese over a Chinese woman. Los Angeles police arrested the participants, who resumed fighting, the police intervened, and two officers were wounded with one white civilian killed. The riot then began, with some police encouraging the violence by offering bribes to the rioters.

When the riot was over Chung Sun was near death, having been seriously beaten and robbed. According to him, he was saved only because he could speak English. He later migrated to the Monterey Bay area in northern California. Nineteen other Chinese were not as fortunate. They were murdered, fifteen being hung from hastily constructed gallows. At least $30,000 in cash and personal property was stolen.

Los Angeles continued to be a hotbed for anti-Chinese rhetoric. In 1873 meetings were held and a chapter of an Anti-Coolie Club was formed. Four years later, after riots in San Francisco, Los Angeles laborers demanded the eradication of the Chinese. They could not accomplish this with violence, so they turned to political action and formed the Workingmen's Club No. 1. Through this political organization, and the Workingmen's Party, anti-Chinese elements were successful in taking over the Los Angeles city government, electing the mayor and twelve out of fifteen city council members in 1880. The new council passed anti-Chinese ordinances authorizing special taxes on Chinese and land-use restrictions in Chinatown. In the early 1880s many Chinese left Los Angeles for Arizona, to work on railroads.[27]

Chung Sun was bitter over his treatment, but at least he survived. He became a laborer, digging ditches in Watsonville for $1.50 per day. At this job, he became friends with C. O. Cummings, the publisher of the *Watsonville Pajaronian*. Cummings printed letters by Chung Sun, who explained his reactions to the riot and the impact it had had on his life. Chung wrote, "Unlearned as you may think us to be, we are not wholly ignorant of your history.... We [Chinese] are taught to believe that the sublime teachings of our own Confucius and other sages of the East are [in the United States] reduced to a practical philosophy, regulating, governing, and harmonizing all your civil and political conduct; . . . that your government is founded and conduced upon principles of pure justice and that all of every clime, race, and creed are here surely protected in person, liberty and property."[28] Chung Sun had left China, as he explained, because he sought in the United States, "freedom and security which I could never hope to realize in my own [country], and now after some months' residence in your great country, with the experience of travel, study and observation, I hope you will pardon me for expressing a painful disappointment. The ill treatment of [my] own countrymen may perhaps be excused on the grounds of race, color, language and religion, but such prejudice can only prevail among the ignorant."[29]

Chung Sun reflected on his lot, "Being a man of education and culture I am capable of other work than digging in the streets, but my philosophy teaches me, any *useful* work is more honorable than idleness. I shall therefore, with patience and resignation, continue to dig with an abiding hope for something better." Chung Sun wrote to the editor for a reason: "I shall try to be charitable as well as just to all mankind, but as a people will hardly correct their faults without knowing them, I write this in a spirit of kindness, notwithstanding my ill treatment, and ask you to publish it."[30]

Another letter from Chung Sun, describing the United States to a friend in China, was published on November 16, 1871. He concluded by observing that "in civility, complaisance, and polite manners [Americans] are wholly wanting and are very properly styled barbarians."[31] His journey proved to be a bitter one. Shortly thereafter Chung Sun went home to China, never to return to Gold Mountain.

The circumstances for Sing Lee and Chong Bing Long did not allow them to return to China alive. Sing Lee was a victim of the Denver riot of 1880, nine years after the assault on Chung Sun in Los Angeles. At least six hundred Chinese lived in Denver by 1880. Many originally came to Colorado to work in the mines, and those who settled in Denver were primarily merchants or workers in restaurants, vegetable and fruit stands, and laundries.[32] Sing Lee worked in a laundry, where life was difficult. Socially, the Chinese were isolated. Work was tedious, dangerous, and physically demanding. Laundries were also a special target of mobs—usually the first Chinese to be attacked were those working in the laundries and the laundry building was the first structure to be destroyed. The laundrymen endured physical persecution; some were stoned or had laundry baskets upset, others were assaulted or murdered.[33]

In Denver, the *Rocky Mountain News* led a campaign to force the Chinese from the city. It trumpeted anti-Chinese rhetoric during the political campaign in the fall of 1880. On the evening of October 30, a political rally was held in Denver, and a particularly hostile, ugly anti-Chinese procession concluded the rally. The next day in a Chinatown tavern two Chinese men and a white man were playing pool. Three or four other whites attacked the three, and news of a potential riot engulfed the city. By 2:00 p.m. a crowd of three thousand, mostly Irish laborers with some other whites and African Americans, had gathered and demanded Chinese blood. Amazingly, Denver's police force chose to do nothing, perhaps because the force numbered only fifteen and no chief had been appointed to fill the recent vacancy. The mayor attempted to disperse the crowd, and upon his failure he called out the fire department. The Denver firemen drenched the mob, whereupon the crowd broke loose and burst into Chinatown.[34]

The mob first attacked the laundries, in one of which they found Sing Lee. Sing was assaulted and dragged into the street, where a rope was placed around his neck and he was lynched. Every laundry in the city was destroyed, and all but two houses owned by Chinese were significantly damaged. To protect the Chinese the Colorado governor ordered the militia to Denver to restore order. The Chinese were rounded up and placed under protective custody in the jails; up to four hundred were housed in Denver's prison facilities.

Once order was restored the Chinese were allowed to return to their Chinatown in Hop Alley. There they found over $50,000 worth of damage to their property. Some Chinese left, but many stayed and rebuilt; none were reimbursed for their losses, and the rioters tried for the murder of Sing Lee were acquitted.[35]

Like Sing Lee, Chong Bing Long worked in a laundry. He lived in Tonopah, in south central Nevada. The turn of the century brought silver strikes in the region and precipitated one of the last mining rushes. Chinese were not allowed to work in the mines, a kind of discrimination that had dogged them throughout the mining frontier. Nevertheless, a number of Chinese moved to Tonopah to work the tailings and worn-out claims, and a small Chinatown was established.[36]

On September 15, 1903, a large mob of white laborers, most out of jobs, attacked the homes and businesses of Tonopah's Chinese. Over one hundred Chinese establishments were burnt, and sixty-six-year-old Chong Bing Long, a longtime resident, was murdered. Fifteen whites were arrested, nine were released, and six were acquitted of all charges. Many Chinese left Tonopah after the riot, but those who escaped to Reno were not safe. Five years later, Reno city officials ordered all buildings in its Chinatown destroyed. In an early example of "urban renewal," many older Chinese were left homeless. These actions in Reno and Tonopah marked the end of the anti-Chinese riots as the West knew them.[37]

The victims of anti-Chinese riots were many throughout the West. Few have left their views, such as Chung Sun, or could have stated how they felt, such as the murdered Chong Bing Long and Sing Lee. Little work has been accomplished by historians identifying an economic and social profile of just who these victims were. Sucheng Chan, in her study of anti-Chinese movements in rural California, has posited the idea that Chinese moving into traditional non-Chinese merchant activities caused greater racial stress than previously thought. Class, therefore, has much to say for it as a causal dimension.[38] This remains to be determined, but what can be said at present is that Chinese victims of anti-Chinese violence ranged throughout the economic spectrum, from the wealthy entrepreneur Chung Sun to the penniless launderer or miner. Thousands of Chinese were assaulted and displaced and hundreds more were lynched and robbed during the five-decade period of anti-Chinese violence.

Conclusion

Much remains to be uncovered about anti-Chinese violence in the American West. All of the previously discussed questions require further amplification, and more information needs to be distilled regarding the role and composition of the perpetrators of the violence, the response of the legal system, including local police and lower-court justices and attorneys, and the primary causal factors behind the violence.

This essay has also examined another important area of anti-Chinese violence—the reaction of its victims to their mistreatment. This, too, is a topic that demands further research. It was not only individuals, such as Chung Sun, who gave vent to their frustration and profound sense of injustice at the violence that was directed toward them. The Chinese community at large reacted not only by organizing for self-help and appealing to the law for protection but also by engaging in subtle acts of cultural resistance. An interesting example that demonstrates this phenomenon, as well as white society's ignorance of and insensitivity to the Chinese experience in America, is the derivation of the word *hoodlum*.

In all of the literature on anti-Chinese violence, those attacking the Chinese are referred to as hoodlums. This term has come to mean a tough, dangerous youth who spends much time on the streets of towns and cities and causes a great deal of trouble. The most recent edition of the *Oxford English Dictionary* notes that *hoodlum* originated as slang in San Francisco about 1870–72 and caught on in American usage by 1877. American newspapers attributed its origin to a lawless group of youths in that city.[39]

Most of the Chinese who moved to San Francisco in the 1850s and 1860s spoke Cantonese Chinese. In the 1830s they had witnessed white persons for the first time in China and called them "hueilum." This was a term meaning "devil" in the Cantonese dialect. When this word emerged cannot be specifically ascertained, but probably it was used no later than the 1830s. For the Chinese, the physical appearance of whites was too strange to be accepted—blue eyes, high noses, yellow or red hair. At first *hueilum* would not necessarily have been derogatory, but with the defeat of the Qing government in the Opium Wars in the 1840s, antiforeign sentiment in China was strong. By then *hueilum* was used not only by Cantonese but by other Chinese to describe the dreaded westerners. The gold rush brought the first Cantonese to San Francisco and it also brought the term to Chinatown. Even today this word can still be heard in San Francisco's Chinatown, and it is no doubt the source of the term *hoodlum*.

In reality the word derives from Chinese discourse and reflects the immigrants' rueful characterization of their detractors. The confusion over the derivation of the word *hoodlum* serves as a symbolic reminder of the ignorance still to be found in the literature surrounding the historical role of the Chinese in the American West.

Appendix
Anti-Chinese Violence In The American West, 1852–1908

ALASKA

Juneau (1893)[40]

ARIZONA

Prescott (1869)[41]
Tubac (1873)[42]
Clifton (1879)[43]
Tucson (1880)[44]
Safford (1884)[45]
Bisbee (1888)[46]
Kingman (1888)[47]
Nogales (1888)[48]
Tombstone (1888)[49]
Yuma (1888)[50]
Flagstaff (1889)[51]

CALIFORNIA

San Francisco (1852, 1859, 1877)[52]
Mariposa (1856)[53]
Shasta (1859)[54]
Los Angeles (1871)[55]
Sacramento (1876)[56]
Truckee (1876)[57]
Chico (1877)[58]
Colusa (1877)[59]
Grass Valley (1877)[60]
Lava Beds (1877)[61]
Rocklin (1877)[62]
Roseville (1877)[63]
Santa Cruz (1877)[64]
Antioch (1878)[65]

Linden (1878)[66]
Arcata (1885)[67]
Crescent City (1885)[68]
Eureka (1885)[69]
Ferndale (1885)[70]
Fresno (1885)[71]
Merced (1885)[72]
Modesto (1885)[73]
Stockton (1885)[74]
Anderson (1886)[75]
Auburn (1886)[76]
Calistoga (1886)[77]
Carson (1886)[78]
Cloverdale (1886)[79]
Dixon (1886)[80]
Gold Run (1886)[81]
Healdsburg (1886)[82]
Hollister (1886)[83]
Lincoln (1886)[84]
Martinez (1886)[85]
Napa (1886)[86]
Nevada City (1886)[87]
Nicolaus (1886)[88]
Oakland (1886)[89]
Pasadena (1886)[90]
Petaluma (1886)[91]
Placerville (1886)[92]
Red Bluff (1886)[93]
Redding (1886)[94]
Saint Helena (1886)[95]
San Buenaventura (1886)[96]
San Jose (1886)[97]
Santa Barbara (1886)[98]
Santa Rosa (1886)[99]
Siskiyou (1886)[100]
Sonoma (1886)[101]

Vallejo (1886)[102]
Ventura (1886)[103]
Wheatland (1886)[104]
Yuba City (1886)[105]
Compton (1893)[106]
Panamint City (1893)[107]
Redlands (1893)[108]
Tulare (1893)[109]
Ukiah (1893)[110]
Vaca Valley (1893)[111]
Visalia (1893)[112]

COLORADO

Caribou (1874, 1879)[113]
Central City (1874)[114]
Leadville (1879)[115]
Denver (1880)[116]
Grand Junction (1883)[117]

HAWAII

Honolulu (1892)[118]

IDAHO

Lewiston (1865, 1883)[119]
Orofino (1867)[120]
Salmon City (1868)[121]
Boise (1869, 1886)[122]
Loon Creek (1872)[123]
Pierce City (1885)[124]
Broadford (1886)[125]
Hailey (1886)[126]
Bonners Ferry (1892)[127]

MONTANA

Cedar Creek (1870)[128]
Butte (1881, 1885, 1888)[129]

Anaconda (1885)[130]
Helena (1887)[131]
Great Falls (1888)[132]
Havre (1888)[133]
Missoula (1892)[134]

NEVADA

Gold Hill (1859)[135]
Virginia City (1865, 1869, 1875, 1876)[136]
Carson City (1867, 1870)[137]
Unionville (1869)[138]
Eureka (1872, 1876)[139]
Elko (1876)[140]
Pioche (1877)[141]
Reno (1878, 1908)[142]
Tuscarora (1878)[143]
Tonopah (1903)[144]

NEW MEXICO

Raton (1885)[145]
Silver City (1885, 1886)[146]
Deming (1888)[147]

OREGON

Oswego (1867)[148]
Baker City (1872)[149]
Portland (1873, 1886)[150]
Aurora (1886)[151]
Jacksonville (1886)[152]
LeGrande (1886)[153]
Mount Tabor (1886)[154]
Newberg (1886)[155]
Oregon City (1886)[156]
Enterprise (1887)[157]

SOUTH DAKOTA

Deadwood (1878)[158]

UTAH

Carbon County (1888)[159]

WASHINGTON

Anacortes (1885)[160]
Auburn (1885)[161]
Bellingham (1885)[162]
Coal Creek (1885)[163]
Everett (1885)[164]
Issaquah (1885 [2])[165]
Olympia (1885)[166]
Port Townsend (1885)[167]
Puyallup (1885)[168]
Seattle (1886)[169]
Tacoma (1885)[170]

WYOMING

Almy (1885)[171]
Carbon (1885)[172]
Cheyenne (1885)[173]
Evanston (1885)[174]
Green River (1885)[175]
Rock Springs (1885)[176]

Notes

Originally published as John R. Wunder, "Anti-Chinese Violence in the American West, 1850–1910," in *Law for the Elephant, Law for the Beaver: Essays in the Legal History of the North American West*, ed. John McLaren, Hamar Foster, and Chet Orloff (Pasadena, CA: Ninth Judicial Circuit Historical Society, 1992): 212–36.

1. Marlon K. Hom, *Songs of Gold Mountain: Cantonese Rhymes from San Francisco Chinatown* (Berkeley: University of California Press, 1987), 48.
2. Individual violence by non-Chinese against Chinese occurred. One can only estimate that it was significant activity, because very little historical work or analysis has been accomplished by historians or others on this subject.
3. Strangely, one author wrote in 1982 that too much had been written about anti-Chinese violence. Randall E. Rohe, in "After the Gold Rush: Chinese Mining in the Far West, 1850–1890," *Montana, Magazine of Western History* 32 (Autumn

1982): 2–19, argues, "Hopefully researchers will move away from the overworked theme of anti-Chinese discrimination and investigate other aspects of the Chinese experience on the western mining frontier" (19). This is not an accurate portrayal of the state of legal historical writing on the anti-Chinese movements. For example, in the heralded book on the history of violence in America by Hugh Davis Graham and Ted Robert Gurr, *Violence in America: Historical and Comparative Perspectives* (New York: Bantam, 1969), anti-Chinese violence is simply ignored.

Roger Daniels, in *Asian America: Chinese and Japanese in the United States since 1850* (Seattle: University of Washington Press, 1988), correctly concludes that "historians have ignored much of the anti-Chinese and anti-Asian violence" (59n66). Richard Maxwell Brown, in "Historiography of Violence in the American West," in *Historians of the American West*, ed. Michael P. Malone (Lincoln: University of Nebraska Press, 1983), 234–69, has only two sketchy paragraphs on anti-Chinese violence (250–51). This is simply because historians have not come to this topic with the same vigor they have used in approaching other kinds of racial violence.

Patricia Nelson Limerick, in her pathbreaking book *The Legacy of Conquest: The Unbroken Past of the American West* (New York: Norton, 1987), has difficulty identifying specific examples of anti-Chinese violence or specific Chinese participants and getting beyond the works of Alexander Saxton and Stuart Miller and the state of California. Future editions will hopefully be able to correct this vacuum.

4. Sucheng Chan, introduction to *Bitter Melon: Stories from the Last Rural Chinese Town in America*, by Jeff Gillenkirk and James Motlow (Seattle: University of Washington Press, 1987), 25.
5. Shih-Shan Henry Tsai, *The Chinese Experience in America* (Bloomington: Indiana University Press, 1986), 68.
6. It is important to stress that this compilation is by no means definitive. Much rural Chinese violence needs to be identified and explored. Only one state, California, in Sucheng Chan's outstanding book *This Bittersweet Soil: The Chinese in California Agriculture, 1860–1890* (Berkeley: University of California Press, 1986), has had its rural areas treated with anything approaching thoroughness, and that treatment is limited in terms of time and scope. Anti-Chinese violence in mining areas has not been discussed in detail. Urban violence has also been ignored. No complete treatment of anti-Chinese violence exists, for example, for San Francisco. Anti-Chinese riots in Los Angeles, Seattle, Tacoma, and Denver have been covered in article form without a comprehensive exploration of either the victims or the perpetrators of the violence.
7. See the appendix to this essay for a specific listing of each outbreak of anti-Chinese violence and its source.
8. Christopher H. Edson, *The Chinese in Eastern Oregon, 1860–1890* (San Francisco:

R and E Research Associates, 1974), 51; David H. Stratton, "The Snake River Massacre of Chinese Miners, 1887," in *A Taste of the West: Essays in Honor of Robert G. Athearn*, ed. Duane A. Smith (Boulder, CO: Pruett Publishing, 1983), 124–25.

9. Murray L. Carroll, "Governor Francis E. Warren, the United States Army and the Chinese Massacre at Rock Springs," *Annals of Wyoming* 59 (Fall 1987): 17–24; Paul Crane and Alfred Larson, "The Chinese Massacre," *Annals of Wyoming* 12 (Fall 1940): 47–55, 153–60. See also Virginia Huidekoper, "Mosaic of a Massacre: The Chinese Experience in Wyoming, 1879–1890," unpublished manuscript prepared for the Wyoming Council for the Humanities.

10. B. P. Wilcox, "Anti-Chinese Riots in Washington," *Washington Historical Quarterly* 20 (1929): 204–11; Jules Alexander Karlin, "The Anti-Chinese Outbreak in Tacoma, 1885," *Pacific Historical Review* 23 (August 1954): 271–83; John R. Wunder, "The Chinese and the Courts in the Pacific Northwest: Justice Denied?," *Pacific Historical Review* 52 (May 1983): 191–211; and Jules Alexander Karlin, "The Anti-Chinese Outbreaks in Seattle," *Pacific Northwest Quarterly* 39 (Spring 1948): 103–29.

11. Elmer Clarence Sandmeyer, *The Anti-Chinese Movement in California* (Urbana: University of Illinois Press, 1973), 48; Susan W. Book, *The Chinese in Butte County, California, 1860–1920* (San Francisco: R and E Research Associates, 1976), 49–57; S. Chan, *This Bittersweet Soil*, 371–74.

12. Lynwood Carranco, "Chinese Expulsion from Humboldt County," *Pacific Historical Review* 30 (November 1961): 329–40.

13. M. Alfreda Elsensohn, *Idaho Chinese Lore* (Cottonwood: Idaho Corporation of Benedictine Sisters, 1971), 116–17.

14. Sandmeyer, *Anti-Chinese Movement*, 42; Robert Seager II, "Some Denominational Reactions to Chinese Immigration to California, 1856–1892," *Pacific Historical Review* 28 (February 1959): 49.

15. See chapter appendix.

16. Larry D. Quinn, "'Chink Chink Chinaman': The Beginning of Nativism in Montana," *Pacific Northwest Quarterly* 58 (April 1967): 84.

17. Lawrence Michael Fong, "Sojourners and Settlers: The Chinese Experience in Arizona," *Journal of Arizona History* 21 (Autumn 1980): 232.

18. For a discussion of San Francisco politics and labor union attitudes of this era, see Gunther Barth, *Bitter Strength: A History of the Chinese in the United States, 1850–1870* (Cambridge, MA: Harvard University Press, 1964); Stuart Creighton Miller, *The Unwelcome Immigrant: The American Image of the Chinese, 1785–1882* (Berkeley: University of California Press, 1969); and Alexander Saxton, *The Indispensable Enemy: Labor and Anti-Chinese Movement in California* (Berkeley: University of California Press, 1971).

19. Sandmeyer, *Anti-Chinese Movement*, 48; William J. Courtney, *San Francisco Anti-Chinese Ordinances, 1850–1900* (San Francisco: R and E Research Associates, 1974), 65.

20. S. Chan, *This Bittersweet Soil*, 370.
21. See Daniels, *Asian America*.
22. Ibid., 59.
23. Russell M. Magnaghi, "Virginia City's Chinese Community, 1860–1880," *Nevada Historical Society Quarterly* 24 (Summer 1981): 149–54; Loren B. Chan, "The Chinese in Nevada: An Historical Survey, 1856–1970," *Nevada Historical Society Quarterly* 18 (Winter 1975): 279–98.
24. Wilcox, "Anti-Chinese Riots in Washington," 205.
25. Ralph James Mooney, "Matthew Deady and the Federal Judicial Response to Racism in the Early West," *Oregon Law Review* 63, no. 4 (1984): 574.
26. L. Chan, "Chinese in Nevada," 295; Patricia K. Ourada, "The Chinese in Colorado," *Colorado Magazine* 29 (Winter 1952): 282–83; Roy T. Wortman, "Denver's Anti-Chinese Riot, 1880," *Colorado Magazine* 42 (Fall 1965): 275–91; William R. Locklear, "The Celestials and the Angels: A Study of the Anti-Chinese Movement in Los Angeles to 1882," in Roger Daniels, ed., *Anti-Chinese Violence in North America* (New York: Arno Press, 1978), 239–56; and Sandy Lydon, *Chinese Gold: The Chinese in the Monterey Bay Region* (Capitola, CA: Capitola Book Company, 1985), 134–35. There is some confusion over the identity of Sing Lee. Ourada says the sole victim of the Denver riot of 1880 was Look Young, while Wortman describes the person as Sing Lee. Because Wortman published his essay thirteen years after Ourada's article appeared in print and because Wortman corrects other discrepancies in Ourada's article, it seems reasonable to conclude that the accurate identity of the casualty of the Denver riot is Sing Lee.
27. Locklear, "Celestials and the Angels," 241–55.
28. *Watsonville Pajaronian*, November 9, 1871, quoted in Lydon, *Chinese Gold*, 134.
29. Ibid.
30. Ibid., 134–35.
31. Ibid., November 16, 1871, quoted in Lydon, *Chinese Gold*, 135.
32. Ourada, "Chinese in Colorado," 278–83; Wortman, "Denver's Anti-Chinese Riot," 275–80.
33. William Hoy, "Tales of the California Chinese," unpublished radio talk, San Francisco, September 16, 1940, as quoted in Paul C. P. Siu, *The Chinese Laundryman: A Study of Social Isolation* (New York: New York University Press, 1987), 50–54.
34. Wortman, "Denver's Anti-Chinese Riot," 285–91. The Denver *Rocky Mountain News* published the preposterous story that the riot was caused by the Chinese. According to the *News*, a Chinese laundry owner demanded ten cents more from a white customer, who refused to pay. The Chinese launderer then purportedly slashed the face of the white man. After a crowd gathered, the Chinese laundry owner fired a gun at the crowd, and this precipitated the riot. Subsequent investigations by historians have proven this explanation a fabrication.
35. Ibid., 287–90; Ourada, "Chinese in Colorado," 278–83.

36. L. Chan, "Chinese in Nevada," 295.
37. Ibid., 295–97, 304. See also Gary P. BeDunnah, *History of the Chinese in Nevada, 1855–1904* (San Francisco: R and E Research Associates, 1973); Gregg Lee Carter, "Social Demography of the Chinese in Nevada: 1870–1880," *Nevada Historical Society Quarterly* 18 (Summer 1975); and Magnaghi, "Virginia City's Chinese Community."
38. Sucheng Chan, "Anti-Chinese Activities in Rural California in the Late Nineteenth Century," paper presented to the one hundredth meeting of the American Historical Association, New York, December 27–30, 1985. Revised versions of this paper were incorporated into Chan's *This Bittersweet Soil.*
39. *The Oxford English Dictionary*, 2nd ed. (Oxford: Clarendon Press, 1989), 7:362. According to Quinn, "the word 'hoodlum' was first used in San Francisco and referred to gangs of toughs employed to beat up the Chinese" ("Chink Chink Chinaman," 84n11).
40. Tsai, *Chinese Experience in America*, 68.
41. Fong, "Sojourners and Settlers," 232.
42. Ibid., 233.
43. Ibid., 241.
44. John R. Wunder, "Law and the Chinese on the Southwest Frontier, 1850s–1902," *Western Legal History* 2 (Summer/Fall 1989): 141.
45. Ibid.
46. S. Chan, introduction, 25.
47. Ibid.
48. Ibid.
49. Ibid.
50. Ibid.
51. Wunder, "Law and the Chinese on the Southwest Frontier," 141.
52. Sandmeyer, *Anti-Chinese Movement*, 42; Seager, "Some Denominational Reactions," 49; Courtney, *San Francisco Anti-Chinese Ordinances*, 65; Saxton, *Indispensable Enemy*, 72–75.
53. Pauline Minke, *Chinese in the Mother Lode, 1850–1870* (San Francisco: R and E Research Associates, 1974), 43–44.
54. Ibid., 45–46.
55. Locklear, "Celestials and the Angels," 239–50.
56. Sylvia Sun Minnick, *Samfow: The San Joaquin Chinese Legacy* (Fresno, CA: Panorama West, 1988), 128–29.
57. Sandmeyer, *Anti-Chinese Movement*, 97–98; S. Chan, *This Bittersweet Soil*, 370–81.
58. S. Chan, *This Bittersweet Soil*, 371–74; Book, *Chinese in Butte County*, 49–57.
59. S. Chan, *This Bittersweet Soil*, 374.
60. Ibid.
61. Ibid.

62. Ibid.
63. Ibid.
64. Lydon, *Chinese Gold*, 119–33.
65. Minnick, *Samfow*, 129.
66. Ibid.
67. Carranco, "Chinese Expulsion from Humboldt County."
68. Ibid.
69. Ibid.
70. Ibid.
71. S. Chan, *This Bittersweet Soil*, 378–39.
72. Sandmeyer, *Anti-Chinese Movement*, 97–98.
73. S. Chan, introduction, 25.
74. Minnick, *Samfow*, 135–62.
75. Sandmeyer, *Anti-Chinese Movement*, 97–98.
76. Ibid.
77. S. Chan, introduction, 25.
78. Sandmeyer, *Anti-Chinese Movement*, 97–98.
79. Ibid.
80. Ibid.
81. Ibid.
82. Ibid.
83. Ibid.
84. Ibid.
85. S. Chan, introduction, 25.
86. Sandmeyer, *Anti-Chinese Movement*, 97–98.
87. Ibid.
88. S. Chan, *This Bittersweet Soil*, 374–75.
89. Sandmeyer, *Anti-Chinese Movement*, 97–98.
90. Ibid.
91. Ibid.
92. Ibid.
93. Ibid.
94. Ibid.
95. S. Chan, introduction, 25.
96. Sandmeyer, *Anti-Chinese Movement*, 97–98.
97. Ibid.
98. Ibid.
99. Ibid.
100. S. Chan, introduction, 25.
101. Sandmeyer, *Anti-Chinese Movement*, 97–98.
102. Ibid.
103. S. Chan, introduction, 25.
104. Sandmeyer, *Anti-Chinese Movement*, 97–98; S. Chan, *This Bittersweet Soil*, 374–75.

105. Sandmeyer, *Anti-Chinese Movement*, 97–98.
106. S. Chan, *This Bittersweet Soil*, 278–79.
107. S. Chan, introduction, 25.
108. S. Chan, *This Bittersweet Soil*, 278–79.
109. Ibid.
110. Ibid.
111. Ibid.
112. Ibid.
113. Ourada, "Chinese in Colorado," 278–79.
114. Ibid., 279.
115. Ibid., 278.
116. Ibid., 282–83; Wortman, "Denver's Anti-Chinese Riot."
117. Christian J. Buys, "Chinese in Early Grand Junction," *Journal of the Western Slope* 2 (Spring 1987): 69–70.
118. Tsai, *The Chinese Experience in America*, 68.
119. Elsensohn, *Idaho Chinese Lore*, 16; John R. Wunder, "The Courts and the Chinese in Frontier Idaho," *Idaho Yesterdays* 25 (Spring 1981): 23.
120. Elsensohn, *Idaho Chinese Lore*, 28.
121. S. Chan, introduction, 25.
122. Elsensohn, *Idaho Chinese Lore*, 90–91.
123. Ibid., 103.
124. Ibid., 29–30; Kenneth Owens, "Pierce City Incident," *Idaho Yesterdays* 3 (Spring 1959): 8–13.
125. S. Chan, introduction, 25.
126. Elsensohn, *Idaho Chinese Lore*, 113.
127. Ibid., 116–17.
128. Quinn, "Chink Chink Chinaman," 86.
129. Ibid., 84–85, 88.
130. Ibid., 88.
131. John R. Wunder, "Law and Chinese in Frontier Montana," *Montana, the Magazine of Western History* 30 (Summer 1980): 20.
132. S. Chan, introduction, 25.
133. Ibid.
134. Quinn, "Chink Chink Chinaman," 85.
135. Carter, "Social Demography," 77.
136. Magnaghi, "Virginia City's Chinese Community," 132, 149–54; L. Chan, "Chinese in Nevada," 297–98.
137. Carter, "Social Demography," 77; Magnaghi, "Virginia City's Chinese Community," 152; L. Chan, "Chinese in Nevada," 270.
138. L. Chan, "Chinese in Nevada," 284–85.
139. Ibid., 284; Carter, "Social Demography," 77.
140. L. Chan, "Chinese in Nevada," 278.
141. Ibid., 289.

142. Ibid., 304; Gary P. BeDunnah, *History of the Chinese in Nevada, 1855–1904* (San Francisco: R and E Research Associates, 1973), 22.
143. Ibid., 280.
144. L. Chan, "Chinese in Nevada," 295.
145. John R. Wunder, "*Territory of New Mexico v. Yee Shun*: A Turning Point in Chinese Legal Relationships in the Trans-Mississippi West," *New Mexico Historical Review* 65 (July 1990): 308.
146. Ibid.; John R. Wunder, "Chinese in Trouble: Criminal Law and Race on the Trans-Mississippi West Frontier," *Western Historical Quarterly* 17 (January 1986): 25–27.
147. Wunder, "*Territory of New Mexico v. Yee Shun*," 307–8.
148. Mooney, "Matthew Deady," 574.
149. Edson, *Chinese in Eastern Oregon*, 43–44.
150. Mooney, "Matthew Deady," 574–75.
151. Ibid.
152. Ibid.
153. S. Chan, introduction, 25.
154. Ibid.
155. Ibid.
156. Ibid., 575.
157. Edson, *Chinese in Eastern Oregon*, 51; Stratton, "Snake River Massacre," 124–25.
158. Watson Parker, *Deadwood: The Golden Years* (Lincoln: University of Nebraska Press, 1981), 147–48.
159. Don C. Conley, "The Pioneer Chinese of Utah," in *The Peoples of Utah*, ed. Helen Z. Papanikolas (Salt Lake City: Utah State Historical Society, 1976), 270–71.
160. Ibid.
161. Wilcox, "Anti-Chinese Riots in Washington," 205.
162. Ibid.
163. Huidekoper, "Mosaic of a Massacre," 94.
164. Ibid.
165. Wilcox, "Anti-Chinese Riots in Washington," 205; Karlin, "Anti-Chinese Outbreak in Tacoma"; John R. Wunder, "The Chinese and the Courts in the Pacific Northwest: Justice Denied?," *Pacific Historical Review* 52 (May 1983): 191–211.
166. Ibid.
167. Ibid.
168. Ibid.; Karlin, "Outbreak in Tacoma," 271; Wunder, "The Chinese and the Courts in the Pacific Northwest," 191–211.
169. Wilcox, "Anti-Chinese Riots in Washington," 208–11; Karlin, "Anti-Chinese Outbreaks in Seattle."
170. Karlin, "Anti-Chinese Outbreak in Tacoma."
171. Carroll, "Governor Francis E. Warren," 18.

172. Ibid., 22.
173. Ibid., 21.
174. Ibid., 18–19.
175. Ibid., 21–22.
176. Carroll, "Governor Francis E. Warren"; Crane and Larson, "Chinese Massacre"; Huidekoper, "Mosaic of a Massacre."

CHAPTER 2

Chinese in Trouble

Criminal Law and Race on the Trans-Mississippi West Frontier

ON THE EVENING of February 24, 1882, at dusk, six Chinese men gathered at the John Lee Laundry in East Las Vegas, New Mexico.[1] This was not an uncommon event for New Town, as the recent addition to Las Vegas was known. The Chinese began settling in this north central New Mexico community in 1879. Many came to work on railroads, in laundries, and at restaurants.[2]

The Chinese reception by non-Chinese had not been gracious in Las Vegas, in New Mexico Territory, or throughout the trans-Mississippi West. The tone of comment was frequently pejorative. The *Las Vegas Optic* noted in October 1883 that "a new gang of Chinese struck the city today. They will find it pretty hard to catch on as our Yu-Lis and Wun Lungs have a corner on the Washee Business."[3] Two years later the same newspaper reported that three Chinese truck farmers who worked a vegetable farm on Nimbrio Creek were massacred, probably by Apaches, on their way to market. This event "created as much alarm and indignation as if the unfortunate victims were white."[4] Perhaps miners at Black Hawk best expressed the feelings of non-Chinese in their formal invitation to the women of Silver City, New Mexico Territory, to attend a dance in the winter of 1884:

'Soy, young ladies are y' wid us?
It's our Ball next Toosdie night

> We're de jolly Black Hawk miners,
> And our mimbers is all white.
> We ain't much as doods, us snoozers,
> But y'betcha coldest Chink
> Da no flies don't die on us, much—
> I should almost blush to blink.
> Well, young ladies, are y' wid us?
> Oh! de boys they're all right
> As I said, no crooks ain't comin'
> To our Ball next Toosdie night.[5]

Anti-Chinese feeling took various forms throughout the trans-Mississippi West in the late nineteenth and the earliest portion of the twentieth centuries. Racial insults dotted editors' perorations and politicians' speeches. Physical violence punctuated the rhetoric; vigilante actions resulted in shootings and lootings, lynchings and massacres. Courts in the West were inevitably called upon to prevent, mediate, or sanction the treatment of the minority Chinese by a majority non-Chinese society.

Here the ambiguities of procedure and process prevailed, representing a significant failure of justice. Even the law proved not to be immune from cultural pressures, and it was in criminal law where anti-Chinese treatment found a firm hold. By providing special circumstances that required the examination of Chinese cultural values against Anglo-American tradition or denying the Chinese direct access to a fair trial, the rules of evidence were reshaped to discourage or prevent Chinese from using the criminal justice system in the trans-Mississippi West.[6]

Specific attention was drawn to Chinese differentness in several evidentiary ways. Challenges to oath taking, testimony against whites, witness incompetency, and dying declarations either denied Chinese full opportunities to use western criminal justice or, more often, clouded trial proceedings with cultural insults and accusations. Western law became infused with racial and cultural requirements; legal doctrine eschewed color blindness or cultural neutrality as a goal for fundamental fairness.

The question of whether a Chinese witness could be bound by an oath was one of several issues that predominated in criminal law in the trans-Mississippi

West during the Gilded Age and oftentimes prevented Chinese defendants and witnesses from achieving equal treatment from the Anglo-American legal system. The establishment of precedents in non-Chinese cases created a context for Chinese litigants, and the focus upon religion and faith made oath taking a particularly sensitive issue. At common law the ability to take an oath was crucial in the admission of any testimony. The oath—a promise to tell the truth or face God's wrath—was dependent upon the witness's religious beliefs. It gained its strength in Protestant England. Very early it was held that non-Protestant witnesses, in this instance Roman Catholics, could not be excluded. Still, witnesses whose religion—cacotheism—sanctioned false testimony might be refused, and certainly such charges could be used to discredit witnesses.[7] Non-Christian adherents and nonwhite litigants were especially susceptible to this challenge.

The first significant court challenge concerning the issue of oath taking and religious beliefs in the American West occurred between Anglo litigants in civil cases over the testimony of non-Chinese. In California in 1861 the California Supreme Court heard a divorce case on appeal. Silas Fuller had sued his wife, Jane Fuller, for divorce on the grounds of extreme cruelty and adultery. Silas offered testimony that Jane had beaten him over the head with a shovel, scratched his face, torn his clothes, assaulted him with a hatchet and a fence rail, called him a dog, bastard, and viper, spat in his face, poured hot tea on him, stolen all his papers, including valuable credit notes, chased him all over Telegraph Hill, and threatened to kill him with a loaded pistol—all incidents that occurred on different occasions. He further produced his fourteen-year-old Chilean servant, James Cruz. Cruz testified, after he denied understanding the meaning of an obligation to an oath to tell the truth and it was explained to him by the trial court judge, that he had seen Jane in bed at the Fuller ranch with Silas's attorney, M. S. Chase. All was denied, but the defendant still lost.[8]

On appeal the testimony of Cruz was attacked as not admissible because Cruz was from Chile and did not have a common religious belief. The appellant alleged that any person swearing to an oath needed to believe in a state of future rewards and punishments. Justices Joseph G. Baldwin and Stephen J. Field were not persuaded. They did not believe that the lower courts had erred. Wrote Baldwin, "The witness seems to have been a foreigner. He was not disqualified by the mere fact that he did not, when first produced, understand the meaning of the word obligation, as applied to an oath. . . . A witness is competent without any respect to his religious sentiments or convictions; the law leaving the matter of *competency* to legal sanctions, or, at least, to considerations independent of religious sentiments or convictions."[9]

Ten years later in Kansas, Jacob Smith sued James H. Brown and eighteen other defendants in an action for ejectment on property known as the "Kansas Half-Breed Indian Lands." Title depended upon testimony given by "a certain Indian" who did not understand the nature of the oath.[10] He stated that he did not know what perjury was but that he knew it was bad to lie. This was sufficient for the trial court to allow Indian testimony and for the Kansas Supreme Court. Chief Justice Samuel A. Kingman, in upholding the lower court decision allowing the Indian testimony, observed, "He was an uneducated Indian, not deficient in understanding, but uninstructed as to the nature of an oath . . . ; yet he knew that it was wrong to speak falsely. . . . Whether he believed that he would be punished in another life was a matter that could not be inquired into under our constitution." Besides, reasoned Kingman, "His evidence afterwards given is such as confirms the opinion we have expressed as to his competency."[11] Thus, from *Fuller* and *Smith*, two jurisdictions in the trans-Mississippi West had withstood a strict common law challenge to testimonial competency.

The first state appellate case to consider the Chinese within the framework of the witness oath issue was *Green v. State of Georgia* (1883).[12] Tom Green was convicted of burglary—he had stolen eighty-five cents that had been left in a store owned by Dorsey Lee, a Chinese resident of Augusta. Lee had testified at Green's trial, but before Lee was sworn he was challenged for competency. Lee stated he "believe the Bible, and believe the God of my religion," that if "man tell lies go to the bad place; go to devil; can't go to heaven, if tell lies." He further stated he did not know about oaths in China. The Georgia high court found that the examination of Lee was acceptable and that this Chinese witness, because he demonstrated an understanding of Christianity and life after death, was competent to testify.[13] Thus far, it would appear that oath taking for Chinese litigants would involve only a quiz on fundamental religious beliefs.

Just one year later the *Yee Shun* case was decided. Here a Chinese, non-Christian witness who merely took an oath to bind his conscience was deemed competent to testify.[14] This landmark case at least allowed Chinese witnesses and defendants onto the witness stands in criminal trials, but there would be human costs involved in the mere establishment of competency.

Returning to John Lee's Laundry in East Las Vegas, New Mexico Territory, on the night of February 24, 1882, the six Chinese men—John Lee, Jo Chinaman, Sam Lee, Ah Locke, Yee Shun, and Jim Lee (also known as Sam Ling King or Frank)—became involved in a legally significant murder trial. During that night Jim Lee was shot twice, receiving a fatal wound to the upper chest. The witnesses agreed that Ah Locke and Sam Lee had come to visit John Lee to encourage him to sell his laundry to them. John Lee throughout the bargaining had remained on the floor in a corner smoking opium. Jo Chinaman was an ironer, and Jim Lee had merely dropped by to talk. All were known to each other except Yee Shun, who had arrived in Las Vegas from Denver that evening and had entered the laundry to ask the whereabouts of a friend, Gum Fing.[15] Yee Shun was twenty years old, 5 feet 3 ½ inches tall, with a "lightish brown yellow" complexion, "straight black" hair, and black eyes. A laborer with no property, he had been born in China and only recently had emigrated to the United States.[16]

A shot was fired, and then another, and Yee Shun, Ah Locke, and Sam Lee ran out the front door. On the floor lay Jim Lee dead. Non-Chinese on the street heard the shots and pursued Yee Shun. He was captured and placed under arrest.[17] On March 10, 1882, Yee Shun was taken before Judge LeBaron Bradford Prince, chief justice of the New Mexico Territory Supreme Court, who was holding district court in San Miguel County, and charged with murder. The next day John Lee was added to the indictment, the first one being dismissed. On March 13, attorneys for Yee Shun and John Lee and the defendants appeared and pleaded not guilty. Sidney Barnes, counsel for John Lee, asked for separate trials, a request that Judge Prince granted. Then the next day the defendants' attorneys asked for a change of venue, but this motion was denied. One day later the defendants requested a postponement, and the court, after argument, agreed to reschedule the separate trials for the fall term.[18]

On August 16, 1882, *Territory of New Mexico v. Yee Shun* began, but with a new judge, recently appointed Chief Justice Samuel B. Axtell. His first order of business was to deny the defendant's request for a continuance. A jury was chosen that consisted of twelve Mexican Americans.[19] The actual trial with testimony began on August 17 and lasted until August 21. The next day the jury found Yee Shun guilty of second-degree murder and recommended life imprisonment. Judge Axtell followed the jury's recommendation. Yee Shun's attorney, T. A. Green, moved for a new trial, which was denied. He then filed notice of appeal to the New Mexico Territory Supreme Court.[20] Meanwhile young Yee Shun was transported to the Kansas State Penitentiary, arriving there on September 28, 1882, to await a hopefully favorable appeal.[21]

At Yee Shun's criminal trial, the key witness for the prosecution proved to be Jo Chinaman. He identified Yee Shun as the killer. Jo Chinaman was a laborer who had come to Las Vegas one year earlier from El Paso, where he had worked on the railroad; prior to his moving to El Paso he had mined gold in California.[22] When Jo Chinaman was sworn, the following exchange occurred between T. A. Green, Yee Shun's attorney; William Breeden, New Mexico Territory attorney general and prosecutor; and Jo Chinaman, aided by an interpreter:

By Mr. Green:
Q. I will ask you if you believe in Chinese worship: their Joss houses do believe in Chinese Joss?
A. I live in a Chinese house.
Q. I will ask you if you believe in the Chinese Joss house where they worship, where they have their religious services? Do you ever go with Chinamen in this country where they worship? Do you understand what a God is?
A. I don't know what it is. Yes, I believe the Chinese religion.
Q. Have you ever changed from Chinese to Christian religion since you came to this country?
A. I am a Chinaman, and believe in the Chinese religion.
Q. Was you ever a witness in Court before?
A. Yes.
Q. Do you know anything about the obligations of an oath under the Christian religion?
A. I don't know it.

By Mr. Breeden through Chinese interpreter:
Q. Ask him if he knows what he is required to do when he takes an oath here as a witness?

A. He come here for a witness to prove that a man got killed.
Q. Ask him what he is to do, or what his duty is in telling his story as a witness? If he knows what his duty is as to telling the truth?
A. I can tell the truth in this case.
Q. Do you know that you are sworn here so that you are to tell the truth?
A. Yes.[23]

Green then objected to the form of oath and the admissibility of any of the witnesses' testimonies. He was overruled, but the incident formed the primary basis of his appeal in Yee Shun's behalf.

In his brief filed with the New Mexico Territory Supreme Court, Green listed six reversible errors, three of which were closely related substantive issues. Green argued that Jo Chinaman did not believe in God, that the witness was a pagan, and that the accuser was "idiotic" and "ignorant." All of these traits necessitated his testimony to be stricken, because the oath had no meaning to the witness.[24] The New Mexico Supreme Court was not persuaded to overrule the trial court. It found that the only question was whether the witness believed the oath to be "binding on his conscience" within the framework of his own religion. Thus, non-Christians could testify in New Mexico courts and take an oath certifying their truthfulness.[25]

What occurred in the Yee Shun case appeared on the surface to be a victory for Chinese litigants. In some ways it was. Chinese non-Christians could testify in criminal trials. However, the New Mexico courts and all other courts in the West required Chinese witnesses to explain their religion and their state of conscience. The Chinese as a group were not summarily allowed to take an oath; they had to accentuate their cultural distinctiveness first in order to testify. The ambiguity in the law encouraged judges and juries to consider Chinese testimony as somehow different from non-Chinese testimony.

Even if a Chinese witness could pass the oath, other restrictions might be imposed. Several courts in the trans-Mississippi West moved toward the exclusion of Chinese testimony based upon the common law concept of infamy. If a witness had been convicted of treason or a crime involving deceit, any testimony would be stricken.[26] A crime of deceit, or the propensity to lie, was of special interest to Oregon courts and Chinese witnesses. Oregon law was interpreted to equate the Chinese with deceit. To allow Chinese testimony meant the witness had to prove he or she was *not* a liar.

In *State v. Mah Jim*, because the lower court allowed testimony from several Chinese witnesses to convict Mah Jim of murdering See Toy at a tong meeting, the Oregon Supreme Court reversed the decision.[27] It reasoned that "experience convinces every one that the testimony of Chinese witnesses is very unreliable, and that they are apt to be actuated by motives that are not honest. The life of a human being should not be forfeited on that character of evidence without a full opportunity to sift it thoroughly."[28] As a point of law after 1886, Chinese witnesses in Oregon court proceedings were deemed belonging to a class whose testimony generally was presumed to be unreliable. Mah Jim received a new trial, but his supreme court decision placed in grave jeopardy any Chinese defendant accused of committing a crime who had only Chinese witnesses to use against the non-Chinese witnesses of the prosecution.

Two years later the Oregon Supreme Court further strengthened this rule in the case of *Ching Ling*. The defendant, along with Chee Gong, Fong Long Dick, Yee Gong, and Chee Son, stood accused of murdering one Lee Yick in the Portland Chinese Theater. All witnesses testifying to the event were Chinese, and they did not agree on who stabbed the mortal blow.[29] The lower court found Chin Ling guilty of murder, but the Oregon Supreme Court reversed. On the basis of testimony offered, the court took judicial notice of an inherent racial quality of the Chinese:

> The object of this testimony evidently was to show that the appellant and other Chinamen charged with the offense bore such malice towards the deceased as to prompt them to commit the homicide. There could have been no other purpose for introducing it. The testimony was not sufficient to have had any weight whatever as against white persons. But very few of them at most could be found credulous enough to believe that *their* race, in consequence of such an occurrence as happened to Chee Gong and his friends, in the affair of their discharge from employment at the restaurant, would have been induced to plan and execute a murder. As to Chinamen, however, it is different. Those among us have exhibited such a peculiarity of temperament, that a circumstance of that character would incite a strong suspicion against them.[30]

Given their infamous nature, a presumption against the innocence of any Chinese person charged with a violent crime was given judicial sanction.

One might assume that Ching Ling had no grounds for reversal, but a greater truth remained to save him. All the prosecution witnesses were Chinese and thereby suspect. The court espoused a higher law: "Juries should be loath to convict a Chinaman of murder in the first degree upon Chinese testimony; not wholly on account of a tender regard for the life of the accused, but also from a respect and reverence for truth and justice. If we were disposed through a dislike of the race to consider the life of a Chinaman as a trivial matter, still we would have no right to immolate justice upon the altar of our prejudice."[31]

In the summer of 1875, L. T. Townsend toured the West and observed that all was not well between Chinese and non-Chinese. "Judging from the present bitter complaints against the Chinaman," Townsend wrote, "it would seem that our friends of the Pacific States are able to see under that 'rat-and-tan complexion' merely an animal of 'sly' and 'peculiar ways.'"[32] Slyness was interpreted by courts as a character flaw that jeopardized Chinese participation in the criminal justice system.

Oregon had the harshest infamy evidential rules in the trans-Mississippi West. Other states and territories modified the rote rules of the common law. Nevertheless, Chinese witnesses had to be examined with reference to religious beliefs in all trans-Mississippi West jurisdictions before they were allowed to testify,[33] and courts allowed admission into evidence the discussion of Chinese mythic propensities to be less than truthful.[34]

The admission of dying declarations into evidence at a trial probably began in early eighteenth-century Britain. The rule quickly traversed the Atlantic Ocean and was refined in the United States. Basically stated, a dying declaration was admitted because of the notion that a person about to die would tell the truth in order to entertain an afterlife and that a person near death may have been the only witness to the lethal assault. It followed that for a dying declaration to be admissible evidence, the declarant had to die and a public prosecution for the specific crime of homicide had to be commenced.[35] All jurisdictions treated the dying declaration as did California in *People v. Sanchez*. "Declarations," held the California Supreme Court in 1864, "of deceased persons, in cases of homicide, stand upon the same footing as the testimony of a witness sworn in the case."[36]

Given the circumstances surrounding dying declarations, Chinese and non-Chinese defendants charged with the murder of Chinese victims challenged the rule governing admissibility. Such defenses first alleged that a Chinese who made a dying declaration must have been a Christian or at least believed in some sort of afterlife in order for the statement to be admitted at a trial. At first it appeared Chinese dying declarations were free from cultural attack. In the case of *People v. Chin Mook Sow*, the defendant was found guilty of stabbing to death Yee Ah Chin. Before he died, Yee Ah Chin identified Chin Mook Sow as his assailant. On appeal the defendant asserted as reversible error the fact that Yee Ah Chin "did not entertain such a belief in a future state as rendered his dying declaration admissible."[37] The California Supreme Court did not agree with the contentions of the defense. It held that evidence of a declarant's lack of belief in Christianity or of a life thereafter would not affect the competency of the declaration. This information, however, was useful to a jury to help it determine the weight it wanted to give to such testimony.[38]

In spite of *Chin Mook Sow*, California continued to grapple with this issue. In *People v. Lim Foon*, the defendant was convicted by a San Joaquin County Court of murdering an elderly Chinese, Yip Suey. Upon arrest, the defendant had been placed in front of Yip Suey, who stated, "Yes, him man shoot me." Yip Suey then expired. After conviction Lim Foon appealed, arguing that the declarant had no religious convictions and had specifically disdained any belief in a spiritual afterlife, thereby making the declaration inadmissible. The California Supreme Court did not agree, but it allowed that the lack of Christian beliefs made dying declarations greatly impaired and subject to incredulity.[39]

Again the cloudy nature of the law allowed for cultural and racial discussions in court. The need for the California court to make such a pronounced anti-Chinese statement in the *Lim Foon* case may have arisen from its own decision made just two years earlier in *People v. Dallen*. Here, on the late afternoon of June 8, 1913, in the small community of Sisson, the town marshal was informed that the "Greek pimp," one Theodore Dallen, had just arrived at a house of ill fame known as the Buckskin. The marshal and his assistant, Andrew Dougherty, went to the bawdy house to arrest the Greek pimp. Dallen evidently heard them, so he jumped out a window and hid under the house. The marshal said he wanted to find the "son-of-a-bitch," and then Dougherty heard something, looked under the house, lit a candle, and was shot in the calf by the Greek pimp. The wounded Dougherty was taken to the home of his half sister, and then on June 10 he was moved to a hospital, where his condition was attended to by one Dr. Legge. He prescribed amputation of Dougherty's leg, but during the probing the physician decided that the gangrenous state was too advanced and halted the operation. Dougherty died on June 13.[40]

Dallen was convicted of murder, and he appealed on many grounds, including the argument that Dougherty's statement implicating Dallen was not admissible because there had been time for the declarant to have been given an oath. The California court refused to adopt this contention, saying that dying declarations require only basic standards for admissibility and that to require more interfered with the province of the jury.[41]

Other trans-Mississippi West jurisdictions also grappled with dying declarations and Chinese interests. The Oregon Supreme Court in *State of Oregon v. Charley Lee Quong, Ah Lee, and Lee John* directly embraced the question of the religious condition of a dying declarant. This dispute involved the premeditated, malicious killing of Chin Sue Ying, a member of the Chinese Mission School in Portland and a recent Christian convert. Chin, the night before he was murdered, had gone to a Chinese joss house where he broke a Chinese "stink-pot" on the floor. A policeman was called, who saw some dark-looking and foul-smelling liquid on the joss house floor, and he heard Lee Quong call Chin, according to court records, a "ki gi," meaning a "man who acts like a prostitute."[42] The officer inquired as to whether he should arrest Chin, but Lee Quong said he should wait until the next morning to swear out a warrant. The next day Chin once again went to the joss house and proceeded to attempt to throw a piece of raw meat on the joss statue, whereupon he was dealt two hatchet blows to the head and two pistol shots to the abdomen.[43]

After the trial of each defendant separately, Ah Lee was convicted and appealed to the Oregon Supreme Court alleging several points of error, including an objection to the admission into evidence of Chin Sue Ying's dying declaration, on the basis that Chin was an imperfect Christian and did not believe in the existence of a Supreme Being. In rejecting this contention, the court took judicial notice of the deceased probably being "a worshipper of Joss, and the heathenish religion of his race," but since he had been attending a Portland missionary school and since he had defaced the joss house, Oregon's general rule was modified to allow this dying declaration to remain as acceptable evidence.[44] A similar conclusion was reached in several cases by Idaho's highest court.[45]

Several years later this same issue was once again taken up by the Oregon Supreme Court. In *State v. Foot You* the defendant had been convicted of second-degree murder for shooting Ching Bo Quang at a Portland bar known as the Temperance Saloon. At the trial the district attorney presented as evidence two written statements signed by the deceased that identified Foot You as his murderer. These statements were sworn to by an interpreter, and another attorney was present when they were signed. Defendant's counsel objected, claiming the dying declaration was orchestrated in a hearing-like setting without opposing counsel's presence. The court ruled that the possible pressure exerted by the prosecution during the dying declaration process was a jury consideration and did not prevent introduction of the dying declaration as valid evidence.[46]

The final Oregon word on Chinese dying declarations occurred in the case of *State v. Yee Gueng* (1910). Here Yee Gueng was convicted of murdering Lee Tai Hoy on a stairway outside an apartment building in downtown Portland. Lee Tai Hoy in a dying declaration identified the defendant as his killer. At the trial, defendant's counsel attempted to have the dying declaration rendered inadmissible because of Lee Tai Hoy's lack of religious belief and membership in a faction of the Bo On Tong Society, both of which affected his ability to be truthful. The judge refused and went one step further. He ordered the jury not to consider any testimony given as to the declarant's religious beliefs. The Oregon Supreme Court, in a significant departure from other jurisdictions, affirmed this position. Chinese religion could not be introduced as mitigating circumstances to dying declarations in Oregon trials. The question of trust and honesty did, however, remain for the jury to weigh.[47]

Where Oregon refused to go, Washington took the step to accept dying declarations from infamous or near-infamous declarants. On August 9, 1895, Edwin Baldwin, Ozro Perkins, and Ulysses Loop beat up Alonzo Wheeler. From these wounds Wheeler died, but before he died he declared the names of the three killers. At the trial where the three defendants were convicted of manslaughter, their counsel sought to expunge the dying declarations because the declarant had been convicted of cattle stealing and had not been pardoned. The trial court refused to sustain the objection and the Washington Supreme Court agreed. The high court strongly suggested that only for perjury could a dying declaration be denied admissibility.[48]

Thus, for nineteenth- and early twentieth-century courts in the trans-Mississippi West, the dying declaration provided significant legal comment and controversy. While justice was sometimes upheld, it provided yet another opportunity for evaluation of the Chinese by non-Chinese and a chance to question and impugn the role Chinese witnesses, defendants, and victims should play in the criminal justice system.

Nowhere would attempts be more concerted to deny Chinese direct access to criminal justice than in California under the development of its racial exclusionary rule.[49] This occurred as a result of an 1854 California Supreme Court decision, *People v. Hall*.[50]

In this case the white defendant was convicted of murder on the basis of testimony from Chinese witnesses. He appealed, asserting that Chinese testimony against a white person was inadmissible per se because a Chinese was a person of color and thereby banned from testifying by criminal statute. This statute, section 14 of California's 1850 Act Concerning Crimes and Punishments, read, "No black or mulatto person, or Indian shall be permitted to give evidence in favor of, or against, any white person."[51] The California Supreme Court agreed with Hall's contention and his conviction was reversed.

The language and reasoning employed by Chief Justice Hugh C. Murray reflected the extremes to which law and race fell in nineteenth-century America. Murray found as a point of law that Indian meant Chinese. He wrote,

> When Columbus first landed upon the shores of this continent, in his attempt to discover a western passage to the Indies, he imagined that he had accomplished the object of his expedition, and that the Island of San Salvador was one of those Islands of the Chinese sea, lying near the extremity of India, which had been described by navigators.
>
> Acting upon this hypothesis, and also perhaps from similarity of features and physical conformation, he gave to the Islanders the name of Indians, which appellation was universally adopted, and extended to the aboriginals of the New World, as well as of Asia.
>
> From that time, down to a very recent period, the American Indians

and the Mongolian or Asiatic, were regarded as the same type of the human species.[52]

Having established the racial link, it remained for Murray to connect Chinese to the intention of the legislature. Murray reasoned, "The evident intention of the Act was to throw around the citizen a protection for life and property, which could only be secured by removing him above the corrupting influences of degraded castes.... The apparent design was to protect the white from the influence of all testimony other than of persons of the same caste."[53] Murray then invoked Chancellor Kent's analysis of whether the Chinese could become citizens of the United States under existing federal statutes. Wrote Kent, "The Act confines the description to 'white' citizens, and it is a matter of doubt, whether, under this provision, any of the tawny races of Asia can be admitted to the privileges of citizenship."[54] Murray then illogically applied this notion to California:

> The same rule that would admit [Chinese] to testify, would admit them to all the equal rights of citizenship, and we might soon see them at the polls, in the jury box, upon the bench, and in the legislative halls.
>
> This is not a speculation which exists in the excited and over-heated imagination of the patriot and statesman, but it is an actual and present danger.[55]

Hysteria then gripped the chief justice's pen. The Chinese, he concluded, are "a race of people marked as inferior, and who are incapable of progress or intellectual development beyond a certain point, as their history has shown."[56] Thus, after *People v. Hall*, the Chinese were denied access to criminal trials strictly on account of their race if a white was a defendant.[57]

The rule in *People v. Hall* was extended to civil cases in 1859,[58] was invoked to formulate a color test covering mixed-bloods, that is, "Chinese Mestizoes,"[59] and was extended to cover specifically the injured party.[60] In this latter case, *People v. Howard*, Chief Justice Stephen J. Field wrote that "it is possible... that instances may arise where, upon this construction, crime may go unpunished. If this be so, it is only [a] matter for the consideration of the Legislature."[61]

Lest there be any doubt, the California legislature acted. In 1863, three years after *Howard*, an amended section 14 expressly included the Chinese in the exclusionary rule: "No . . . Chinese [as well as mulattos and Indians] shall be permitted to give evidence in favor or against, any white man."[62]

There were limits to the testimonial exclusion. In *People v. Awa*, a Chinese man was convicted of manslaughter. At his first trial, he offered as evidence a Chinese witness. The testimony was disallowed on the basis of the exclusionary rule. On appeal the California Supreme Court reversed, concluding that the state—the People—were not exclusively white.[63] Then, in *People v. Jones*, the defendant was convicted of stealing four ounces of gold from Ah Po. There was no admissible evidence except from the victim. The trial court had instructed the jury, "If the best evidence cannot be produced, then secondary evidence is admissible. In the present case Ah Po [the victim] . . . would be the best witness to prove the robber. But the law precludes his testimony, and hence what would be secondary testimony in ordinary cases becomes the best evidence in the case at bar."[64]

On appeal the California Supreme Court reversed, but it urged a legislative reconsideration: "It does not appear to us reasonable that a less measure of proof, or testimony of a less persuasive character, should be required to convict a man of the crime of robbery, when committed upon a Chinaman, than when committed upon a citizen of California, merely because a Chinaman is an incompetent witness; and for that reason it might be impossible to prove the body of the offense in accordance with the rules of evidence well established in the law."[65]

Relief appeared to be coming to Chinese criminal victims and defendants. In 1866 in an attempt to make it easier to prosecute prostitution, the legislature lifted the ban, allowing Chinese testimony in such cases.[66] That same year the Civil Rights Act was passed, but in *People v. Washington* the California Supreme Court narrowly limited the act to apply only to blacks. In this case George Washington, a mulatto, was convicted of robbing Ah Wang on the testimony of Chinese witnesses. This conviction was reversed under the federal Civil Rights Act; black was now white, which disallowed Chinese testimony against blacks in California.[67] One year later Chinese testimony against a white, this time under the Fourteenth Amendment, was disallowed by the same California Supreme Court.[68]

The California Chinese exclusionary rule eventually was stricken during codification reforms of the 1870s. Section 1321 of the Penal Code of 1872 formally ended the racial exclusionary rule.[69] No other state or territory adopted the California position, although Nebraska, Minnesota, and Washington retained racial exclusions upon Native American testimony, and Nebraska in *Pumphrey v. State* was asked to adopt *People v. Hall* with reference to Japanese testimony, but it declined.[70] A foremost specialist on evidence, John Henry Wigmore, in 1904 attempted to understand the policy behind California's Chinese exclusionary rule. "The condition of public feeling in that community against the economic encroachments of Chinese laborers," wrote Wigmore, "explains and extenuates (while it may not excuse) this blunder in the policy of the testimonial law."[71]

In order for the Chinese to participate in the American criminal justice system, they clearly needed more than constitutional amendments and federal laws. Left to state and territorial legislatures and courts, they were indeed in trouble. Chinese willing to come to a trial or those unfortunate enough to be charged with a crime frequently risked cultural insults and, worse, legally sanctioned discrimination. Challenges to oath-taking abilities, questions of near-infamy disqualifications, and adherence to a racial testimonial exclusion discouraged Chinese cooperation in criminal cases and denied to the Chinese fundamental forms of fairness in criminal law. Ambiguities allowed non-Chinese to pass judgments upon the culture of the Chinese during an era of intolerance. The criminal justice system in the West became for Chinese what the criminal justice system of the South represented for blacks in immediate post–Civil War America.

But what happened to Yee Shun, the young Chinese involved in a murder in Las Vegas, New Mexico Territory? He had been transported to the Kansas State Penitentiary to await word of his appeal from the New Mexico Territory Supreme Court. Finally, during the January term, 1884, the court issued its opinion denying his appeal.[72] Yee Shun's attorney, T. A. Green, no doubt delayed sending the bad news to his client, who had already served two years in prison. Perhaps when Yee Shun heard the decision, it proved too much for the twenty-two-year-old. On September 11, 1884, Yee Shun took drastic action, which was recorded the next morning in the *Leavenworth (KS) Times*: "Yee Shun, a Chinaman, confined in the penitentiary on a life sentence from New Mexico, hanged himself yesterday morning in his cell. He committed the deed with a small cord that he had taken from his bed."[73]

Notes

Originally published as John R. Wunder, "Chinese in Trouble: Criminal Law and Race on the Trans-Mississippi West Frontier," *Western Historical Quarterly* 17 (January 1986): 25–41.

1. *Territory of New Mexico v. Yee Shun* (1992), trial transcript, 27, 51–53, 87, San Miguel County District Court Records, New Mexico State Archives, Santa Fe.
2. F. Stanley, *The Las Vegas Story* (Denver, CO, 1951), 179.
3. *Las Vegas Optic* (New Mexico Territory), October 9, 1883.
4. *Las Vegas Optic*, November 1885, as reported in *Silver City* (New Mexico Territory) *Enterprise*, November 27, 1885.
5. *Las Vegas Optic*, February 1, 1884.
6. Law and race in nineteenth-century America have been the subject of recent scholarly scrutiny, most effectively concerning blacks and Native Americans. See John R. Wunder, "The Chinese and the Courts in the Pacific Northwest: Justice Denied?," *Pacific Historical Review* 52 (May 1983): 191–211, for a brief listing of relevant significant works.

    However, it is important that research on the Chinese and law be governed not exclusively by comparative models. There will be useful common elements, but the Chinese experience must be considered on its own merits.

    Chinese and the law in the American West have been discussed in far fewer sources. Overviews are limited to indirect treatments in Elmer C. Sandmeyer, *The Anti-Chinese Movement in California* (Urbana: University of Illinois Press, 1939); Alexander P. Saxton, *The Indispensable Enemy: Labor and the Anti-Chinese Movement in California* (Berkeley: University of California Press, 1971); Milton R. Konvitz, *The Alien and the Asiatic in American Law* (Ithaca, NY: Cornell University Press, 1946); and Stan Steiner, *Fusang: The Chinese Who Built America* (New York: Harper & Row, 1979).

    For more specific coverage, see also *The Chinese Texans* (San Antonio, 1978); William J. Courtney, "San Francisco Anti-Chinese Ordinances, 1850–1900" (PhD diss., University of San Francisco, 1956); Susan W. Book, *The Chinese in Butte County, California, 1860–1920* (San Francisco: R and E Research Associates, 1976); Gary P. BeDunnah, "A History of the Chinese in Nevada, 1855–1904" (MA thesis, University of Nevada, Reno, 1966); Christopher H. Edson, *The Chinese in Eastern Oregon, 1860–1890* (San Francisco: R and E Research Associates, 1974); Edward C. Lydon, *The Anti-Chinese Movement in the Hawaiian Kingdom, 1852–1886* (San Francisco: R and E Research Associates, 1975); John R. Wunder, "Law and Chinese in Frontier Montana," *Montana, the Magazine of Western History* 30 (Summer 1980): 18–31; M. Alfreda Elsensohn, *Idaho Chinese Lore* (Cottonwood: Idaho Corporation of Benedictine Sisters, 1971); Robert Edward Wynne, "Reaction to the Chinese in the Pacific Northwest and British Columbia, 1850 to 1910" (PhD diss., University of Washington, 1964); and Roger Daniels, ed., *Anti-Chinese Violence in North America* (New York: Arno Press, 1978).

7. Whitebread's Trial, 7 How. St. Tr. 311, 361, 379 (1679); and John Henry Wigmore, *A Treatise on the System of Evidence in Trials at Common Law* (Boston: Little, Brown, 1904), 646–47. Cacotheism in seventeenth-century England was interpreted by the courts to mean a heretical or "harsh" theology. Cacotheists are not religiously prevented from taking oaths; inability to swear to an oath because of one's religious belief is a separate evidential problem.
8. *Fuller v. Fuller*, 17 Cal 605 at 606–7 (1861).
9. Ibid., 612.
10. *Smith v. Brown et al.*, 8 Kan 409 (1871).
11. Ibid., 415.
12. *Green v. State of Georgia*, 71 Ga 487 (1883).
13. Ibid., 489–90, 492–93.
14. *Territory v. Yee Shun*, 3 NM 100 (1884).
15. *Yee Shun*, District Court Records, 133–35, 143–68.
16. Prisoner Ledgers A & E, Number 2763, Kansas State Penitentiary Records, Kansas State Archives, Topeka.
17. *Yee Shun*, District Court Records, 1–15.
18. Criminal Record Book A, US District Court of New Mexico Territory, San Miguel County, New Mexico State Archives, 88, 90, 91, 95, 99, 101, 115. See also Walter J. Donlon, "LeBaron Bradford Prince, Chief Justice and Governor of New Mexico Territory, 1879–1893" (PhD diss., University of New Mexico, 1967).
19. Criminal Record Book A, 115–16, 145, 160–61. The jurors were Blas Martinez, Manuel Tagaija, Runaldo Archibeque, Alsolinario Almanzar, Jose Leon Martinez, Hijinio Garcia, Marcos Tagoya, Ysidro Torres, Manuel Jimenes, Manuel Urioste, Juan Chavez, and Juan E. Sena.
20. Ibid., 163–64, 166, 170, 172–73, 176–77. See also Civil/Criminal Court Index, District Court, San Miguel County, 1847–1882, New Mexico State Archives.
21. Prisoner, Kansas Penitentiary Records. New Mexico Territory transported felons to Kansas to house for a fee. This agreement preceded adequate and secure prison facilities in New Mexico.
22. *Yee Shun*, District Court Records, 49–50.
23. Ibid., 50–51.
24. T. A. Green, Appellant Brief, in *Territory of New Mexico v. Yee Shun* (1883), manuscript court records, Book 153–59, New Mexico Supreme Court Archives, Santa Fe.
25. *Territory v. Yee Shun*, 3 NM 100, 2 Pac 84–85 (1884). See also Simon Greenleaf, *A Treatise on the Law of Evidence* (Boston: Little and Brown, 1842), sec. 370–71, 414–17.
26. Edward W. Cleary, ed., *McCormick's Handbook of the Law of Evidence* (St. Paul, MN: West Publishing, 1972), 142.
27. *State v. Mah Jim*, 13 Ore 235 (1886). For a further discussion of this case and *State of Oregon v. Ching Ling* within a regional context, see Wunder, "The Chinese and the Courts in the Pacific Northwest," 204–5.

28. *State v. Mah Jim*, 13 Ore 235 at 236–237 (1886).
29. *State of Oregon v. Ching Ling*, 16 Ore 419 (1888).
30. Ibid., 423.
31. Ibid., 425. See also *State of Oregon v. Chee Gong and Fong Long Dick*, 16 Ore 534 (1888). Elmer Sandmeyer has observed, "In some cases the charge against the Chinese was simply that they were dishonest and unreliable, and that the entire business life of China was permeated by the idea that every person who handled a transaction should take his share of graft. More specifically, they were accused of having no regard for the sanctity of an oath." Sandmeyer, *Anti-Chinese Movement*, 34.
32. Luther Tracy Townsend, *The Chinese Problem* (Boston, 1876; repr., San Francisco: R and E Research Associates, 1970), 58. For black anti-Chinese attitudes, see Leigh Dana Johnsen, "Equal Rights and the 'Heathen Chinee': Black Activism in San Francisco, 1865–1875," *Western Historical Quarterly* 11 (January 1980): 57–68.
33. In the following trans-Mississippi states and territories, religious belief could not deny testimonial oath taking: Arizona, Ariz. Rev. Statutes, sec. 1866 and 2037 (1877); Colorado, Colorado Constitution, art. II, sec. 4 (1876), Colo. Annot. Statutes, sec. 4821 (1891); Idaho, Idaho Constitution, art. I, sec. 4 (1899); Iowa, Iowa Constitution, art. 1, sec. 4 (1857); Montana, Montana Constitution, art. III, sec. 4 (1889); Nebraska, Nebraska Constitution, art. I, sec. 4 (1875), Neb. Comp. Statutes, sec. 5939 (1899); Nevada, Nevada Constitution, art. I, sec. 4 (1864), Nev. Gen. Statutes, sec. 4578 (1885); New Mexico, N. M. Comp. Laws, sec. 3015 (1897); North Dakota, North Dakota Constitution, art. I, sec. 4 (1899); Oklahoma, Okla. Statutes, sec. 4229 (1893); Oregon, Oregon Constitution, art. I, sec. 6, 7 (1859); South Dakota, South Dakota Constitution, sec. 86 (1889); Texas, Texas Constitution, art. I, sec. 5 (1876); Tx. P.C., sec. 776 (1895); Utah, Utah Constitution, art. 1, sec. 4 (1895); and Wyoming, Wyoming Constitution, art. I, sec. 18 (1889).

    In the following trans-Mississippi West states, no witness could deny the being of God: Arkansas, Arkansas Constitution, art. XIX, sec. 1 (1874); and Louisiana, La. C. Pr., sec. 478 (1894).

    In the following trans-Mississippi West states, non-Christians, such as many Chinese witnesses, were to be sworn to oaths according to "peculiar ceremonies": Arkansas, Ark. Statutes, sec. 2924 (1894); California, Cal. C.C.P., sec. 2096 (1872); Kansas, Kan. Gen. Statutes, chap. 95, sec. 351 (1897); Minnesota, Minn. Gen. Statutes, sec. 5665 (1894); Missouri, Mo. Rev. Statutes, sec. 8842 (1899); and Washington, Wash. C. and Statutes, sec. 6057 (1897).

    See also Wigmore, *Treatise Evidence*, 3:2365–71.
34. See also *State v. Lu Sing*, 34 Mont 31 (1906). In *Fernandez v. State*, 16 Ariz 269 (1914), the testimony of an elderly Apache-Mohave was accepted by her merely promising not to tell a lie.

    For exclusion of testimony in federal courts based upon tests of infamy, see

U.S. v. Biebusch, 1 F. 213 (1880), and particularly perjury, see *State v. Harras*, 22 Wash 57 (1900).
35. Wigmore, *Treatise Evidence*, 2:1798–819.
36. *People v. Sanchez*, 24 Cal 17 at 26 (1864).
37. *People v. Chin Mook Sow*, 51 Cal 597 at 599 (1877).
38. Ibid., 599–600.
39. *People v. Lim Foon*, 155 Pac 477 (1915).
40. *People v. Dallen*, 132 Pac 1064 (1913).
41. Ibid.
42. *State of Oregon v. Charley Lee* (indicted under the name of Charley Lee Quong) and *Ah Lee* (indicted under the name of Lee Jaw), jointly indicted with *Lee John*, 7 Ore 237 at 249 (1879). The invective was probably *k'ai-ai*, meaning homosexual.
43. Ibid., 258.
44. *State of Oregon v. Ah Lee*, 8 Ore 214 at 217 (1880). For a further discussion of these cases, see Wunder, "The Chinese and the Courts in the Pacific Northwest," 197–98.
45. See *People v. Ah Too*, 2 Idaho 47 (1884); Appellant's Brief, *People v. Ah Too*, filed January 29, 1884, Respondent's Brief, *People v. Ah Too*, filed January 31, 1884; Blaine County District Court trial transcript, *State v. Yee Wee*, June 29, 1899, all in Idaho State Archives, Boise; and *State v. Yee Wee*, 7 Idaho 188 (1900). See also John R. Wunder, "The Courts and the Chinese in Frontier Idaho," *Idaho Yesterdays* 25 (Spring 1981): 23–32.
46. *State v. Foot You*, 24 Ore 61 (1893).
47. *State v. Yee Gueng*, 57 Ore 509 (1910).
48. *State v. Baldwin et al.*, 15 Wash 15 (1896).
49. J. A. C. Grant, "Testimonial Exclusion Because of Race: A Chapter in the History of Intolerance in California," *UCLA Law Review* 17 (November 1969): 192–201.
50. *People v. Hall*, 4 Cal 399 (1854).
51. Cal. Statutes, chap. 99 (1850).
52. *People v. Hall*, 4 Cal 399 at 400 (1854).
53. Ibid., 403.
54. Ibid., 404.
55. Ibid., 404–5.
56. Ibid., 405.
57. Jack Chen, *The Chinese of America* (New York: Harper Collins, 1981), 45; and Daniel Chu and Samuel Chu, *Passage to the Golden Gate: A History of the Chinese in America to 1910* (Garden City, NY: Doubleday, 1967), 84.
58. *Speer v. See Yup Company*, 13 Cal 73 (1859).
59. *Sanchez v. Stout*, 1 D. C. R. (Labatt) 241 (Cal App. 1857), as cited in Grant, "Testimonial Exclusion," 196; and *People v. Elyea*, 14 Cal 145 (1859).

60. *People v. Howard*, 17 Cal 64 (1860).
61. Ibid., 65.
62. Cal. Statutes, chap. 70 (1863).
63. *People v. Awa*, 27 Cal 639 (1865).
64. *People v. Jones*, 31 Cal 566 at 572 (1867).
65. Ibid.
66. Grant, "Testimonial Exclusion," 197.
67. Ibid., 198–201; and *People v. Washington*, 36 Cal 568 (1869).
68. *People v. Brady*, 40 Cal 198 (1870).
69. Grant, "Testimonial Exclusion," 200–201. See also *People v. McGuire*, 45 Cal 56 (1872).
70. Nebr. Comp. Statutes, sec. 4734, 5902; Minn. Gen. Statutes, sec. 2007; Wash. Annot. Code and Statutes, sec. 6940, 7316; and *Pumphrey v. State*, 84 Neb 636 (1909).
71. Wigmore, *Treatise Evidence*, 1:645–46.
72. *Territory of New Mexico v. Yee Shun*, 3 NM 100 (1884).
73. Prisoner, Kansas Penitentiary Records; and *Leavenworth (KS) Times*, September 12, 1884, p. 4, col. 2.

California

CHAPTER 3

People v. Hall (Cal, 1854) Revisited

THE CLOSE OF November 18, 1853, left California District Court judge William T. Barbour one frustrated man. That autumn he had presided over a contentious murder trial in Nevada City, California, a trial that had provoked the town and the entire Sierra Nevada mining community. Three white miners, Samuel Wiseman and two brothers, George W. and John Erastus Coble Hall, had been accused of killing a Chinese miner, Ling Sing, below the forks of the Bear River in Nevada County, and a jury on October 14, 1853, after protracted deliberations well into the night, had found one of them, young George Hall, a recent immigrant from Ohio, guilty of murder.[1]

A month later, after plenty of local talk and some demonstrations seeking Hall's release, Judge Barbour had arrived at Nevada City's courthouse to pass sentence. And to make matters worse, the defendant seemed to have no remorse. When given his chance to speak by the judge, Hall spoke bitterly: "I have never had a difficulty with anyone. It seems hard that because I was so unlucky as to be there when that Chinaman was killed, I should be put down as his murderer!" Hall, warming to his protested innocence, next contradicted himself. "Those Chinamen," he snarled, "because I had a difficulty with one of them, swore my life away. I must now leave my wife and friends and all I hold dear because I was so unlucky as to have trouble with them." Hall then finished his retort: "I have other witnesses I can produce if I am allowed a new hearing. That is all I have to say."[2]

At the trial Judge Barbour had heard testimony from Chinese male witnesses that was corroborated by white male testimony, and he had sat through the introduction of strong circumstantial evidence. That the jury convicted Hall had not surprised him. The judge turned to Hall and murmured that the strength of the accusations "would not have permitted the most incredulous to form any other conclusion" than a guilty verdict. Barbour's voice strengthened as he began to sentence an angry and frustrated gold rush panner and lecture a troubled community and a racist society from the "densely crowded" courtroom.[3]

Barbour himself was relatively new to California. In his early thirties, having read for the bar in Missouri before his arrival in the Golden State with the first wave of rushers in 1850, Barbour had attained a judgeship with his election to the district court bench in 1851. No stranger to uproars, Judge Barbour stood tall.[4] The judge intoned, "In the intendment and contemplation of the law, the lives of all men are held strictly sacred, without distinction; be he in high or low position, rich or poor, good or bad, his life belongs to his country and his God, and no self constituted authority can with impunity deprive him of the right." Directly facing young Hall, Judge Barbour admonished the recently convicted murderer and his neighbors: "You must unfortunately have participated in a delusion, which has prevailed to an alarming extent in California. Many persons here have supposed it less heinous to kill a Negro, an Indian or a Chinaman, than a white person. This is a gross error. The law of our country throws the aegis of its protection upon all within its jurisdiction, it knows no race, color, or distinction."[5] Judge Barbour then swiftly sentenced George W. Hall to be hung on December 30, 1853, and left the courtroom, perhaps anticipating a California racial catharsis.

The delusions of race, as Judge Barbour so eloquently summarized California's, and indeed the American West's, dilemma, constituted any number of strong crosscurrents in the rivers of nineteenth-century American legal history. To document and analyze the history of race relations, particularly in the diverse American West, retains a historical and contemporary resonance, although during the past several decades significant attention has been devoted to this subject. The legal rights of the Chinese have attracted mention, and the seminal case of *People v. Hall* (1854) has even merited discussion in several treatments.[6] But strangely no full history of this important legal decision has been dug out from the legal pilings of gold rush California. Let us then consider the facts, the nuances of law, the holdings, and the legal significance of California's tortured contribution to mid-nineteenth-century racial understanding.

The Place, the Times, and the People

The discovery of gold in 1848 set off a stampede to California the likes of which had never before been experienced in the American West. Thousands upon thousands of people virtually overnight set off for Gold Mountain. They came from Europe and the American East Coast via ships sailing around South America or up from the Panamanian isthmus. Stops on South America's edge brought more potential immigrants from Chile and Peru. More sailed directly across the Pacific from Australia and China. They also came on foot and by wagon from Mexico or the American South, New England, and the Midwest. Over fifty thousand in 1850 braved the hardships of the Oregon Trail to make it to the California cutoff and then scale the Sierra Nevadas for gold country.[7]

Hundreds explored the nooks and crannies of California's interior, and the Sierra Nevada foothills became their temporary home, soon the third-largest metropolitan area of the new state. So rapid was the population rush that the state government in Sacramento named the new settlement of Nevada (renamed Nevada City once neighboring Nevada achieved statehood, so as not to cause confusion) the county seat of the new county of Nevada, drawn in 1851.[8] Nevada County, shaped like post–World War II Czechoslovakia, lies nuzzled between Yuba, Sierra, and Placer Counties and borders on the southeast the Bear River and on the northwest the middle fork of the Yuba River. The rolling terrain contained numerous creeks, lakes, forests, and potential gold strikes.[9]

Nevada City grew up around Deer Creek, where "ounce" diggings yielded rich gravel strikes. Its first building constructed in 1849 housed a general store owned by one Dr. A. B. Caldwell. This busy entrepreneur already operated another store four miles farther down Deer Creek. News of Nevada County gold strikes brought thousands from the Sacramento area. By 1851 an estimated thirty-five thousand men conducted placer mining in and around Nevada County, and fourteen hotels plus 150 stores and gambling places located in Nevada City that year.[10]

Not all was well in Nevada County. A drought persisted in 1850 and 1851, and the initial placer strikes near Nevada City showed signs of decline. On March 11, 1851, the first of several great fires hit Nevada City, wiping out half of the city. Their community having been built in a pine forest without bricks and mortar, Nevada Citians were fortunate the entire settlement did not burn. Nevertheless, the settlers resolved to rebuild. A Whig newspaper called the *Nevada Journal*, the first for Nevada County, located in Nevada City and offered its first issue in April 1851.[11] The miners who had congregated in Nevada City soon spread out, finding more placer and quartz gold strikes throughout the county, or moved on. One of the strikes made was at the confluence of Greenhorn Creek and Bear River.

So anxious were the multitudes for further gold strikes that in 1852 Anthony Chabot adapted a stream of water to a canvas hose to wash gravel into his sluice box, and in 1853 Edward Matteson added a nozzle to the hose, pointing the pressurized water to the hillside. The first hydraulic mining in California evolved out of placer mining in Nevada County. Thus, almost simultaneously, placer, quartz, and hydraulic mining drew throngs to what was by 1853 a remote yet urbanized outpost.[12]

Although county organization came to this California region, not everyone was ready for law and order. In March 1851 an unidentified man was hung at Kentucky Bar for highway robbery and horse stealing. It was reported that Judge Lynch infrequently visited Nevada County during the early 1850s. Still, law arrived in Nevada City. Niles Searls opened his law practice in 1850, and he built one of the first brick buildings in the county for his law office. He planned to stay. Young William M. Stewart arrived on the Yuba River to pan for gold, but he soon lost interest and became one of the first to read law in Nevada County, studying with the new county district attorney, John R. McConnell, who had arrived in 1850. Stewart eventually served as Nevada County district attorney from 1853 to 1854.[13]

Censuses, of course, were notoriously inaccurate during the early gold rush years. People moved around, some didn't want to be bothered, and some deliberately avoided being counted. Nevertheless, population statistics give us a sense of Nevada County. When in 1852 California took a special census, it found 21,365 people living in Nevada County. This total included 3,886 Chinese and 3,226 Indians.[14] Although people continued to migrate to Nevada County, by 1853 more miners were leaving the area than were coming in. The official federal census in 1860 found 16,146 residents in Nevada County, including 2,147 Chinese. Nevada City's township numbered 3,679. with 480 Chinese, and Little York Township on the Bear River, site of the murder of Ling Sing in 1853, was home to 1,035 the day the census taker came to call, including only 82 Chinese. Ten years later, in 1870, Nevada County's population had increased modestly, but the statistics also reflected changes in the mining industry moving from placer to quartz mining. The 1870 census revealed 19,134 residents, including 2,627 Chinese, in all of Nevada County. Urban townships such as Nevada City and Grass Valley had significantly increased in population, while Little York Township had dropped to 868 total residents but with a 150 percent increase in Chinese, to 128. Only 9 Indians remained in Nevada County.[15]

The residents of early Nevada County reflected California's diversity. The indigenous of the Yuba River watershed, the southern Maidu or Nisenan, had resided in the Sierra Nevada foothills for at least three hundred years and perhaps longer. Most Nisenans lived in extended families of fifteen to twenty in villages of three to seven multifamily houses. They moved for the change of seasons, following animals, fish, and plant harvests. Black oak acorns constituted the primary source of food for the Nisenans.

Native Americans who suddenly found their homelands invaded after 1848 at first attempted to adjust. They witnessed the new foods, the large animals non-Indians brought with them, and the attractive trade goods. To obtain these items required mining, and Nisenans became miners. An 1848 report noted that more than half of California's Indians were involved in mining. Most worked as laborers for a small share, but some Indians became independent miners. One white miner in Nevada City in 1849 commented that traders liked Indians who brought their gold dust in to barter because they would buy out the entire inventory. Most of the Nisenan miners were women.

California's Indians also tried to negotiate with their new ruler, the United States. Previously, most had been able to ignore first Spain and then Mexico, but the gold rush altered everything. In 1851 and 1852 a number of treaties were agreed upon between federal representatives and California's Indigenous peoples that included the sale of some of their lands and the protection of other land, but the US Senate refused to ratify the treaties.

The Nisenans soon found that they would not be able to negotiate or adjust to the new conditions in their homelands. Diseases brought by the outsiders proved lethal. By 1852 a smallpox epidemic had killed over 20 percent of the Nisenans in the Nevada City area. Mining tore up the land, muddied the streams, and destroyed the oak trees. Furthermore, environmental damage to the ecological system increased exponentially with the development of hydraulic mining. Miners also brought significant violence to the region. When Nisenans resisted incursions, they were killed. Violence, starvation, and disease decimated the Nisenans so that, within a decade, what few survived abandoned Nevada County.[16] During the early 1850s, who might have suspected that the California Supreme Court would rule as a matter of law that the Chinese who came to Nevada County were really Nisenan Indians and the Nisenans Chinese?

A majority of the population invading Nevada County by 1850 arrived from one of two directions. From the west, many who migrated to San Francisco via ship journeyed to Sacramento, the gateway to the Sierras. From there, they then found their way to Nevada County. These immigrants included, among many others, Europeans and white Americans who had traveled to New York or Boston to catch a ship bound for California. Upon their arrival in San Francisco, many were broke. Some took jobs, like George Dornin, who worked first as a sign painter, then a wallpaper hanger, and then as an upholsterer at ten dollars a day. After a few months and with sufficient resources saved, most took a boat from San Francisco to Sacramento, and then they boarded a stage to Nevada City, a trip that took several days. Dornin set Nevada City as his destination when he heard that he could raffle merchandise there from a single shipment for up to $10,000. Such was the excitement of the mines.[17]

A number of Jews came to Nevada County in this migration. All arrived from Europe and most from Germany, where they had been the victim of anti-Semitic laws limiting the number of Jewish marriages and had chosen the wrong side in the Revolution of 1848. Some came to participate in the gold rush, such as "a Jew named Heyman" who panned for gold in Grass Valley in 1852. Others arrived to become merchants, to supply miners with necessities such as food, clothing, tobacco, hardware, and equipment. A sufficient number of Jews had arrived in Nevada City by the fall of 1852 to celebrate the High Holidays. By 1854 the Nevada Hebrew Society had acquired a cemetery, and in 1855 the Hebrew Benevolent Society of Grass Valley raised money to help those who had suffered losses in a fire. Other Jews joined and created civic organizations and became leading county citizens.[18] No records indicate that Samuel Wiseman, a gold miner like Heyman and involved in the Ling Sing murder, came from one of the Jewish families of Nevada County.

The Chinese also arrived in San Francisco in significant numbers. In 1849 only fifty-four Chinese had come to California, but by 1852 over twenty thousand had migrated. News of the Gold Mountain discoveries along with the Tai Ping Rebellion, floods, drought, and famine combined to encourage migration. A credit system caused many Chinese to owe a person or company for their passage, and they too had to work in order to make it to the mines. Once they had some resources or if their work contracts required them to report to mining country, the Chinese took river and road transportation from San Francisco to the Sierra Nevada foothills and Nevada County.

By 1860 Chinese constituted 13 percent of the Nevada County population. The numbers of Chinese in Nevada County placed it seventh highest in the population of Chinese among all counties in California. Most Chinese in Nevada County told federal census takers they worked in mining. For example, in 1860 of the 320 Chinese in Grass Valley, 272 listed their occupations as miners, 13 as cooks, 13 as laundrymen, 7 as self-employed, and 14 as unemployed. Since most Chinese were in the field, settlement in towns evolved gradually. Chinese quarters eventually developed in Nevada County, but not until the late 1860s. Such Chinatowns, as in Nevada City, contained general stores, a temple or joss house, gambling halls and brothels, laundries, boardinghouses, herbalists, restaurants, and assay offices and gold buyers.

Of course, the Chinese in California had to overcome more than many others in the gold rush to be successful. A Foreign Miner's License Tax of 1852 in the northern mines required payments of from three to six dollars per month, and it was almost exclusively collected from Chinese. In Nevada County, miners paid $103,250 in foreign miners taxes between 1854 and 1870. Chinese were also prevented from owning land or mining claims. Most Chinese then either worked leftover or abandoned claims, independent claims in remote areas, or dummy claims owned by whites, or hired out as general laborers in hydraulic mines. In these rural areas, Chinese suffered violence. An 1862 report by the California legislature noted the high number of Chinese murdered and robbed that year in mining country, including eleven known to have been murdered by collectors of the Foreign Miner's Tax.[19] It seems likely that Ling Sing, probable placer miner on an abandoned claim near the junction of Greenhorn Creek and Bear River in Little York Township, followed this route to his fatal demise.

Still others journeyed to Nevada County overland. They did so by traveling the Truckee Route of the California Trail. This trail crossed a forty-mile desert in northwestern Nevada and then climbed through Reno Valley. At what is now the town of Truckee, California, the trail split into several paths, including two following the Yuba and Bear Rivers. Thousands of young men from America's heartland, some even with families, traversed the Truckee Route.

The first immigrants to the Bear River Valley found a scattering of settlers. In 1850 Cyrus Loveland wrote, "This valley has a large creek running through it and contains three or four trading posts."[20] That same year when John Steele traveled down the Bear, he was surprised by what he saw: "Here we found a restaurant, built of logs and covered with pine boughs."[21] On October 2, 1850, Micajah Littleton recorded in his diary, "This day we made 18 miles to Cold Spring[.] [F]or 2 miles after you leave Bear Val[1]ey you have the steepest hill and the longest one perhaps on the rout[e][.] [O]ne mile from where you come into the Val[1]ey you come to the forks of the road[:] one goes down Steep hollow to the left and the other by Nevada City."[22] Others recorded the difficulty of traveling the western foothills of the Sierras, but by 1852 people on the California Trail knew about Nevada County, and for many it represented their destination.

In *Days of Gold: The California Gold Rush and the American Nation*, Malcolm Rohrbough explains the motivations and the deprivation for American families that the gold craze brought. Most of the would-be miners were young men. Many were married, and they left wives and children behind. Some traveled with relatives. Two brothers from Maine, William and George Farnsworth, obtained permission from their parents to make the journey. After two years, George, who was married and had children, returned to Maine. Two brothers from Mississippi, William and Willis Dixon, took to the trail, but Willis died before they could journey across the Plains.[23]

Leaving a wife behind oftentimes proved problematic. When John Eagle from Pennsylvania decided to go to California, he and his wife made the decision together. Others went against the wishes of wives and relatives.

William Swain from New York deliberately ignored his wife's pleadings to stay at home with her and their infant daughter. Many Argonauts who left their loved ones missed them dearly, and they frequently made reference to them in their letters and journals.

No one region had a monopoly on California immigrants, but Ohio sent many of its native sons. Elisha Perkins deserted his pregnant wife and a losing business in Marietta to join the Harmar Company, whose investors sponsored twenty young Ohioans to go to California. Five men from Logan County, Ohio, including John Gish, signed an agreement whereby they pledged to support each other on the arduous trip, and to make the agreement all the more compelling, each contributed $200 to guarantee the contract. Many a native of the Buckeye State set his dreams upon California in the 1850s.[24]

We do not know a great deal about the Hall brothers. We do know that George and John were young white men, probably in their late twenties when they left Ohio for California. They arrived in Nevada County during the summer of 1852. That George left a wife behind and that the brothers most likely traveled together over the Truckee Route is established, but how the Hall brothers met up with Samuel Wiseman is unknown.

The Murder and the Trial

Reconstructing the events that led to the California Supreme Court opinion of *People v. Hall* (1854) is not an easy task. In the California State Archives supreme court files is a copy of the grand jury indictment brought against the Hall brothers and one "Lemuel" Wiseman, the defendants' demurrer, the objection of Samuel Wiseman that he is incorrectly named in the legal record, the order to hold separate trials for Wiseman and each of the Halls, and a brief summary of the proceedings of the Hall brothers' one trial. While the Hall trial is not covered verbatim in the *Nevada Journal*, the sentencing hearing is, with complete coverage of Judge Barbour's speech from the bench. Nevertheless, from some hints found in the *Nevada Journal* and the grand jury indictment, the circumstances leading to the murder can be discerned. What should be emphasized, however, is the mere fact that this particular case went to trial, let alone its surprising verdict.

On the night of August 9, 1853, Ling Sing surprised three white men as they were trying to rob his cousin Chin Ying and his sluice box on Greenhorn Creek near its intersection with Bear River. They shot Ling Sing. Just four days earlier, the *Nevada Journal* had reported a Chilean having been hung by a vigilance committee for being a party to the murder of another Chinese miner elsewhere in the county.[25] On August 12, the three men who were said to have robbed and beaten Chin Ying and shot Ling Sing were arrested at the Little York camp. Charged with "shooting and dangerously wounding a Chinaman" while he and several other Chinese tried to prevent the robbery, the suspects were transported to Nevada City.[26] Then one week later, the paper noted Ling Sing had died and that the Hall brothers and another miner, one Wiseman, had been indicted for Ling Sing's murder. The next week another Chinese miner reportedly was murdered near Weber Creek and robbed of $500–$600.[27]

The grand jury indictment gives some indication of the murder circumstances. After Ling Sing surprised the would-be robbers, the three men assaulted Ling Sing and threw him to the ground. George Hall, described in the *Nevada Journal* as five foot, ten inches tall and "about thirty years of age, with dark complexion, black hair, and blue eyes,"[28] then calmly loaded his gun with gunpowder and buckshot and aimed the gun at Ling Sing, who remained face down on the ground. George's two companions stood by and encouraged him to shoot. Using both his hands, George raised and discharged his gun into the back of Ling Sing, causing at least fifteen wounds, several of which were judged to be mortal. Ling Sing died some time after the shot, and the three men fled. George Hall was charged with committing a murder with malice aforethought, and his brother John Hall and "Lemuel" Wiseman were both charged with aiding and abetting the murder. Witnesses to this event included Chin Ying, a cousin of the deceased. Chin Ying had also been beaten, but he did not testify to the grand jury. Those who did included three other Chinese miners, Jo, Au Yo, and Ho Chow. A white witness, probably a miner named John Bowin, was also listed. New district attorney William Stewart signed the indictment, and the legal process began.[29]

On September 22, 1853, Judge William Barbour opened court with a formal reading of the indictment to the three defendants, and he then asked if "they were indicted by their true names." Perhaps surprising the prosecution team of Stewart, James Churchman, and H. C. Gardiner, Wiseman spoke up and stated that his name was not "Lemuel" but Samuel C. Wiseman and that therefore the indictment should be dismissed. Judge Barbour ignored this request and ordered the name of "Lemuel Wiseman" placed in the indictment. The judge then set one week later as the time for the commencement of the trial.[30]

Those anticipating the trial date had to wait one more day after the defendants' attorneys—John R. McConnell, the former district attorney, and three other lawyers from his law firm, Stanton Buckner, John C. Palmer and James S. Carpenter—filed several demurrers in an effort to dismiss the case. First, McConnell noted that the three charges in the indictment were inconsistent. In the first and third charges, George Hall was named as the murderer and his brother John was charged with aiding and abetting, but in the second charge John was also charged with murder. Next, McConnell alleged that the indictment did not conform to California state statutes as to proper form because it didn't list which court would hear the prosecution, nor did it clearly and carefully describe the actual murder act. And third, John Hall and "Lemuel" Wiseman were charged with murder in the introductory preamble to the indictment but then not shown to have committed that crime in the indictment itself.[31]

Clearly, the indictment was poorly drawn. No doubt Judge Barbour knew this to be the situation. After all, the twenty-seven-year-old district attorney Stewart had just been certified as a lawyer and elected to his post. His mentor, J. R. McConnell, now called him on his mistakes. It would have been easy for the judge to dismiss the case, but he did not. This was certainly not an ordinary case, given the attraction to it from a budding twenty-member Nevada County bar.

On September 30 court was once again in session, and the defendants pleaded not guilty. Next John Hall's attorneys moved that he be tried in a separate trial, but Judge Barbour overruled the motion, which was excepted by counsel. Now it was time to consider the demurrers. After hearing arguments from both Stewart and McConnell, the judge overruled all of the demurrers and again defendants' counsel excepted. At this point Stewart and McConnell announced that they had agreed to try each of the defendants separately in defiance of Judge Barbour's previous ruling, and they were ready to begin immediately with Samuel Wiseman's trial.[32] No doubt Judge Barbour must have been surprised by this development.

What next transpired is not explained in the legal record. The *Nevada Journal* reported on October 7 that Wiseman's trial had concluded with his acquittal. Thus, somewhere between September 30 and October 7 the Wiseman trial proceedings were initiated. We do know that a second trial began October 4, but this trial did not separate the Hall defendants. Brothers George and John would face the prosecution together.[33]

On October 4, 1853, Judge Barbour impaneled a jury to hear murder charges against George and John Hall. Ten jurors were chosen, exhausting the existing jury panel, so the judge ordered the sheriff to select twenty-one more potential jurors. The next day two more jurors were sworn, as were four prosecution witnesses and two official interpreters, the Reverend William Speer and Ho Clem. Of the twelve jurors impaneled, three were listed in the 1852 California state census for Nevada County: Moses Brown, age thirty, miner; Isaiah Moody, age twenty-six, miner; and Thomas Wright, age forty-one, teamster. With this limited information, one might conclude that the jury had at least some members who would be sympathetic to the defendants.

Prior to the trial, William Stewart traveled to San Francisco to talk with the Reverend Speer. He and Judge Barbour were concerned about how to appropriately swear in the Chinese witnesses. Speer told Stewart that burning paper was sufficient, that one did not have to cut off a chicken's head. So impressed was Stewart with his interviewee that he invited the Presbyterian missionary to come to Nevada City to be a translator for the trial. Reverend Speer crusaded throughout California for better treatment for the Chinese. He just happened to be lecturing about China on September 30 at the Nevada City Presbyterian Church, and as someone who had been a missionary in China and was fluent in Chinese, Speer made himself available to the court.[34]

Unfortunately, the trial record is very brief. Beginning on October 5, Judge Barbour and the jury heard a series of prosecution witnesses, but they are only listed as testifying rather than having their testimony recorded. Chinese witnesses included Chin Ying, Nu On, and Nau Koo. These witnesses had not testified before the grand jury. John R. McConnell objected to Chin Ying testifying about how Sing Ling's body was handled and what happened after the shooting, but Judge Barbour overruled the objections and the defendants' counsel excepted. What is important here is what the defendants' counsel did not do. No objections were raised as to whether or not

Chinese witnesses could testify. McConnell questioned only selected portions of their actual testimony.[35]

The next day Judge Barbour considered the testimony of four white witnesses for the prosecution: the foreman of the grand jury, W. C. Ferguson; a doctor whose last name is not readable from the record; one William Burlington; and a "Captain" Bowin, a miner. Prosecution witnesses continued on October 7 with statements from Elijah Tompkins and Tarbuck Ballard. Defendants then produced sixteen white witnesses, including Samuel Wiseman, attorney Stewart, and miners W. Reaves, age thirty; a Mr. Thorn, age thirty-five, and John Curley, age twenty-seven. A. Palmer, age twenty-one and listed as a mechanic, also testified for the Halls. Again we have no knowledge about the subject of their testimony. No objections were made by counsel.[36]

The trial had moved quickly. Saturday morning, October 8, Judge Barbour convened the court to hear summary arguments. The jury then departed under the watchful eye of Sheriff W. H. Endicott. There was some urgency to reaching a verdict, as it was the weekend and also the end of the court term. The jury debated all afternoon and evening, and finally at 2:00 a.m. Sunday morning they announced they had reached a verdict and returned to Judge Barbour's courtroom. No doubt he was pleased that a verdict had been reached, but the timing probably left him weary. The jury then announced that they had found John Hall not guilty, but they had concluded that George Hall was guilty of murdering Ling Sing. Not missing a beat, Judge Barbour ordered John freed immediately and George returned to the jail to be held for sentencing on November 19, when the judge would next return to Nevada City.[37]

As the weeks passed, Nevada City residents began to sense the specialness of this case. The local paper tried to contain the growing nervousness. On October 28 the *Nevada Journal* reported that a Chinese miner had been lynched near Diamond Springs. Whipped and his queue cut off, the young man had been rescued from death by other miners. The newspaper also editorialized that violence against the Chinese in San Francisco should be punished, and the editor applauded courts that enforced the law.[38] Then, on November 18, the day before the sentencing of George Hall, the *Nevada Journal* seemed to equivocate when it published this admonition: "The difficulty in rendering sentence [in *People v. Hall*] consists in the fact that the verdict was not brought in by the jury till after 12 o'clock midnight on the last day of the term, and it is contended a new trial (as held by some) should therefore be granted." No doubt John R. McConnell had visited the editor. Stating the obvious, the paper concluded, "The decision of the court is looked for with great interest."[39]

On November 19 Judge Barbour pronounced sentence on George Hall. The judge did not show mercy to the defendant. "George W. Hall," addressed the judge, "at the last September term of this court you were tried under an indictment for murder by a jury of your countrymen who were of your own selection. They, after a protracted and patient investigation of the case, rendered a verdict of 'guilty' as against you, and 'not guilty' as to your codefendant."[40] At this point the *Nevada Journal* reported that the prisoner was "greatly overcome by distress" in the standing-room-only courtroom. He righted himself, however, long enough to speak his mind. He gave no ground and maintained his innocence, vowing to introduce new evidence that would clear him if he was allowed and explaining his presence at the murder as bad luck and his conviction as prejudice against him by the lying Chinese witnesses.[41]

Judge Barbour was not impressed. "Of all things, the law is most regardful of the lives whom it governs; otherwise, there would be but little need of human laws to govern us in a state of society. They are instituted among mankind, the better to protect life, liberty, and property!" philosophized the judge. "Life is the immediate gift of God, and the right to enjoy this sacred and divine donation must ever remain inviolable with a free and well-governed people."[42] He sentenced George Hall to be hung on the morning of December 30, 1853.[43] Facing Hall, Judge Barbour offered no sympathy: "You have with malice and premeditation taken the life of Ling Sing, a Chinaman, for which the law imposes the penalty of death. This alone will satisfy the demands of the laws of your country, and expiate this offense with earthly requirements."[44]

He then challenged the young Ohioan. His hanging, the judge admonished, "will not satisfy or appease the wrath of that God who created you both [meaning Ling Sing and George Hall]. Mark it well! It is repentance, true and sincere repentance alone, [that] can entitle you to his mercy. I beseech you, to improve diligently the time left you, and seek forgiveness from that Divine Being who can alone pardon and save!"[45] Perhaps Judge Barbour was warning the defense lawyers as well, but they had none of his bluster. Four days later they filed notice of appeal, and Nevada County Clerk

W. S. Patterson sent off the trial record, such as it was, to the California Supreme Court in Sacramento.[46]

The California Supreme Court's Decision

Within days of Judge Barbour's sentence announcement, the citizenry of Nevada County stirred to action. The tone of local commentary turned bitter. "It is probable," projected the *Nevada Journal*, "a movement will be made by the court and the bar to obtain a commutation of the sentence." The *Journal* noticeably changed its language. It now referred to the Chinese as "celestials" and no longer viewed them as hard-working miners but as "well disposed" and frequently possessing fraudulent mining licenses.[47]

The new year brought no news regarding George Hall's appeal. It seemed to many that the California Supreme Court was dawdling and neglectful of justice. By August a petition was circulating in Nevada County urging the governor to pardon Hall. And the *Journal* worried about the health of the young murderer. He had already served a year in the county jail, and most of the community now seemed sympathetic to his plight. Many had forgotten the crime. The editor described the prisoner as "wasting away—dying by inches" and having "lost his sensibilities to humanity."[48]

Given this growing empathy for Hall, the *Nevada Journal* reminded its neighbors that a pardon was not appropriate because Hall could not be exonerated. Moreover, asking for a new trial with new evidence was insensitive and costly. Nevada County would no doubt be charged $3,000 for another trial of Hall, and the county had footed the bill for his incarceration since the initial trial at a cost of $100 a month. The public seemed restless and frustrated.[49]

Perhaps the California Supreme Court found itself in a dilemma. The trial record did not afford many opportunities for reversal. John R. McConnell, counsel for the defendant, had objected to the indictment in traditional ways, suggesting there were fundamental errors. But the objections left no means to embrace a broad policy, and the majority on the court wanted to take a stand against the Chinese. As a general history of Nevada County so perceptively observed in 1880, "No exception was taken to the admission of the testimony of the Chinese witnesses at the trial, and the record contained no evidence, except the Chinese names, that Chinamen had sworn in the case." Nevertheless, Chief Justice Hugh C. Murray would not be deterred, and together with Justice Solomon Heydenfelt, the court issued an opinion that assumed "the only question in the case was whether or not Chinese testimony was admissible."[50]

The California State Archives has no copies of any briefs prepared or notes of any lawyerly communications or oral arguments. All that remains is the seven-page opinion authored by Justice Murray and a brief one-sentence dissent from Justice Alexander Wells. The opinion, however, represents the utter depths to which the California Supreme Court, or perhaps any American court, would go to in order to oppress a racial minority, and it is worthy of careful analysis.

The very first sentence contains two possible errors, one of commission and one of omission. George W. Hall is termed "a free white citizen of this State." Hall had only recently arrived in California from Ohio. Attaining California citizenship in 1853 definitely was not a refined legal concept, but perhaps the court was thinking figuratively. He, according to the Court, "was convicted of murder upon the testimony of Chinese witnesses."[51] Yes, there is no doubt that Chinese material witnesses testified in Hall's trial, but so did white witnesses, and the record does not reveal what the witnesses said. No one on the jury stated it was the Chinese witnesses who swayed them. In the second paragraph, Chief Justice Murray reveals his agenda. "The point involved in this case, is the admissibility of such evidence," or in other words, whether Chinese could testify in American courts of law against whites.[52] The California Supreme Court ultimately determined that the Chinese did not have this right.

How the court reached this conclusion involves six pages of tortured logic. Justice Murray immediately established the statutory precedent for his holding. California laws in both civil and criminal proceedings prohibited Indians and African Americans from testifying as witnesses for or against a "white man." Mulattos were also prohibited from offering testimony against whites in criminal proceedings. Next the justice sought to explore what the California legislature meant by the racial terms *black*, *Negro*, *mulatto*, *Indian*, and *white*. After quickly dismissing four of the five categories, Justice Murray then spent two pages on the history and an amazing ethnology even for 1853 of American Indians.[53]

For the chief justice, Indians were Asians and more than likely Chinese. This was because Columbus thought he had landed on the island of San Salvador in the Chinese Sea. Since Columbus thought he was near India and the Native peoples he met physically resembled Mongolians, "Indians" seemed the correct term. Moreover, from 1492 to the present, "American Indians and the Mongolian, or Asiatic, were regarded as the same type of the human species."[54]

Shifting ground, Justice Murray then moved to a discussion of migration. He established as fact that Asiatics crossed the Bering Strait and eventually inhabited Mexico and South America. He considered the Indigenous of the Aleutian Islands and how they "resemble, in a remarkable degree, in language and appearance, both the inhabitants of Kamtschatka (who are admitted to be of the Mongolian type), and the Esquimaux [Eskimo], who again, in turn resemble other tribes of American Indians."[55] Thus the justice concluded that the name *Indian* meant the "Mongolian race."

Having concluded that the Chinese were in fact American Indians, the Chinese then could be prohibited under current California law from testifying against whites. But Chief Justice Murray went further and revealed his underlying prejudices in his concluding paragraphs. "The same rule which would admit them [the Chinese] to testify," worried the jurist, "would admit them to all the equal rights of citizenship, and we might soon see them at the polls, in the jury box, upon the bench, and in our legislative halls."[56] This, concluded Justice Murray, was a most serious business and "not a speculation which exists in the excited and over-heated imagination of the patriot and statesman, but it is an *actual and present danger*."[57] Chief Justice Hugh C. Murray was manning the barricades to stop the onward march of the Chinese to equality and citizenship.

Finally, the chief justice embraced the virulent racism growing exponentially within early California. The Chinese, he wrote in his last full paragraph of the opinion, represented the

> anomalous spectacle of a distinct people, living in our community, recognizing no laws of this State, except through necessity, bringing with them their prejudices and national feuds, in which they indulge in open violation of law; whose mendacity is proverbial; a race of people whom nature has marked as inferior, and who are incapable of progress

or intellectual development beyond a certain point, as their history has shown; differing in language, opinions, color, and physical conformation; between whom and ourselves nature has placed an impassable difference, is now presented, and for them is claim[ed], not only the right to swear away the life of a citizen, but the further privilege of participating with us in administering the affairs of our Government.[58]

Loners, violent, biased, liars, retarded, misshapen, and discolored, these miscreant aliens ought not be allowed to take away the life of an American citizen, reasoned California's highest-ranking judge, let alone participate in our democracy. Although they never met, George Hall had a friend and ally in Chief Justice Hugh Murray.

Justice Alexander Wells dissented, stating, "From the opinion of the Chief Justice, I most respectfully dissent."[59] Less than a month later, Justice Wells died in San Jose from an internal hemorrhage. The *Nevada Journal* noted his passing with as much venom as previously displayed by Chief Justice Murray: "The political and judicial course of this gentleman had so much lessened him [in] public opinion in this county that no regret has been expressed by any party of any shade of opinion." Rather, his death "has been looked upon as a providential partial purification of the Supreme Bench."[60]

Reaction to the California Supreme Court's decision varied. The *Nevada Journal* duly recorded that the clerk of the district court received a telegraphic dispatch from Sacramento announcing the reversal and possible retrial. S. W. Fletcher told the local paper that he likely would enter a *nolle prosequi* for the case. The primary white witness to the murder had died, and no Chinese testimony could be taken in a retrial. Thus George Hall essentially achieved his freedom. Editorialized the *Journal*, "Hall has had a severe lesson, and we trust it will be a profitable one to him. He is suddenly raised as if to life again, and has [an] opportunity to wipe out by a life of good conduct, the single yet deep stain of his former one."[61] And in case its readers had forgotten, Nevada City's weekly reminded them that the defendant had spent over a year in county jail, and court action, including the appeal to the supreme court, had cost thousands of dollars for the county.

What subsequently happened to the main participants in this legal drama? George Hall stayed in California and perhaps never returned to Ohio to see his family. He died in 1876. Whether he took the advice of Judge Barbour to heart is not known. His younger brother, John, was the subject of a civil lawsuit, probably in the 1860s, and was still listed as a miner in the *Nevada County Mining and Business Directory* in 1895. What happened to Samuel Wiseman is unknown. William Stewart resigned as Nevada County district attorney in 1854 and moved to the state of Nevada, where he embarked upon a very successful political career that took him to Washington, DC, as Nevada's "silver" senator. Judge Barbour, however, had numerous problems.

After *People v. Hall*, many in Nevada County wanted to rid themselves of their district judge. Because the area was fairly evenly balanced in terms of Whigs and Democrats, the next election seemed difficult. Moreover, Barbour had provoked a young, ambitious attorney in a case before his court, one Stephen J. Field, and in 1853 they nearly fought a deadly duel. Barbour opted to avoid the confrontation he had chosen. Thus the leading members of the bar and the county circulated a petition to create a new judicial district. This eventually moved Judge Barbour to Yuba County, where he continued to be very controversial. Judge Barbour in many ways was his own worst enemy, reportedly because of fits of alcoholism and debauchery. He became so difficult to work with and so unable to handle the demands of his position that he avoided making judicial pronouncements. When Judge Niles Searls took over the district court in Nevada County in 1855, he discovered a huge backlog of cases. Moreover, Judge Barbour himself was indicted for attempted murder and assault on a reporter who had called attention to his inabilities, and although he successfully dodged a California jail, he was forced from office in 1859 and reportedly left the state.[62]

What happened to the Chinese witnesses and particularly Chin Ying remains subject to conjecture. As for *People v. Hall*, Chinese merchants in San Francisco reacted strongly. They sought to separate themselves from Indians while at the same time admonishing the views of Chief Justice Murray. In a published broadside, the Chinese authors noted that the opinion of *People v. Hall* concluded, "We Chinese are the same as Indians and Negroes, and your courts will not allow us to bear witness." To this they objected, because Indians "know no mutual respect; they wear neither clothes nor shoes; they live in wild places and in caves." Instead the Chinese were known, they argued, for their advanced civilization, their dynasties of emperors, and their intelligence and enlightenment.[63]

California commentators recognized the weaknesses inherent within the opinion. In a letter to the editor of the *Nevada Journal* from one Oberon, the interested party asks, "Has a Chinaman any rights under our constitution?" The letter writer reiterates at length how wrongly California law has been interpreted with reference to the Chinese. "These wretched Asiatics," comments Oberon, "are made the victims under the color of law, of tyranny and oppression so flagrant, and outrageous, as to excite the indignation of the [sorr]iest serf in Christendom. They are beaten, abused, and, _____ I had almost said robbed, by the myrmidons of the law, and every avenue to redress is from the antipathies of the whites, remorselessly closed against them."[64]

Several decades later, historians preparing a Nevada County history boldly asserted that the *People v. Hall* decision was legally flawed and embarrassing. The court, wrote the historians, "without aid from the record," created a question about California law that had not been asked on appeal. Moreover, the justices then had complicated the issue with a self-serving racial ideology. "The ethnological reasoning by which the Court arrived at its conclusions," observed the unknown authors, "reads curiously enough, but this decision is standing evidence that the influx of Chinese was looked upon at that early day as a menace to our institutions."[65]

The Significance of *People v. Hall* (1854)

The impact of *People v. Hall* lasted for generations. In Nevada County and throughout California, Chinese found working within the American legal system difficult although not impossible. Having gone down the race road, California's highest court soon would be confronted with interpreting the Fourteenth Amendment for Chinese and African American relationships, and Nevada County again offered a complicated fact pattern. Moreover, just as in the twentieth century, Californians prideful of being on the cutting edge of societal developments set a standard that some states attempted to emulate in preventing accessibility for minorities to the American legal system. Eventually California confronted this grievous opinion and attempted to work out its race relationships, including rather than excluding the Chinese.

Those residing at the origins of *People v. Hall* knew well that adjusting to this opinion would mean miscarriages of justice. David Beesley, in his meticulous tracing of Chinese history in Nevada County, discovered two cases where crimes against Chinese men were dismissed because no white witnesses could be found. Another involved the murder of a Chinese woodcutter, Ah Ling, by a group of five whites who successfully prevented other whites from testifying against them.[66] Beesley examined a wide variety of county legal documents dating from 1850 to 1920, and he found the Chinese continued to interact with the legal system at the local level, particularly in criminal and civil law cases, marriage certifications, and business law. Here local justices and leaders within the legal system tried to move around *People v. Hall* when they could so in order to afford Chinese fairness. While acts of violence against the Chinese in Nevada County all too often went unprosecuted, the Chinese who continued to migrate until the 1880s refused passivity and pursued their rights.[67]

Elsewhere in California and the American West, *People v. Hall* provided meaningful legal precedent for anti-Chinese actions. California observers noted that the 1854 decision of the California Supreme Court was directly responsible for "many of those lawless and unjust acts that have furnished such a disgraceful chapter in the history of the state."[68] The Chinese had no protection in courts of law, and this spread throughout county and municipal governments. In short, "unprincipled whites" committed crimes against the Chinese with abandon, as long as there were no other but Chinese witnesses.

The California Supreme Court soon found itself in demand to refine its skewed concepts of race relations. The *Hall* ruling was first extended to civil cases in 1859,[69] and then, to determine a color test for mixed-bloods in 1860, the court defined the concept of "Chinese mestizoes." In *People v. Howard*, new chief justice Stephen J. Field, who would go on to fame on the US Supreme Court, embraced *People v. Hall* and noted harshly, "It is possible... that instances may arise where, upon this construction, crime may go unpunished. If this be so, it is only [a] matter for the consideration of the Legislature."[70]

Finally, in 1863 the California legislature did act, codifying *People v. Hall* into statutory law. In an amendment to the previous exclusionary act, new language—"No Chinese shall be permitted to give evidence in favor or against any white man"—accomplished Justice Murray's dicta.[71] This, however, had to be amended, and the California Supreme Court met that challenge when it ironically was called upon once again by an appeal from Nevada County.

In 1867 an African American named George Washington attempted to rob several Chinese miners near the settlement of Grass Valley southwest of Nevada City. The Chinese overcame him, and when his case came to trial, Washington claimed that as a citizen of the United States and because of the Fourteenth Amendment and *People v. Hall*, Chinese witnesses could not testify against him. District Court judge T. B. McFarland agreed with this argument, and on appeal to the California Supreme Court the justices sustained the lower court decision.[72] Now the court determined that black Californians were in fact white Californians under the new Civil War amendments and the Civil Rights Act, and thus African Americans were also covered under the *Hall* doctrine. California for legal purposes had determined that Chinese were Indians and blacks were whites.

Other states in the American West also succumbed to the anti-Chinese hysteria of the 1870s to 1890s, and they too passed laws putting special restrictions on Chinese abilities to give testimony in courts. When challenged, these states could always argue that they had adopted reasonable restrictions rather than total exclusion, as had California. No other state adopted California's *Hall* doctrine for the Chinese, but Minnesota, Washington, and Nebraska prohibited Native American testimony against whites, and when the Nebraska Supreme Court was asked to adopt *People v. Hall* as a precedent for a case involving Japanese testimony, it refused to do so.[73]

Eventually even California reversed *People v. Hall*. It did so with changes in its law codes in the 1870s. Section 1321 of the Penal Code of 1872 ended the racial exclusionary rule. California altered its restrictions on Chinese testimony only after a federal district court judge in San Francisco interpreted the Fourteenth Amendment to allow Chinese to testify against whites.[74]

After the explosion of anti-Chinese violence throughout the American West and the US Congress's passage of Chinese exclusion legislation in 1882, 1892, and 1902, John Henry Wigmore, the leading Gilded Age legal thinker on the laws of evidence, tried in 1904 to explain why California adopted the legal conclusions in *People v. Hall*, subsequently passed related statutes, and issued further judicial interpretations. Wrote Wigmore, "The condition of public feeling in that community against the economic encroachments of Chinese laborers explains and extenuates (while it may not excuse) this blunder in the policy of the testimonial law."[75] The fallout and legal impact of an 1853 murder in the goldfields of Nevada County, California, had truly stretched beyond reason the legal underpinnings so essential to the building of a harmonious multiracial society in the nineteenth-century American West.

Appendix

People v. Hall
4 Cal 399 (1854)

THE PEOPLE, respondent, V. GEORGE W. HALL, appellant. [399]

WITNESS—PERSONS INCOMPETENT.—Section 394 of the Civil Practice Act provides: "No Indian or Negro shall be allowed to testify as a witness in any action in which a white person is a party."

[76]IDEM. —Section 14 of the Criminal Act provides: "No Black, or Mulatto person, or Indian shall be allowed to give evidence in favor of, or against a White man." *Held*, that the words, Indian, Negro, Black and White, are generic terms, designating race. That, therefore, Chinese and all other peoples not white, are included in the prohibition from being witnesses against Whites.

Mr. Ch. J. MURRAY delivered the opinion of the Court. Mr. J. HEYDENFELDT concurred.

The appellant, a free white citizen of this State, was convicted of murder upon the testimony of Chinese witnesses.

The point involved in this case is the admissibility of such evidence.

The 394th section of the Act Concerning Civil Cases provides that no Indian or Negro shall be allowed to testify as a witness in any action or proceeding in which a White person is a party.

The 14th section of the Act of April 16th, 1850, regulating Criminal Proceedings, provides that "No Black or Mulatto person, or Indian, shall be allowed to give evidence in favor of, or against a white man."

The true point at which we are anxious to arrive is the legal signification of the words "Black, Mulatto, Indian and White person," and whether the Legislature adopted them as generic terms, or intended to limit their application to specific types of the human species.

Before considering this question, it is proper to remark the difference between the two sections of our statute, already quoted, the latter being more broad and comprehensive in its exclusion, by use of the word "Black," instead of Negro.

[400] *Conceding, however, for the present, that the word "Black," as used in the 14th section, and "Negro," in 394th, are convertible terms, and that the former was intended to include the latter, let us proceed to inquire who are excluded from testifying as witnesses under the term "Indian."

When Columbus first landed upon the shores of this continent, in his attempt to discover a western passage to the Indies, he imagined that he had accomplished the object of his expedition, and that the Island of San Salvador was one of those Islands of the Chinese Sea, lying near the extremity of India, which had been described by navigators.

Acting upon this hypothesis, and also perhaps from the similarity of features and physical conformation, he gave to the Islanders the name of Indians, which appellation was universally adopted, and extended to the aboriginals of the New World, as well as of Asia.

From that time, down to a very recent period, the American Indians and the Mongolian, or Asiatic, were regarded as the same type of the human species.

In order to arrive at a correct understanding of the intention of our Legislature, it will be necessary to go back to the early history of legislation on this subject, our statute being only a transcript of those of older States.

At the period from which this legislation dates, those portions of Asia which include India proper, the Eastern Archipelago, and the countries washed by the Chinese waters, as far as then known, were denominated the Indies, from which the inhabitants had derived the generic name of Indians.

Ethnology, at that time, was unknown as a distinct science, or if known, had not reached that high point of perfection which it has since attained by the scientific inquiries and discoveries of the master minds of the last half century. Few speculations had been made with regard to the moral or physical differences between the different races of mankind. These were general in their character, and limited to those visible and palpable variations which could not escape the attention of the most common observer.

The general, or perhaps universal, opinion of that day was that there were but three distinct types of [401] the human species, which, in their turn, were subdivided into varieties of tribes. This opinion is still held by many scientific writers, and is supported by Cuvier, one of the most eminent naturalists of modern times.

Many ingenious speculations have been resorted to for the purpose of sustaining this opinion. It has been supposed, and not without plausibility, that this continent was first peopled by Asiatics, who crossed Behring's Straits, and from thence found their way down to the more fruitful climates of Mexico and South America. Almost every tribe has some tradition of coming from the North, and many of them, that their ancestors came from some remote country beyond the ocean.

From the eastern portions of Kamchatka, the Aleutian Islands form a long and continuous group, extending eastward to that portion of the North American Continent inhabited by the Esquimaux. They appear to be a continuation of the lofty volcanic ranges which traverse the two continents, and are inhabited by a race who resemble, in a remarkable degree, in language and appearance, both the inhabitants of Kamtschatka (who are admitted to be of the Mongolian type), and the Esquimaux, who again, in turn, resemble other tribes of American Indians. The similarity of the skull and pelvis, and the general configuration of the two races; the remarkable resemblance in eyes, beard, hair, and other peculiarities, together with the contiguity of the two continents, might well have led to the belief that this country was first peopled by the Asiatics, and that the difference between the different tribes and the parent stock was such as would necessarily arise from the circumstances of climate, pursuits, and other physical causes, and was no greater than that existing between the Arab and the European, both of whom were supposed to belong to the Caucasian race.

Although the discoveries of eminent archeologists, and the researches of modern geologists, have given to this continent an antiquity of thousands of years anterior to the evidence of man's existence, and the light of modern science may have shown conclusively that it was not [402] people by the inhabitants of Asia, but that the Aborigines are a distinct type, and as such claim a distinct origin, still, this would not in any degree, alter the meaning of the term, and render that specific which was before generic.

To argue such a proposition would be an insult [403] to the good sense of the Legislature.

We have adverted to these speculations for the purpose of showing that the name of Indian, from the time of Columbus to the present day, has been used to designate, not alone the North American Indian, but the whole of the Mongolian race, and that the name, though first applied probably through mistake, was afterwards continued as appropriate on account of the supposed common origin.

That this was the common opinion in the early history of American legislation cannot be disputed, and, therefore, all legislation upon the subject must have borne relation to that opinion.

Can, then, the use of the word "Indian," because at the present day it may be sometimes regarded as a specific, and not as a generic term, alter this conclusion? We think not; because at the origin of the legislation we are considering, it was used and admitted in its common and ordinary acceptation, as a generic term, distinguishing the great Mongolian race, and as such, its meaning then became fixed by law, and in construing statutes the legal meaning of words must be preserved.

Again: the words of the Act must be construed in *pari materia*. It will not be disputed that "White" and "Negro" are generic terms, and refer to two of the great types of mankind. If these, as well as the word "Indian," are not to be regarded as generic terms, including the two great races which they were intended to designate, but only specific, and applying to those whites and Negroes who were inhabitants of this continent at the time of the passage of the Act, the most anomalous consequences would ensue. The European white man who comes here would not be shielded from the testimony of the degraded and demoralized caste, while the Negro, fresh from the coast of Africa, or the Indian of Patagonia, the Kanaka, South Sea Islander, or New Hollander, would be admitted, upon their arrival, to testify against white citizens in our courts of law.

The evident intention of the Act was to throw around the citizen a protection for life and property, which could only be secured by removing him above the corrupting influences of degraded castes.

It can hardly be supposed that any Legislature would attempt this by excluding domestic negroes and Indians, who not infrequently have correct notions of their obligations to society, and turning loose upon the community the more degraded tribes of the same species, who have nothing in common with us, in language, country or laws.

We have, thus far, considered this subject on the hypothesis that the 14th section of the Act Regulating Criminal Proceedings and the 394th section of the Practice Act, were the same.

As before remarked, there is a wide difference between the two. The word "black" may include all negroes, but the term "negro" does not include all black persons.

By the use of this term in this connection, we understand it to mean the opposite of "white," and that it should be taken as contradistinguished from all white persons.

In using the words "no black or mulatto person, or Indian shall be allowed to give evidence for or against a white person," the Legislature, if any attention can be ascribed to it, adopted the most comprehensive terms to embrace every known class or shade of color, as the apparent design was to protect the white person from the influence of all testimony other than that of persons of the same caste. The use of these terms must, by every sound rule of construction, exclude every one who is not of white blood.

The Act of Congress, in defining what description of aliens may become naturalized citizens, provides that every "free white citizen," etc., etc. In speaking of this subject, Chancellor Kent says that "the Act confines the description to 'white' citizens, and that it is a matter of doubt, whether, under this provision, any of the tawny races of Asia can be admitted to citizenship." (2 Kent's Com. 72.)

We are not disposed to leave this question in any [404] doubt. The word "white" has a distinct signification, which *ex vi termini*, excludes black, yellow, and all other colors. It will be observed, by reference to the first section of the second Article of the Constitution of this State, that none but white males can become electors, except in the case of Indians, who may be admitted by special Act of the Legislature. On examination of the constitutional debates, it will be found that not a little difficulty existed in selecting these precise words, which were finally agreed upon as the most comprehensive that could be suggested to exclude all inferior races.

If the term "white," as used in the Constitution, was not understood in its generic sense as including the Caucasian race, and necessarily excluding all others, where was the necessity of providing for the admission of Indians to the privilege of voting, by special legislation?

We are of the opinion that the words "white," "negro," "mulatto," "Indian," and "black person," wherever they occur in our Constitution and laws, must be taken in their generic sense, and that, even admitting the Indian of this continent is not of the Mongolian type, that the words "black person," in the

14th section, must be taken as contradistinguished from white, and necessarily excludes all races other than Caucasian.

We have carefully considered all the consequences resulting from a different rule of construction, and are satisfied that even in a doubtful case, we would be impelled to this decision on grounds of public policy.

The same rule which would admit them to testify, would admit them to all the equal rights of citizenship, and we might soon see them at the polls, in the jury box, upon the bench, and in our legislative halls.

This is not a speculation which exists in the excited and over-heated imagination of the patriot and statesman, but it is an actual and present danger.

The anomalous spectacle of a distinct people, living in our community, recognizing no laws of this State, except through necessity, bringing with them their prejudices and national feuds, in which they indulge in open violation of law; whose mendacity is proverbial; a race of [405] people whom nature has marked as inferior, and who are incapable of progress or intellectual development beyond a certain point, as their history has shown; differing in language, opinions, color, and physical conformation; between whom and ourselves nature has placed an impassable difference, is now presented, and for them is claimed, not only the right to swear away the life of a citizen, but the further privilege of participating with us in administering the affairs of our Government.

These facts were before the Legislature that framed this Act, and have been known as matters of public history to every subsequent Legislature.

There can be no doubt as to the intention of the Legislature, and that if it had ever been anticipated that this class of people were not embraced in the prohibition, then such specific words would have been employed as would have put the matter beyond any possible controversy.

For these reasons, we are of opinion that the testimony was inadmissible.

The judgment is reversed and the cause remanded.

Mr. Justice WELLS dissented, as follows:

From the opinion of the Chief Justice, I most respectfully dissent.

Notes

I am most grateful for the research advice, writings, manuscript materials, and thoughtful conversations of Wallace Hagaman, Nevada City, California, a first-rate historian of the Chinese experience in America, and for financial support from the Rawley Fund of the Department of History, University of Nebraska-Lincoln.

1. The *Nevada (CA) Journal*, August 9, 1853, first reported the murder of Ling Sing on the very day the body was discovered. Subsequent issues sparsely covered the trial, and the November 25, 1853, issue includes a unique complete accounting of the sentencing. See also David Beesley, "More Than *People v. Hall*: Chinese Immigrants and American Law in a Sierra Nevada County, 1850-1920," *Locus* 3 (Spring 1991):123-39, esp. 123-26; and David Allan Comstock, *Brides of the Gold Rush: The Nevada County Chronicles, 1854-1859* (Grass Valley, CA: Comstock Bonanza Press, 1987), 144-45, 162-72.
2. *Nevada Journal*, November 25, 1853.
3. Ibid.
4. Comstock, *Brides of the Gold Rush*, 162.
5. *Nevada Journal*, November 25, 1853. Also quoted in part in Comstock, *Brides of the Gold Rush*, 145.
6. For example, Patricia Nelson Limerick gives due attention to *People v. Hall* in *The Legacy of Conquest: The Unbroken Past of the American West* (New York: Norton, 1987), 261-62. Chinese legal rights, without mention of this landmark case, are considered in other recent surveys, such as Lawrence M. Friedman, *A History of American Law*, 2nd ed. (New York: Simon and Schuster, 1985), 350-51, 509-10; Kermit L. Hall, *The Magic Mirror: Law in American History* (New York: Oxford University Press, 1989), 146-49, 157, 248, 264; Richard White, *"It's Your Misfortune and None of My Own": A New History of the American West* (Norman: University of Oklahoma Press, 1993), 282-84, 323; Roger Daniels, *Asian America: Chinese and Japanese in the United States since 1850* (Seattle: University of Washington Press, 1988); and Gordon Morris Bakken, ed., *Law in the Western United States* (Norman: University of Oklahoma Press, 2000), 496-505.
7. For two of the best of several recent publications documenting and analyzing the history of the California gold rush, see Susan Lee Johnson, *Roaring Camp: The Social World of the California Gold Rush* (New York: W. W. Norton, 2000); and Malcolm J. Rohrbough, *Days of Gold: The California Gold Rush and the American Nation* (Berkeley: University of California Press, 1997). See also Juanita Kennedy Browne, *Nuggets of Nevada County History*, 5th ed. (Nevada City, CA: Nevada County Historical Society, 1992), 1-6.
8. Aaron Augustus Sargent, *1848-1851, 150 Years Ago, "A Sketch of Nevada County,"* reprint arranged, illustrated, and annotated by David Allan Comstock (Grass Valley, CA: Nevada County Sesquicentennial, 1998), 1-2, 5-6.

9. Hank Meals, *Columbia Hill: Nevada County, California, an Interpretive History* (Nevada City, CA: Susan Lamela, 1998), 5–6.
10. Ibid., 25–27; Harley M. Leete Jr., *Sketches of the Gold Country*, reprint with additional text by Robert M. Wyckoff (1938; Nevada City, CA: Nevada City Publishers, 1998), 7–10.
11. Sargent, *1848–1851*, 8–11; Meals, *Columbia Hill*, 35–36; Gil Richards, *Historic Sites of the California Mother Lode* (Redwood City, CA: Copperline, 1998), 50–51.
12. Meals, *Columbia Hill*, 29–31; Paul D. Morrison, ed. and comp., *Placer Gold Deposits of the Sierra Nevada* (Baldwin Park, CA: Gem Guides Book Co., 1997), 106–7.
13. *Thompson and West's History of Nevada County, California, with Illustrations, 1880*, reprinted with an introduction by W. Turrentine Jackson (Berkeley, CA: Howell North Books, 1970), 104–5; Sargent, *1848–1851*, 8–11; Meals, *Columbia Hill*, 35–36; and Richards, *Historic Sites*, 50–51.
14. Meals, *Columbia Hill*, 13; Browne, *Nuggets of Nevada County History*, 28; and *Nevada City, California, Chinese Quarter* (Tahoe National Forest, Nevada County Arts Council, and Nevada City Chinese Quarter Society, 1999). The 1852 California census totals for Nevada County do not match the actual manuscript census totals. The manuscript census totals 19,498 persons with 6,909 readable names, 7,098 unreadable names, 5,407 Chinese not specifically named, 81 African Americans, and 3 Indians. This is a substantially different total. See David Allan Comstock and Ardis Hatten Comstock, eds., *Nevada County Vital Statistics, 1850–1869*, Nevada County Pioneer Series, vol. 1 (Grass Valley, CA: Comstock Bonanza Press, 1996).
15. US Census, *Eighth Census, Population of the U.S. in 1860*, table 3, "Population of Cities and Towns," 31; US Census, *Ninth Census*, table 3, "Population of Civil Divisions Less than Counties," 91, quoted in Thomas Arthur Deeble, "A History of Two Chinatowns in Grass Valley and Nevada City" (MA thesis, San Francisco State College, 1972), table 10, "Townships in Nevada County and Their Populations," 73; Browne, *Nuggets of Nevada County History*, 28.
16. Meals, *Columbia Hill*, 8–17; Browne, *Nuggets of Nevada County History*, 23–28; Tanis Chapman Thorne, preface to "Indians of Nevada City in 1854," typescript pamphlet of letter, W. P. Crenshaw, Navada [sic] City, CA, to F. J. Henley, superintendent of Indian affairs, Washington, DC, December 16, 1854, National Archives, record group 75, microfilm 234, Letters Received by Office of Indian Affairs, 1824–1881, roll 64.
17. George D. Dornin, *Thirty Years Ago, 1849–1879: Gold Rush Memories of a Daguerreotype Artist*, ed. Peter E. Palmquist (Nevada City: Carl Mautz, 1995), 44–47.
18. Robert E. Levinson, "The History of the Jews of Grass Valley, Nevada City and Vicinity," *Nevada County Historical Society Bulletin* 25 (July 1971): 1–8.
19. Meals, *Columbia Hill*, 103–6; *Nevada City, California, Chinese Quarter*; David

Beesley, "The Chinese and the Nevada County Narrow Gauge Railroad," *Nevada County Historical Society Bulletin*, Special Chinese Collection no. SC-1 (1993), 1–2; Wallace R. Hagaman, *Chinese Temples of Nevada City and Grass Valley, California, 18690–1938* (Nevada City, CA: Cowboy Press, 1999), 4–6; Silvia Anne Sheafer, *Chinese and the Gold Rush* (Glendale: Historical California Journal Publications, 1998), 22–23; Patrick Tinloy, "Nevada County's Chinese in Two Parts: Part I—Prior to 1900," *Nevada County Historical Society Bulletin* 25 (January 1971): 2–3; Lucile Eaves, "A History of California Labor Legislation with an Introductory Sketch of the San Francisco Labor Movement," *University of California Publications in Economics* 2 (August 1910): 105–13.

20. Olive Newell, *Tail of the Elephant: The Emigrant Experience on the Truckee Route of the California Trail, 1844–1852* (Nevada City, CA: Nevada County Historical Society, 1997), 255.
21. Ibid. See also pages 141, 258, 275, 278, 312, and 346 for other immigrant experiences in the Bear Valley and on Greenhorn Creek.
22. Ibid., 256.
23. Rohrbough, *Days of Gold*, 38–39.
24. Ibid., 39, 43, 73.
25. *Nevada Journal*, August 5, 1853; Beesley, "More Than *People v. Hall*," 123.
26. *Nevada Journal*, August 12, 1853.
27. Ibid., August 19 and 26, 1853.
28. Ibid., November 25, 1853; also quoted in Beesley, "More Than *People v. Hall*," 123.
29. "The People of the State of California against George W. Hall, John E. C. Hall, and Lemuel Wiseman in the Court of Sessions of the County of Nevada, August Term of Said Court, 1853," grand jury indictment, 1–4, Nevada City, CA, Index to Records of California Supreme Court Cases, H–Q Defendants, 47, in *People v. George W. Hall*, box 148, file 7158, California State Archives, Sacramento (hereinafter referred to as George W. Hall Collection, California State Archives).
30. "People of the State of California v. George W. Hall, John E. C. Hall, and Lemuel Wiseman," preliminary hearing, Tenth Judicial District Court, Judge William Barbour presiding, September 22, 1853, Nevada City, CA, in George W. Hall Collection, California State Archives. See also Comstock, *Brides of the Gold Rush*, 144.
31. "People of the State of California v. George W. Hall, John E. C. Hall, and Lemuel Wiseman," demurrers prepared by James R. McConnell, Buckner S. Hill, and J. S. Carpenter, formally filed with the Tenth Judicial District Court, September 30, 1853, 1–2, in George W. Hall Collection, California State Archives.
32. "People of State of California v. George W. Hall, John E. C. Hall, and Lemuel Wiseman," demurrers hearing, September 30, 1853, Nevada City, CA, in George W. Hall Collection, California State Archives.

33. *Nevada Journal*, October 7, 1853; "People of the State of California v. George W. Hall and John E. C. Hall," murder trial record, October 4, 1853, Nevada City, CA, in George W. Hall Collection, California State Archives.
34. California State Census, 1852, Nevada County, in Comstock and Comstock, *Nevada County Vital Statistics*, 92, 100, 126; *Nevada Journal*, August 26, 1853; "People of the State of California v. George W. Hall and John E. C. Hall," October 5, 1853, Nevada City, CA, in George W. Hall Collection, California State Archives.
    Hopefully Speer's translations were more accurate than his recollections of the testimony he sent to a friend: "Two brothers named Hall (from Illinois or Indiana) and a person named Wiseman were 'prospecting' on Bear River. Near sundown, on the 9th of August, they came upon a Chinese camp. The Halls, with little or no provocation, fell upon and cruelly beat one of the Chinese whom they met alone, and as he says, searched him for gold, though without obtaining any. The man, as soon as released, fled crying for help 'to save his life.' The Americans started upon his track, carrying their baggage and rifles. As they passed by some tents at a little distance, the cousin of the man, hearing his cries, ran out, and was immediately shot down by the elder Hall." This factual description of the murder contradicts virtually all other sources, including the indictment. See Comstock, *Brides of the Gold Rush*, 144–45.
35. "People of the State of California v. George W. Hall and John E. C. Hall," October 5, 1853, Nevada City, CA, in George W. Hall Collection, California State Archives.
36. Ibid., October 6–7, 1853; Comstock and Comstock, *Nevada County Vital Statistics*, 52, 57, 88, 93, 121–23.
37. "People of the State of California v. George W. Hall and John E. C. Hall," October 8–9, 1853, Nevada City, CA, including jury verdict, in George W. Hall Collection, California State Archives.
38. *Nevada Journal*, October 28, 1853.
39. Ibid., November 18, 1853.
40. Ibid., November 25, 1853.
41. Ibid.
42. Ibid.
43. "People of the State of California v. George W. Hall," death sentence, November 19, 1853, Nevada City, CA, in George W. Hall Collection, California State Archives.
44. *Nevada Journal*, November 25, 1853.
45. Ibid.
46. "People of State of California v. George W. Hall," notice of appeal by J. R. McConnell, receipt by William Stewart, November 23, 1853, Nevada City, CA, and receipt of records sent to the California state supreme court by clerk W. S. Patterson, November 30, 1853, Nevada City, CA, in George W. Hall Collection, California State Archives.
47. *Nevada Journal*, November 25, and December 9, 1853.
48. Ibid., August 4, 1854.

49. Ibid.
50. *Thompson and West's History of Nevada County*, 103.
51. *People v. George W. Hall*, 4 Cal 399–405 at 399 (1854).
52. Ibid.
53. Ibid., 399–400.
54. Ibid., 400.
55. Ibid., 401.
56. Ibid., 404.
57. Ibid., 405, italics added.
58. Ibid., 405.
59. Ibid.
60. *Nevada Journal*, November 3, 1854.
61. Ibid., October 7, 1854.
62. Comstock, *Brides of the Gold Rush*, 144–45, 162–64, 171, 184, 220, 392, 397–400, 409; David Allan Comstock, *Gold Diggers and Camp Followers* (Grass Valley, CA: Comstock Bonanza Press, 1982), 337.
63. *Remarks of the Chinese Merchants of San Francisco* (San Francisco: Whitton, Towne, 1855), 5–6.
64. *Nevada Journal*, October 30, 1857.
65. *Thompson and West's History of Nevada County*, 103.
66. *People v. G. W. Getchell et. al.*, Searls Historical Library, Nevada City, CA, Cab. 5-4263, noted in Beesley, "More Than *People v. Hall*," 125–26.
67. Ibid., 138–39.
68. Eaves, "History of California Labor Legislation," 114.
69. *Speer v. See Yup Company*, 13 Cal 73 (1859). See also John R. Wunder, "Chinese in Trouble: Criminal Law and Race on the Trans-Mississippi West Frontier," *Western Historical Quarterly* 17 (January 1986): 25–41.
70. *People v. Howard*, 17 Cal 64 at 65 (1860).
71. Cal. Statutes, chap. 70 (1863). See also J. A. C. Grant, "Testimonial Exclusion Because of Race: A Chapter in the History of Intolerance in California," *UCLA Law Review* 17 (November 1969): 192–201.
72. *People v. Washington*, 36 Cal 568 (1869). See also Beesley, "More Than *People v. Hall*," 126–27; Grant, "Testimonial Exclusion," 198–201; and Wunder, "Chinese in Trouble," 40.
73. For a full discussion of these legal points, see Wunder, "Chinese in Trouble," 32–40, with particular reference to notes 33 and 70.
74. Grant, "Testimonial Exclusion," 200–201; Wunder, "Chinese in Trouble," 40; Eaves, "History of California Labor Legislation," 114, quoting California, *Code of Civil Procedure* (1872), 493–94.
75. John Henry Wigmore, *A Treatise on the System of Evidence in Trials at Common Law* (Boston: Brown, 1904), 646–47.
76. Cited in *Speer v. See Yup Co.*, 13 Cal 73; *People v. Elyea*, 14 Cal 146. See *People v. Washington*, 36 Cal 658; *People v. Brady*, 40 Cal 198; *People v. McGuire*, 45 Cal 56.

CHAPTER 4

The Chinese and California

A Torturous Legal Relationship

John R. Wunder and Clare V. McKanna Jr.

NINETEENTH-CENTURY CALIFORNIA WAS not an easy place to live for most Chinese. The industrialized society emerging in the post–Civil War American West dictated sacrifices on the part of many westerners, and for Californians, the Chinese represented a group whose presence required physical and legal sacrifices. Chinese were found throughout California in both rural and urban settings. The greatest concentration of Chinese were in two cities, San Francisco and Sacramento, and it is here where the legal battles were most intense.

The history of American law and the Chinese is a relatively new topic for scholarly investigation. Recently a number of articles have been published on Chinese American legal history, and several monographs have appeared that deal with specific events, although they are approached primarily as immigration and labor history. The most comprehensive book to date on the legal treatment of the Chinese at the state and local level is Charles J. McClain's *In Search of Equality: The Chinese Struggle against Discrimination in Nineteenth-Century America* (Berkeley: University of California Press, 1994). It is this book and the treatment of Chinese in California's legal system at the state and local level that are the subject of this review essay.

Chinese immigrants in America came first to California. It was here where most Chinese chose to stay, and it was here where the Chinese experienced the first discriminatory actions of a majority society and the first of what would be a series of legal battles to obtain equality.

Charles McClain describes in detail how these struggles were met by the Chinese. His meticulous research, some of which utilizes sources never before consulted by American scholars, establishes two much-needed purposes for his book. Of primary importance is the correction of the historical distortions of Chinese reactions to legal discrimination. Writes McClain, "The conventional wisdom concerning the Chinese and their supposed political backwardness needs to be stood on its head."[1] McClain shows how Chinese litigants, Chinese merchant organizations, and the Chinese consulate in San Francisco were closely involved in legislative debates at the local and state levels and in litigation, including important tests before the US Supreme Court and the California Supreme Court. Because of this sophisticated political action, Chinese in California and elsewhere avoided even worse treatments than were accorded them by legal bodies. "To ignore Chinese legal initiatives is, as well, to ignore an important facet of US constitutional history in general," explains McClain.[2]

A related objective for McClain is placing legal battles involving the Chinese within a historical framework that includes the Chinese. This framework elevates the Chinese perspective. Past treatments of American constitutional history rarely if ever considered the Chinese role or motivation behind such test cases as *Yick Wo v. Hopkins*, for example, and this requires a correction in order to understand the full story.

McClain thus offers a kind of legal history never before written. He shows how the Chinese in California and particularly in San Francisco attempted to confront legal discrimination and extralegal violence. *In Search of Equality* is divided into four parts. The first explores the initial Chinese responses to California's anti-Chinese laws. Part 2 considers the crucial decade of anti-Chinese violence and legislation in California, the 1880s. The focus then shifts to laundry litigation, where the Chinese sought to defeat anti-Chinese forces. The third part continues a discussion of the legal developments of the 1880s, combining local California resistance to national legislation, particularly the exclusion acts. Anti-Chinese violence in San Francisco is addressed. The final section considers two separate discriminatory actions on the part of California and San Francisco authorities: attempts to segregate Chinese residents and actions to destroy Chinatown under the guise of sanitary ordinances and a bubonic plague scare.

Thus, this is a most welcome book.[3] *In Search of Equality* represents a pathbreaking scholarly analysis of the Chinese legal historical experience in urban California. Other recent works have helped explain rural legal experiences, such as Sucheng Chan's *This Bittersweet Soil: The Chinese in California Agriculture, 1860–1910* and Sandy Lydon's *Chinese Gold: The Chinese in the Monterey Bay Region*, and Lucy Salyer's recently published book treats fully the Chinese immigrant experience with federal immigration officials and the federal district court in San Francisco.[4] Yet the urban legal experience has received less attention. How state and local governments sought to restrain the Chinese in Sacramento and San Francisco are important aspects of this story.

An inflammatory headline reading "A Highbinder War / Two Mongolians Laid Out in the Battle / The City Prison Filled with Murderous Mongols" appeared in the June 1892 *Sacramento Bee*.[5] It reveals the racial prejudice against Asians harbored by newspaper editors and the general public in nineteenth-century Sacramento. This and numerous other racially charged headlines helped create a myth—the Asian as barbarian.[6] Newspaper editors and reporters used a number of terms to characterize the Chinese as a criminal element, but *highbinder* appeared to be their favorite.[7]

The story accompanying the headline suggested that the Chinese involved in a homicide that occurred on Third Street between I and J Streets in Sacramento were members of a secret society employed to kill two Chinese businessmen. Homicide seemed to be a common occurrence and, in this case, a fight between two rival Chinese groups ended with Yee Kie and Lee Gong lying dead on a Sacramento street.[8] This type of "secret society" killing,[9] however, was not a typical Asian homicide in California during the nineteenth century.

Recent research has opened a dialogue on the fairness accorded Asians within criminal justice systems in the American West.[10] While there is scholarship on the treatment of Chinese in California, especially during the gold rush,[11] and their experiences within the criminal justice system, the treatment of Asians accused of homicide during the nineteenth century remains largely undocumented.[12] The notoriety of homicide points to rich sources on criminal behavior—coroner's inquests, court indictments, criminal records, and newspaper accounts. Relying mainly on statistical data collected from these records in Sacramento County, California; an assessment of the treatment of Asians accused of homicide during the period 1850–1900;

the treatment of non-Asian defendants accused of killing Asians; and a comparison of Sacramento County aggregate homicide rates with similar data for three other California counties—Calaveras, San Joaquin, and Tuolumne—will provide a wider context for evaluation of the Chinese experience with American law.[13]

The city of Sacramento lies in the Great Valley where the American and Sacramento Rivers join before flowing westward to the San Francisco Bay. During the mid-nineteenth century, Sacramento served as a major supply center for miners headed for the gold camps. Sparked by the gold rush and the later development of the transcontinental railroad, the city's population grew rapidly, from 9,087 in 1850 to 24,142 by 1860. Sacramento's population stabilized before jumping significantly to 34,390 in 1880 and then increased gradually to 45,914 by the end of the nineteenth century. The population within Sacramento County included a significant segment of Asians (table 4). Although comparatively small during the first two decades, the Asian population grew to 13.4 and 14.2 percent of the total population, respectively, for the decades 1870 and 1880. By 1900 the Asian percentage had declined to 9.7 percent.

In Sacramento County, Asians were more likely than any other racial group to kill within their own race. Of thirty-eight cases involving Asians as perpetrators in Sacramento County, only one involved a non-Asian victim, and the perpetrator in that case was never specifically identified.[14] Fifty-eight Asians were indicted for murder in these thirty-eight cases, but charges against twenty defendants were dismissed. This high number of indictments that ended in dismissals reflects the tendency by law enforcement officials to "round up the usual suspects." Indictment information and newspaper accounts suggest that Sacramento police often arrested any suspicious-looking Chinese within the vicinity of the crime.[15]

The typical Asian homicide almost always occurred in Sacramento's Chinatown,[16] tended to be an affair between two males,[17] and was accomplished with a handgun.[18] For example, around 11:00 a.m. on March 1, 1873, Ah Fat met Ah Quong on the southwest corner of I and Third Streets and quarreled over an Asian woman who had allegedly been abducted. Ah Fat pulled a revolver and shot Ah Quong, who died within minutes. Police in the vicinity quickly apprehended Ah Fat, seized his weapon, and placed him in jail. With the aid of eyewitnesses, a jury found Ah Fat guilty and sentenced him to life in prison.[19] A similar shooting occurred in the same vicinity a month later involving Ah Ow, a cousin of Ah Quong. In this case one or more assailants met Ah Ow on I Street between Second and Third and fired several shots. They immediately turned and ran down I Street. Eventually, police arrested Ah Toy, Ah King, Ah Yan, and Ah Lue.[20] Although arrested and detained, none of the alleged assailants were indicted for the killing.

On October 10, 1881, a group of Chinese met at a house on Third Street between I and J, where they celebrated. During the party an altercation occurred that ended with Yee Ah Pong pulling a revolver and killing Yee Ah Gee. With a large number of witnesses present, the prosecutor was able to make a strong case that ended in the conviction of Yee Ah Pong.[21] In another case that occurred at Third and I Streets on August 8, 1889, Ah Heong and another unnamed assailant accosted Suey Kay. Ah Heong pulled a revolver and shot him twice. When police arrived, Suey Kay claimed that he had been robbed.[22] With witnesses and a dying declaration by the victim, the prosecutors were able to gain a conviction and life sentence for Ah Heong.[23]

These cases that ended in conviction, however, were the exception. In most of the cases involving Asian perpetrators and victims, the prosecutors were unable to gain convictions. Police and prosecutors often encountered great difficulty in dealing with Chinese homicide cases because of the language barrier and the tendency for Asians to deal internally with their own problems. Although they indicted fifty-eight defendants involving thirty-eight homicide cases, prosecutors were able to convict only fourteen, or 24 percent (figure 1). Thirty-eight percent of the defendants were found not guilty, and an additional 35 percent were dismissed.[24] In other words, 76 percent of those Asians indicted were released from custody by the criminal justice system.

Possibly fearing reprisals, many Asians refused to testify against other Asians accused of homicide. In other cases, Asian victims were listed as killed by "persons unknown," a common euphemism used by the coroner when he was unable to locate eyewitnesses. Since most of these homicides with unknown assailants occurred within the Sacramento Chinatown section, it can be assumed that the perpetrators were also Asian.[25] Those Asian homicides that occurred outside of Sacramento's Chinatown present some difficulty in determining the race of the perpetrators.

Chinese in Sacramento were more likely to be victims than perpetrators (thirty-eight cases). Whites and African Americans killed thirteen and two

TABLE 4. Asian Population, Sacramento County, 1860–1900 (Percentage of Total Population)

	1860	1870	1880	1890	1900
Asian	7.1	13.4	14.2	10.9	9.7

Source: US Department of Commerce, Bureau of the Census, *Eighth through Twelfth Census, 1860–1900*.

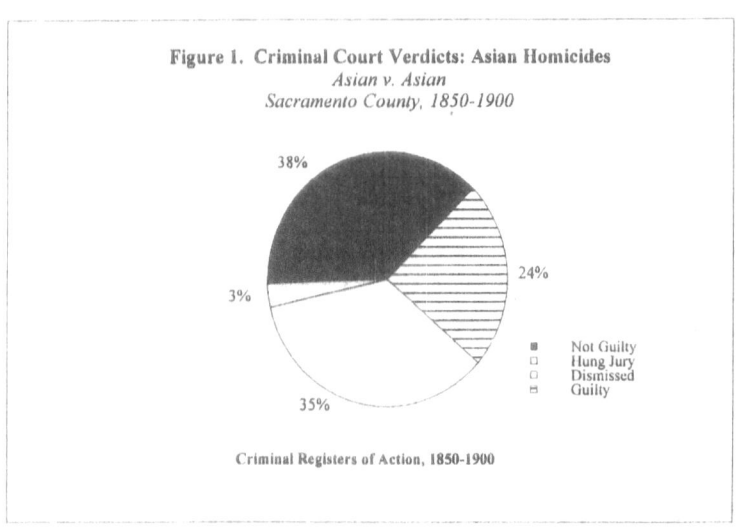

Figure 1. Criminal Court Verdicts: Asian Homicides
Asian v. Asian
Sacramento County, 1850–1900

Criminal Registers of Action, 1850–1900

Asians, respectively, while the identity of the killers of eight other Asian victims could not be determined. The killing of Asians by whites took a variety of forms, including lynching. Some nineteenth-century white commentators treated lynchings as an acceptable means of "controlling lawlessness" on the frontier.[26] There is no doubt that lynchings were homicides, yet all of the perpetrators of these crimes avoided criminal prosecution. Few white citizens perceived this kind of retributive punishment as a crime; rather, it appeared to them to be a reasonable response to any serious crime allegedly committed by others. For example, on November 12, 1861, white miners lynched a Chinese man in the vicinity of Prairie City, several miles east of Sacramento. A newspaper story contained the following details: "The body, all over it, bore marks of brutal violence, and the rope by which it was hanged had been dripping blood. The probable facts are these: A Chinaman was detected in stealing gold from the claim of four white persons. The culprit was taken by about twenty miners and whipped, beat, kicked and dragged around the village of Prairie City and thrown and left in a creek, from which he was taken by four men and hanged to a tree."[27] In this and another Asian lynching case that occurred on October 18, 1858, there was no attempt by law enforcement officers to apprehend the guilty parties.

Five cases involved Asians either attempting to rob whites or in the process of taking property from white stores, farms, or ranches. All except one of the white perpetrators used a shotgun to kill their victims. In all five cases prosecutors refused to indict the white perpetrators.[28] Three other cases, however, revealed quite different circumstances. On June 21, 1858, a man named Mike Davis drowned Chim Yow in Sutter Lake. Even though Davis was identified, the prosecutor brought no indictment against him.[29] In May 1866 a white man entered a cabin on Coloma Road, a mile from Folsom, and began to slash several Chinese who were living there. He seriously wounded one and killed another. Law enforcement officials were unable to locate a suspect.[30]

On June 22, 1872, Edward Robinson, an African American waiter working at the Grand Hotel, began an argument in the kitchen with the cook, Ah Lee. Robinson claimed that when he ordered breakfast for the hotel bookkeeper, Ah Lee threatened him with a knife and a meat cleaver. Robinson reached up on a shelf, retrieved a revolver, and shot the cook. Before dying Ah Lee told a different story. He claimed that Robinson attacked him and when Ah Lee tried to escape, Robinson shot him.[31] A little over two decades later John Green, an African American, shot and killed an Asian who attempted to escape from the house of Green's employer, Robert Coons. One week earlier Coons's brother had been poisoned by whiskey given him by an Asian. The local constable believed that Green had acted appropriately.[32]

Prosecutors brought charges against nine of the thirteen whites and both African Americans accused of killing Asians. Thomas Powell and Henry Kramer (white suspects) were tried and found not guilty, and Simon Raten was found not guilty by reason of insanity. The six other white defendants had charges against them dismissed. Juries simply would not convict whites accused of killing Asians. In the two cases involving African American perpetrators, a jury found Edward Robinson guilty of murdering Ah Lee, while, not surprisingly, a jury found John Green not guilty of murdering an unknown Asian.

A comparison of homicide conviction rates between Asians and whites in Sacramento, San Joaquin, Calaveras, and Tuolumne Counties may help to explain the operation of the criminal justice system for the Chinese in nineteenth-century California. Within these four counties, prosecutors indicted a total of 437 whites and 100 Asians for murder. Although they varied somewhat, white guilty verdicts averaged 43 percent for the four counties (figure 2). There is, however, a significant disparity between the guilty verdicts for Asian defendants. From a low of 24 percent in Sacramento, they double for San Joaquin, increase another 9 percent in Calaveras, and jump to 80 percent in Tuolumne. Whether this indicates better legal representation, an alert Chinese community in Sacramento, or more hostile juries in rural areas is not clear, but further analysis of the sentencing sheds more light on the criminal justice system.

In Calaveras County thirteen Asians were found guilty, for a conviction rate of 59 percent. In Tuolumne County not a single Asian received a not guilty verdict, indicating that once the trial process began Asian defendants were in trouble (figure 3). White juries in Tuolumne would not find Chinese not guilty. Justice appeared to be much harder for Asian defendants in the gold camp counties of Calaveras and Tuolumne and in San Joaquin than in Sacramento. On the other hand, white not guilty verdicts averaged about 35 percent, reaching a high of 41 and 40 percent, respectively, for San Joaquin and Tuolumne. Only Sacramento and Calaveras County Asian defendants had not guilty verdicts over 30 percent, with 38 and 36 percent, respectively.

The data suggest that there was some chance for Asian defendants before the trial began. Dismissal rates reached 34 percent in Sacramento and 30 percent in San Joaquin, and dropped to 20 and 5 percent, respectively, for Tuolumne and Calaveras Counties (figure 4). Nevertheless, the Sacramento County figures are misleading because law enforcement officers usually rounded up and prosecutors often indicted large numbers of Asian "suspects." Prior to the trial, however, it became clear to the prosecutors that they could not make a case against many of the defendants. Consequently, they had to dismiss the charges against them. Whites charged with murder averaged about a 20 percent dismissal rate.

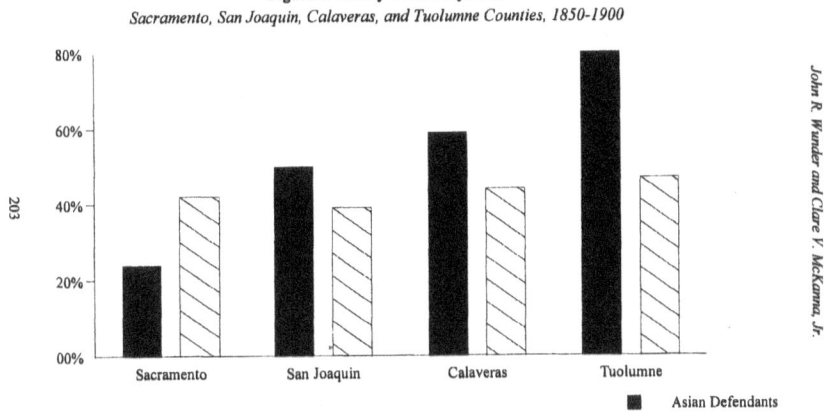

Figure 2. Guilty Verdict by Race
Sacramento, San Joaquin, Calaveras, and Tuolumne Counties, 1850-1900

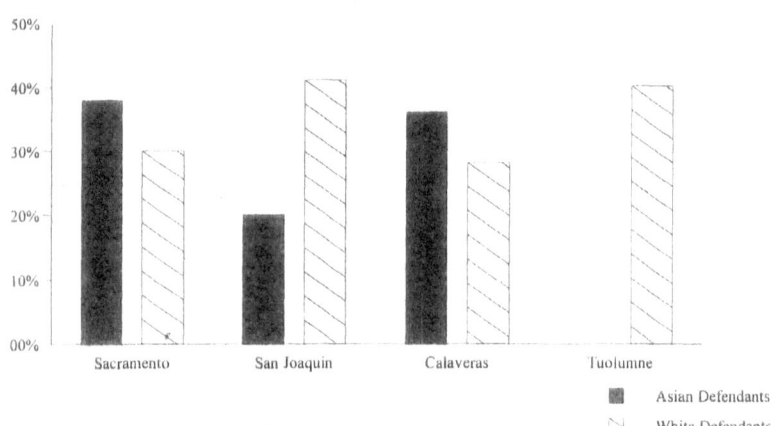

Figure 3. Not Guilty Verdict by Race
Sacramento, San Joaquin, Calaveras, and Tuolumne Counties, 1850-1900

The aggregate data suggest that Asian defendants had a better chance in the courts of Sacramento and San Joaquin Counties, while in the gold camp counties of Calaveras and Tuolumne justice could be harsh. Of the thirteen convictions of Asians in Calaveras County, nine Asian defendants were sentenced to death and an additional three defendants received life in prison. Tuolumne juries convicted eight Asian defendants. Five of these Asian

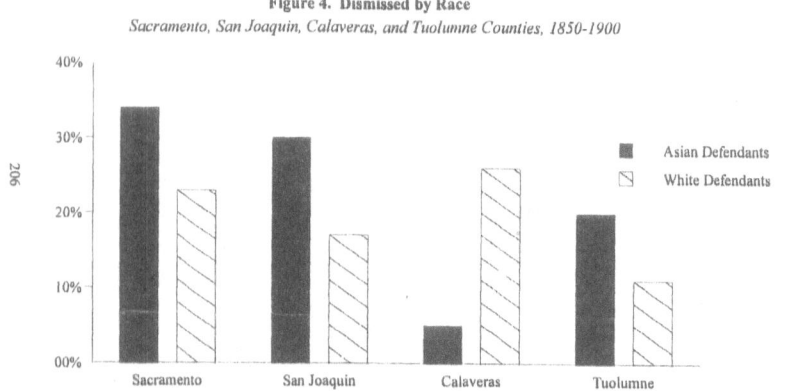

Figure 4. Dismissed by Race
Sacramento, San Joaquin, Calaveras, and Tuolumne Counties, 1850-1900

defendants received death sentences, and one obtained a life sentence. Only one of the death penalty cases involved a white victim (Tuolumne); the rest of the victims were Asian.

The Sacramento data confirm that Asian perpetrators tended to kill within their own racial group, with virtually all of their victims being Asian (table 5). However, Sacramento County had a significant number of cases involving whites killing Asians. Whites killed 21 percent of the Asian victims (thirteen cases). The aggregate data reveals twenty-three cases involving whites killing Asians. Although twelve white defendants were indicted, not a single white defendant was convicted of killing an Asian.

What, then, accounts for the 76 percent (not guilty, hung jury, and dismissed) release of Asian defendants by Sacramento County's criminal justice system? One explanation would be the legal representation available to Asian defendants. Most Asians belonged to one of the Six Companies established to provide benefits for Chinese workers. The Six Companies were well-established in Sacramento's Chinatown by 1855 and operated to aid Chinese citizens by providing food, lodging, entertainment, employment opportunities, medical treatment, and legal representation when needed.[33] Unlike other minorities, who had difficulty obtaining counsel, Asians had immediate access to legal representation.[34] This can be verified by the lack of plea bargaining (a common method employed by prosecutors against indigents) among Asian defendants, as well as in the conviction rates for Asians in Sacramento County.[35]

The failure of Chinese witnesses to testify against other Chinese also may

TABLE 5. Perpetrator-Victim Relationship, Sacramento County, 1850–1900

Perpetrator/Victim	%	N
Asian/Asian	61.6	37
White/Asian	21.6	13
Black/Asian	3.3	2
Unknown/Asian	13.3	8

Source: Sacramento County coroner's inquests, 1850–1900.

have been an important factor in the low conviction rates. Several of the homicides suggest that there may have been clan loyalty involved and retribution taken against earlier homicides.[36] For example, in 1897 one prosecutor complained, "My experience has taught me that, in dealing with this class of people, the crime of murder is committed as a matter of revenge—not so much as against the individual, but as against some individual who is a member of the 'tong' or society to which they belong; and that the killing of one Chinaman usually results in the killing of another, in order to satisfy this spirit of revenge that exists among them as individuals and as members of the organizations to which they belong."[37]

What can we conclude from this discussion of race and homicide in Sacramento? During the last half of the nineteenth century, California experienced considerable social turmoil caused by the gold rush that in turn stimulated rapid population growth. The intermixing of racial groups created tensions that were reflected by interracial killings. Chinese seldom killed outside of their racial group, but interracial homicides involving white perpetrators and Chinese victims always ended with not guilty verdicts or dismissals. Intraracial killings, however, were a different matter, with whites receiving guilty verdicts that averaged 43 percent for the four counties. The guilty verdicts for Asians varied significantly among the four counties, ranging from a low of 24 percent in Sacramento to a high of 80 percent in Tuolumne. The data clearly demonstrate that there were two standards of justice—one for whites and another for Chinese. Although the results are somewhat mixed, the conviction rates, life sentences, and death sentences show that Asians received "harsher" justice than whites.

Homicide studies of California are just beginning to be done by legal historians. Sacramento is the first city to have a specific study of Chinese and homicide. No comparable data have been compiled for San Francisco. Charles McClain, however, has analyzed the reception of the Chinese in San Francisco based upon attempts by the majority to use local ordinances to force Chinese to leave. This was done to prevent Chinese from making a living, to force Chinese to concentrate in specific parts of the city, and to blame the Chinese for urban diseases. Similar studies have not been done for Sacramento.

In McClain's book, he offers three important chapters that trace the history of the Chinese within San Francisco's legal system. The first is chapter 4, "The Laundry Litigation of the 1880s,"[38] wherein McClain unravels the intricate legal framework constructed by those who wanted to force the Chinese from San Francisco and the skillful opposition of the Chinese to these laws and their enforcement.

The first action to restrict Chinese laundry operations came in 1873 and 1876, when special fee legislation was passed by San Francisco's Board of Supervisors. Chinese fought these new laws in local courts with some success. Next the board passed legislation aimed at restricting the building construction of laundries, requiring brick and one-story constructions. These were aimed at the Chinese, who frequently had many people living in their wooden buildings. Legal sparring continued on both sides, culminating in the important dispute *Yick Wo v. Hopkins*, which required a US Supreme Court interpretation of San Francisco's laws. Although these ordinances were struck down by the court, opponents of the Chinese did not stop their efforts to discourage the Chinese from staying in San Francisco and other cities.

The 1880s mark the high water of anti-Chinese violence in the American West. There had been significant hostility demonstrated toward the Chinese in San Francisco and California before the 1880s, and after this fateful decade it continued on a lesser basis. Further efforts to force the Chinese out turned away from laundry regulation to housing discrimination.

McClain shows in chapter 9, "Challenging Residential Segregation: The Case of *In re Lee Sing*,"[39] how Chinese in San Francisco tried to stop removal of the Chinese from the city. He tells of a report prepared for the San Francisco Board of Supervisors that refers to the Chinese section of the city as "a moral cancer" and as a place home to "a Mongolian vampire sapping [San Francisco's] vitals."[40] The solution, the supervisors concluded, was to force a dispersal of the Chinese. They chose to begin this harassment by passing an ordinance that prevented Chinese from moving into Chinatown.

This caused the Chinese government to become involved. It challenged the local law in federal court. Indeed, the federal courts in San Francisco were busy hearing Chinese cases throughout the last half of the nineteenth century. Circuit judge Lorenzo Sawyer invalidated the ordinance, finding it to be a blatant attempt at discriminatory legislation. This did not stop the city from enacting other ordinances aimed at residential segregation or the state from attempting to force Chinese into residential patterns they did not wish to accept.

The last chapter in McClain's excellent book concerns the amazing attempt by San Francisco officials to force Chinese out by concocting a scheme based upon medical hysteria. Chapter 10, "Medicine, Race, and the Law: The Bubonic Plague Outbreak of 1900,"[41] shows to what length law can be used for a nefarious end. When a Chinese man was found dead in March 1900 and it was determined that the cause of his death was bubonic plague, San Francisco local leaders decided to use this event as a means to force the Chinese to evacuate Chinatown. The strategy was to blockade Chinatown and enforce a quarantine, and then officials considered razing Chinatown. The Chinese fought back successfully in the courts and on diplomatic fronts. Eventually the disease ran its course, but the impact of this episode on San Francisco's Chinese would remain.

Thus, race and law were a most important dual factor in the history of San Francisco in the last half of the nineteenth century. The Chinese were singled out for discriminatory treatment, but they successfully defended themselves. Although they were able to resist their removal, the toll was great.[42] For the Chinese in California, constant vigilance was needed just to keep jobs and retain homes.

The tale of two California cities, Sacramento and San Francisco, although presented on different levels because of diverse historical sources and research, is quite similar. The nineteenth century was a time of singular persecution and harassment for their Chinese residents.

Whether it was the constancy of arrest for crimes that Chinese had not committed or the branding of racist epithets in the local media, the Chinese in Sacramento found their lives to be that of living on the brink. Similarly, the Chinese in San Francisco had to be committed to the monitoring of local officials, who used ordinances and legal maneuvers to try to prevent the Chinese from making a living or to force the removal of the Chinese.

In each circumstance, the Chinese resisted the use of American law for discriminatory ends. It did not matter whether the laws or the courts were federal, state, or local. The Chinese fought to prevent their people from being victims, and in that process they made law and provided a basis for twentieth-century legal breakthroughs toward making California and the United States a fairer society.

Charles J. McClain has shown us what can be done with thoughtful, comprehensive research in this area of legal history. His work is a model for future studies and raises many other issues. Thanks to *In Search of Equality*, the story of the Chinese in California and in the American West is beginning to be told.

Notes

Originally published as John R. Wunder and Clare V. McKanna Jr., "The Chinese and California: A Torturous Legal Relationship," *California Supreme Court Historical Society Yearbook* 2 (1995): 195–214.

1. Charles J. McClain, *In Search of Equality: The Chinese Struggle against Discrimination in Nineteenth-Century America* (Berkeley: University of California Press, 1994), 3.
2. Ibid., 4.
3. As one of us has written elsewhere, "It offers a significant departure from previous studies, and it raises numerous areas for further investigation just by its own far-reaching analysis and pathbreaking research." John R. Wunder, review of *In Search of Equality: The Chinese Struggle against Discrimination in Nineteenth-Century America*, by Charles J. McClain, *Western Historical Quarterly* 26 (Spring 1995): 97–98.
4. See Sucheng Chan, *This Bittersweet Soil: The Chinese in California Agriculture, 1860–1910* (Berkeley: University of California Press, 1986); Sandy Lydon, *Chinese Gold: The Chinese in the Monterey Bay Region* (Capitola, CA: Capitola Book Company, 1985); Lucy Salyer, *Laws Harsh as Tigers: Chinese Immigrants and the Shaping of Modern Immigration Law* (Chapel Hill: University of North Carolina Press, 1995).
5. *Sacramento Bee*, June 1, 1892.
6. On June 2, 1892, the *Sacramento Bee* once again used bold type to headline a homicide that had occurred the previous day: "THE MONGOLIAN MAFIA / The Insignia of a Highbinder's Headquarters." The story suggested that the police and coroner had discovered records involving the "highbinders."

Not to be outdone, the *Sacramento Daily Record-Union* (June 1, 1892) trumpeted, "SHOWER OF BULLETS! / Chinese Highbinders Fight a Battle in the Streets / ABOUT FIFTY SHOTS FIRED." For further documentation of such inflammatory headlines, see *Sacramento Bee*, November 12–14, 1883.

7. Originally used to describe Irish immigrants accused of criminal activity in New York, the term *highbinder* first appeared as an epithet to characterize Chinese as criminal in the *San Francisco Call*, March 27, 1876. It has mainly been used to attack Chinese "secret societies" in San Francisco and elsewhere in the United States. See *The Oxford English Dictionary* (Oxford: Clarendon Press, 1989), 7:223.

8. Two days later, the *Sacramento Bee* announced with the blaring headline "COATS OF MAIL. Formidable Shields Worn by Chinese Highbinders" that police had raided the Bing Ting Hong "secret society" and also had captured trophies, including "two ponderous coats of mail" weighing twenty pounds each. Presumably they were used for protection. See *Sacramento Bee*, June 3, 1892.

The following day the *Bee* changed the story, claiming that it was the Bang Kong Tong that had been raided. Court records indicate that the perpetrator belonged to the Bing Kong Tong. See *People of the State of California v. Chin Hane and Hoey Yen Sing*, California, Sacramento County, Superior Court, *Criminal Case Files, 1850–1900*. Sacramento Historical Society Archives. Lee Heong, the victim, was alleged to be a member of the Chee Hong [sic] Tong. In the daily coverage of the homicide, the *Bee* misspelled the assailant Chin Hane's name as Ching Hing, Ching Hing Hane, and Chin Hing. Indeed, the language issue as well as other facts were very fuzzy.

9. See Stanford M. Lyman, "Chinese Secret Societies in the Occident: Notes and Suggestions for Research on the Sociology of Secrecy," *Canadian Review of Sociology and Anthropology* 1 (1964): 79–102.

10. See John R. Wunder, "The Chinese and the Courts in the Pacific Northwest: Justice Denied?," *Pacific Historical Review* 52 (May 1983): 208. See also John R. Wunder, "Law and Chinese in Frontier Montana," *Montana, the Magazine of Western History* 30 (Summer 1981): 18–31.

11. See, for example, Alexander Saxton, *The Indispensable Enemy: Labor and the Anti-Chinese Movement in California* (Berkeley: University of California Press, 1971); David D. DuFault, "The Chinese in the Mining Camps," *Southern California Quarterly* 41 (1959): 155–70; Stanford M. Lyman, *Chinese Americans* (New York: Random House, 1974); Elmer C. Sandmeyer, *The Anti-Chinese Movement in California* (Urbana: University of Illinois Press, 1939); and Robert F. Heizer and Alan F. Almquist, *The Other Californians* (Berkeley: University of California Press, 1971).

12. See John R. Wunder, "Chinese in Trouble: Criminal Law and Race on the Trans-Mississippi West Frontier," *Western Historical Quarterly* 17 (January 1986):

25–41; Charles J. McClain Jr., "The Chinese Struggle for Civil Rights in Nineteenth Century America: The First Phase, 1850–1870," *California Law Review* 72 (1984): 548–50; Paul Takagi and Tony Platt, "Behind the Gilded Ghetto: An Analysis of Race, Class and Crime in Chinatown," *Crime and Social Justice* 9 (1978): 2–25; and Charles A. Tracy, "Race, Crime and Social Policy: The Chinese in Oregon, 1871–1885," *Crime and Social Justice* 12 (1980): 11–25.

See also John R. Wunder, "*Territory of New Mexico v. Yee Shun*: A Turning Point in Chinese Legal Relationships in the Trans-Mississippi West," *New Mexico Historical Review* 65 (July 1990): 305–18; and Robert H. Tillman, "The Prosecution of Homicide in Sacramento, California, 1853–1900," *Southern California Quarterly* 68 (1986): 167–81.

13. These counties display regional, economic, and ethnic variety that provide an important cross-section of nineteenth-century California society.
14. *Sacramento Bee*, November 19, 1858.
15. See California, Sacramento County, *Criminal Registers of Action, 1850–1900*, Sacramento Historical Society Archives.
16. See Willard B. Farwell, "Chinatown in Sacramento," in *The Chinese at Home and Abroad* (San Francisco: A. L. Bancroft, 1885), 97–114.
17. Only two Asian female victims and no female perpetrators appeared within the statistics. See *Sacramento Union*, February 9, 1856.
18. Fifty percent of the Asian assailants used handguns in the commission of their crime, followed by 24 percent who employed knives in their attacks. See California, Sacramento County, *Coroner's Inquest, 1850–1900*, Sacramento Historical Society Archives.
19. *People of the State of California v. Ah Fat*, California, Sacramento County, District Court, *Criminal Case Files, 1850–1900*.
20. *Sacramento Bee*, April 15, 1873. It is possible that this and the previous homicide were related to tong rivalry, but the evidence is too sketchy to draw any firm conclusions. See *Sacramento Bee*, March 3 and April 15, 1873.
21. *Sacramento Bee*, October 11, 1881; and *People of the State of California v. Yee Ah Pong*, California, Sacramento County, Superior Court, *Criminal Case Files, 1850–1900*.
22. *Sacramento Bee*, July 9, 1889.
23. See *People of the State of California v. Suey Kay*, in California, Sacramento County, Superior County, *Criminal Case Files, 1850–1900*.
24. California, Sacramento County, *Registers of Criminal Action, 1850–1900*.
25. Only five cases involving Asian victims killed by alleged Asian perpetrators occurred outside of the Chinatown section of Sacramento. Two were committed in Folsom Prison by Asian inmates and the other three occurred in Chinese mining camps. See California, Sacramento County, *Coroner's Inquests*, December 14, 1861, September 12, 1881, August 8, 1883, May 6, 1885, and August 9, 1892.

26. See, for example, Hubert Howe Bancroft, *Popular Tribunals*, vol. 1 (San Francisco: History Company, 1887); and Thomas J. Dimsdale, *The Vigilantes of Montana* (Norman: University of Oklahoma Press, 1953).
27. *Sacramento Bee*, November 16, 1861.
28. For the cases involving white defendants and Asian victims, see California, Sacramento County, District and Superior Courts, *Criminal Case Files*, defendants Michael O'Neil, Thomas Powell, Henry A. Kramer, Simon Raten, Jack English, James Ryan, John McDuff, Charles Denman, William Johnson, and William Davis; *Sacramento Bee*, January 4, 1873, March 31, 1875, May 3, 1880, February 24, 1882, and July 19, 1884; and California, Sacramento County, *Coroner's Inquests, 1850–1900*.
29. *Sacramento Bee*, June 23, 1858.
30. Ibid., May 7, 1866.
31. Ibid., June 22, 1872.
32. Ibid., November 26, 1897.
33. See Mary Roberts Coolidge, *Chinese Immigration* (New York: Henry Holt, 1909), 402–7; Shih-Shan Henry Tsai, *China and the Overseas Chinese in the United States, 1868–1911* (Fayetteville: University of Arkansas Press, 1983), 124–29; and Chinese Consolidated Benevolent Association California, *Memorial: Six Chinese Companies, an Address to the Senate and House of Representatives of the United States, December 8, 1877* (Repr., San Francisco: R and E Research Associates, 1970).
34. In the nineteenth century, indigents accused of murder found themselves in a difficult predicament. California law provided for legal representation at the trial stage in felony cases but did not give legal counsel for preliminary hearings. California Indians, who did not know their legal rights, often confessed to sheriffs or police officers. Prosecutors had the upper hand and demanded that the accused either plead guilty or risk long terms of imprisonment or even execution. See, for example, *People of the State of California v. Augustin Castro*, in California, San Diego County, District Court, April 1872, San Diego Historical Society Research Archives.
35. California Indians, and to a lesser extent Hispanics, had high plea bargain rates compared to white and Asian defendants. See Clare V. McKanna Jr., "Interracial Homicide: A Tale of Seven California Counties, 1850–1900," unpublished manuscript.
36. See *People of the State of California v. Ah Fat*, in California, Sacramento County, District Court, *Criminal Case Files, 1850–1900*; and *Sacramento Bee*, March 3 and April 15, 1873.
37. *People of the State of California v. Ling Ying Toy (alias Quong Sing) and Ching Gow Duey (alias Chin Ah Gow Nuey)*, p. 3, August 1897, in California, Sacramento County, Superior Court, *Criminal Case Files, 1850–1900*.

38. McClain, *In Search of Equality*, 98–132.
39. Ibid., 223–33.
40. Ibid., 224.
41. Ibid., 234–76.
42. The record was parallel in these respects to Chinese litigants' experiences with immigration administration. See, for example, Salyer, *Laws Harsh as Tigers*.

CHAPTER 5

Chinese Laundries and the Fourteenth Amendment

Yick Wo v. Hopkins, 118 US 356 (1886)

In the summer of 1885, Yick Wo and over 150 other Chinese residents of San Francisco deliberately violated two ordinances in order to challenge an infringement on what they considered a basic right: the right to engage in economic activity. The San Francisco county and city ordinances, passed in May and July 1880, placed restrictions on laundry operators that were applied to prevent Chinese laundries from functioning. This challenge eventually was resolved by the US Supreme Court in a unanimous decision, *Yick Wo v. Hopkins*.

The period from 1820 to 1882 was a time of free Chinese immigration, and hundreds of Chinese moved to California. By 1870 over forty-nine thousand Chinese lived in California, and that number increased to over seventy-five thousand by 1880. This amounted to nearly 10 percent of California's population. Approximately 40 percent of all Chinese in California lived in the six counties of the San Francisco Bay area.

Many Caucasian and Hispanic Californians did not like this influx of Chinese. As a result, laws were passed that discriminated against them. The first California anti-Chinese law passed was the Foreign Miner's License Tax Act of 1852, which required a head tax of four dollars per month to mine. In 1860 a Foreign Fishing License Tax Act of four dollars per month was passed, and two years later the Chinese police tax charged those not engaged in mining with a monthly $2.50 fee.

The legal assault on Chinese living in San Francisco became especially acute in the 1870s. The city and county passed such ordinances as the "Queue Ordinance" of 1876, which required the hair of Chinese prisoners to be cut, and the "No Special Police for Chinese Quarter Ordinance" of 1878, which singled out the Chinese to deny them police protection for their homes and businesses. Also, an 1876 ordinance required all hand laundries with horse-drawn delivery vehicles to pay a new license fee of $2.25 per month.

Outright banning of the Chinese from certain economic activities also started in the 1870s. In 1879 Chinese were prohibited from working for state, county, or city governments. This provision was placed in the new California Constitution. The next year the California legislature made it a misdemeanor for any corporation chartered in California to employ Chinese workers. Thus these state laws and local ordinances made life extremely difficult for the Chinese in California. One historian concluded that "so severe and strident were the local laws that sought to banish the Chinese people from American life that in some ways they equaled the slave ordinances of the South."

Anti-Chinese feeling manifested itself nationally in 1876 when a committee of California legislators memorialized Congress to restrict Chinese immigration. Six years later, Congress successfully passed the first of several exclusion acts aimed at halting Chinese from coming to the United States. These laws were enforced, and Chinese immigration was significantly curtailed.

Simultaneously, political agitation and violence struck California. In 1877 Denis Kearney led the Workingmen's Party in protests against the Chinese in San Francisco. This group eventually took over the California Democratic Party, which embraced anti-Chinese rhetoric and actions. It was this group that played an important role at the California Constitutional Convention by inserting anti-Chinese sections into the new constitution. It also took over local San Francisco government with the election of Isaac Kalloch as mayor of San Francisco in 1879. Political agitation eventually led to the expulsion of the Chinese from Eureka and Truckee and the first organized massacre of Chinese at Rock Springs, Wyoming.

Federal and local laws and anti-Chinese violence caused many Chinese to abandon rural areas and to congregate in Chinatowns in urban areas. The Chinese were also forced to leave farming, mining, manufacturing, railroading, and the professions for self-employment in marginal and noncompetitive occupations. In 1881–82 a Trades' Assembly labor census was taken in San Francisco.

Chinese labor was concentrated in four areas: cigar making (8,500 Chinese, or 97 percent of all persons working at this occupation), boot and shoe making (5,700 Chinese, or 84 percent), clothes making (7,510 Chinese, or 88 percent), and laundry operation (5,107 Chinese, or 89 percent).

The Chinese did not go into laundry work by choice. It was a difficult job, which caused social isolation from the Chinese community because the laundry owner had to do business primarily with hostile non-Chinese customers. Chinese laundries were not liked by many whites as well. Missionaries believed them to be centers of moral perversion. Visions of white females captured by Chinese and forced into prostitution operations headquartered at Chinese laundries were readily propagated. Such was the fear and loathing that California mobs began attacking isolated laundries in the 1870s. Even so, the laundry business attracted many Chinese. It afforded a modest and steady income. Few skills, little capital, and minimal English-speaking skills were needed. To some degree, the outreach to selected portions of the white community cushioned the violence of the anti-Chinese era.

Most laundries were family operations, and three kinds evolved. The hand laundry with one or two persons was most common. The other two types required specialization and a greater investment: shirt-processing firms specialized in ironing only, and wet-washing firms only washed clothes. All of these laundries required back-breaking labor, and they operated throughout the day and night.

Yick Wo knew this life. He had been in the laundry business for twenty-two years prior to his arrest. He had arrived in California in 1861 and never became a US citizen, a process that in the 1860s and 1870s would have been most difficult for him. As the owner of a laundry, Yick Wo was quite familiar with the ordinances monitoring laundry operations in San Francisco. He had a license dated March 3, 1884, from the board of fire wardens certifying that his stoves, irons, and washing machines were safe. He also had a certificate from the health officer stating that his laundry was sanitary and that it drained properly. His city license to operate his laundry was to expire on October 1, 1885.

To comply with local law, Yick Wo, on June 1, 1885, applied to the Board of Supervisors for renewal of his general license to operate his laundry. The board rejected his request on July 1. The ordinance that allowed the board to grant laundry licenses was first passed in 1880. This local law provided that all persons who established a laundry within the San Francisco city limits had to obtain the consent of the Board of Supervisors. Violation of the ordinance would result in a misdemeanor conviction and a fine of up to $1,000, a county jail sentence of not more than six months, or both. The ordinance also prohibited certain scaffoldings. Laundries found in brick buildings did not need the license, whereas laundries in wooden buildings did. This allowed the Board of Supervisors to claim that the ordinance was necessary as a fire-protection measure.

Yick Wo was not the only Chinese laundry owner who was denied a license by the board. The petitions of two hundred other Chinese owners had also been denied. Eighty laundry licenses had been granted, all but one to non-Chinese owners. The only exception was a permit given to May Meagles, and no doubt this exception had missed the board's attention. The lack of permits issued to Chinese laundry owners did not seem to be correlated to the structure of the buildings. Of the 320 laundries listed for San Francisco in 1880, 310 were in wooden buildings. Chinese owners constituted approximately 240 laundries. By 1885, 200 of the 240 Chinese-owned laundries were denied licenses to operate.

Shortly after his license request was denied, Yick Wo was arrested for operating a laundry without a license. He was taken to a San Francisco police court, where he was found guilty and fined ten dollars. Yick Wo refused to pay the fine, and he was jailed for ten days. He then petitioned California's highest court, the California Supreme Court, for a writ of habeas corpus. When his petition was denied, he appealed to the US Supreme Court, naming Sheriff Hopkins in his suit.

Yick Wo had a difficult case. He knew that San Francisco would argue that the ordinances in question were designed to protect the health and safety of its residents. Yet clearly the result of enforcing this law was discriminatory. Thus he had to address this twofold problem in his argument.

In a masterful defense, Yick Wo's attorneys, led by prominent San Francisco Republican Hall McAllister, conceded that the state and city had the right to regulate certain businesses that posed potential health and safety problems. Laundries fell under this framework. However, laundries were not dangerous or unhealthy per se, and therefore they could not be prohibited. They argued that the best evidence for this conclusion was the ordinances themselves, which regulated rather than banned laundry operations. The purpose of the statutes was to ensure the health and safety of San Francisco's residents *and* the continued operation of laundries.

The plaintiff next cited the results from the enforcement of the ordinances. What had in effect happened was the curtailment of the laundry business through a blatant discriminatory practice of not granting licenses to Chinese laundry owners. Statistics presented to the court showed that, of the 280 license petitions received by the Board of Supervisors, 80 were granted. Only 25 percent of the laundries in San Francisco could operate, and only one of the 201 Chinese applicants was granted a license. Thus, in a bold move, pre-Brandeis brief and pre–*Brown v. Board of Education* (1954), statistical evidence was presented before the court.

Having proven the discriminatory result of the administering of these ordinances, Yick Wo then claimed this state action violated China's 1880 treaty with the United States and the Fourteenth Amendment. More specifically, he argued that the due process clause of the Fourteenth Amendment had been abrogated by the ordinances and their enforcement.

San Francisco claimed it was only practicing a traditional right of every governing body: the duty to protect the health and safety of its citizens. This police power, it argued, was "indestructible and inalienable," and it had been granted at the beginnings of American governance. Thus, to the defendant, it was too late to question the existence of the police power, even with the Fourteenth Amendment. The police power was sufficiently strong so as to allow discriminatory interpretations.

It was a haughty argument. San Francisco virtually dared the Supreme Court to limit the police powers of state and local government. It tried to force the court to choose between abolishing police power and ratifying any police power. If the court could find a middle ground, it would have to adopt a position never before taken—extending the Fourteenth Amendment to prevent discriminatory municipal actions, and this is precisely what it did.

On May 10, 1886, Justice Stanley Matthews read the unanimous opinion of the court. He began by dismissing the issue of the plaintiff's imprisonment, his jail term having expired. The court might have stopped there, but Matthews asserted that the "meaning of the ordinances" of San Francisco had attracted the court's concern.

The court found that the ordinances were so vague as to vest a power broader than police power in the Board of Supervisors. This power constituted "a naked and arbitrary power to give or withhold consent, not only as to places, but as to persons." Thus the court saw this power as discriminatory, a form of class legislation prohibited by the Fourteenth Amendment.

To reach this conclusion the court specifically noted that the Fourteenth Amendment applies to all persons, citizens and aliens alike. Moreover, Matthews developed a test for legislation to see whether it was prohibited by the Fourteenth Amendment. Legislation must specifically regulate an economic activity in terms of safety and health practices, and such laws must be applied fairly. For Yick Wo, the San Francisco ordinances failed both tests, but the court was most offended by the discriminatory application by the Board of Supervisors. Wrote Matthews, "The very idea that one man may be compelled to hold his life, or the means of living, or any material right essential to the enjoyment of life, at the mere will of another, seems to be intolerable in any country where freedom prevails, as being the essence of slavery itself." Thus the court ruled the ordinances unconstitutional. The actions of the Board of Supervisors were discriminatory and violated the due process clause of the Fourteenth Amendment.

The significance of this case was especially important to the evolution of constitutional law and to the Chinese. The court in its opinion expanded the Fourteenth Amendment. In one motion of the pen, Matthews limited state police powers, activated the due process clause to prohibit discriminatory action, broadly construed the coverage of the Fourteenth Amendment to include aliens, and placed state and local governments on notice that the Fourteenth Amendment would be applied to actions not previously associated with slavery and the Civil War.

The effect of this case on the anti-Chinese movement in California and throughout the West was profound. The Supreme Court answered the question posed by Yick Wo's attorneys: "That it [the enforcement of the ordinances] does mean prohibition, as to the Chinese, it seems to us must be apparent to every citizen of San Francisco who has been here long enough to be familiar with the cause of an active and aggressive branch of public opinion and of public notorious events. Can a court be blind to what must be necessarily known to every intelligent person in the State?" The Supreme Court was not blind, and by condemning the official actions of the city of San Francisco, it placed public officials on notice that the anti-Chinese agitations of Californians and other westerners would no longer be tolerated. One reason why the anti-Chinese movements lessened in the next decade can be attributed to the stand taken by the *Yick Wo* court.

Yick Wo v. Hopkins did not, however, achieve an immediate end to discrimination, nor did it activate the Fourteenth Amendment. Shortly after 1886 the Supreme Court's composition changed and the new court saw the Fourteenth Amendment more as a vehicle to prevent broad social change. It extolled property rights, and attempts by states and localities to use regulatory powers to restrict property rights and economic activities were thwarted. The Fourteenth Amendment became a haven for substantive economic theory protected by the due process clause. *Yick Wo* would reassert itself in the twentieth century when the Fourteenth Amendment was reactivated to destroy the Jim Crow system of discrimination against blacks that had been erected in the border states and the South after the Civil War.

Note

Originally published as John R. Wunder, "Chinese Laundries and the Fourteenth Amendment," in *Historic U.S. Court Cases, 1690–1990: An Encyclopedia*, ed. John W. Johnson (New York: Garland 1992), 437–40.

Selected Bibliography

Barth, G. *Bitter Strength: A History of the Chinese in the United States, 1850–70*. Cambridge, MA: Harvard University Press, 1964.

Cheng-Tsu W., ed. *"Chink": A Documentary History of Anti-Chinese Prejudice in America*. New York: World Publishing, 1972.

Konvitz, M. R. *The Alien and the Asiatic in American Law*. Ithaca, NY: Cornell University Press, 1946.

Kung, S. W. *Chinese in American Life: Some Aspects of Their History, Status, Problems, and Contributions*. Seattle: University of Washington Press, 1962.

Miller, S. C. *The Unwelcome Immigrant: The American Image of the Chinese, 1785–1882*. Berkeley: University of California Press, 1969.

Saxton, A. *The Indispensable Enemy: Labor and the Anti-Chinese Movement in California*. Berkeley: University of California Press, 1971.

Shih-Shan Henry Tsai. *The Chinese Experience in America*. Bloomington: Indiana University Press, 1986.

Steiner, S. *Fusang: The Chinese Who Built America*. New York: Harper & Row, 1979.

Pacific Northwest

CHAPTER 6

The Chinese and the Courts in the Pacific Northwest

Justice Denied?

"CHINAMAN CLINGS TO his idolatry and heathenism with the tenacity of life; lives upon less than the refuse from the table of a civilized man, and devotes his sister to the basest lust of humanity, and makes her an unsexed prostitute to disseminate disease among the devotees of base passions."[1]

Such was the view in 1871 of a Montana editor toward the latest immigrants, the Chinese. His attitude was shared by many non-Asians in the United States during the nineteenth century, and it had been commonplace since the arrival of the first Chinese.

The Chinese began migrating to the United States in the 1840s, during the California gold rush. Economic motives apparently prompted most to take the voyage, although a significant number in later periods came to the New World under duress. Population data available from the US census indicate that the number of Chinese increased rapidly until 1890, the first count following enactment of national exclusionary legislation in 1882. The Chinese had never constituted more than 0.2 percent of the total population of the United States, but their economic impact was considerably more significant than mere numbers indicate. Almost all were adult males who were concentrated in the West, especially in California and the Pacific Northwest (Washington, Oregon, Idaho, Montana, and Wyoming). As early as 1870, 28.5 percent of all Idahoans and 9.5 percent of all Montanans were Chinese; in 1880, approximately one person out of every twenty in Oregon, Washington, and Wyoming was Chinese.[2]

TABLE 6. Chinese Population in the United States, 1860–1890

POPULATION BY STATE				
	1860	1870	1880	1890
United States	34,933*	63,199	105,465	107,475
California	34,933*	49,277	75,132	72,472
Idaho	N.I.	4,274	3,379	2,007
Montana	N.I.	1,949	1,765	2,532
Oregon	N.I.	3,330	9,510	9,540
Washington	N.I.	234	3,186	3,260
Wyoming	N.I.	143	914	465

PERCENTAGE OF POPULATION				
	1860	1870	1880	1890
United States	0.1*	0.2	0.2	0.2
California	9.2*	8.8	9.8	6.0
Idaho	N.I.	28.5	11.6	2.4
Montana	N.I.	9.5	5.0	1.9
Oregon	N.I.	3.7	5.8	3.0
Washington	N.I.	0.1	4.7	0.9
Wyoming	N.I.	1.5	4.7	0.8

* Figures available only for all Asians in the United States.
N.I. = No information available.

In the late 1850s through the 1870s increased numbers of Chinese went to the Northwest in response primarily to mining discoveries in Idaho and Montana and jobs in railroad construction throughout the area. Oregon and Washington Territory greeted these new Americans with xenophobia and head taxes. In Wyoming Territory the hostility led to an outbreak on September 4, 1885, known as the Rock Springs Massacre. White coal miners, attempting to force all Chinese from the territory's mines, killed twenty-eight of them. Three days later, thirty-five Chinese hop workers in the Issaquah Valley of Washington Territory were attacked; three were murdered. In September and October 1885, violence throughout northwestern rural areas forced the Chinese to flee to Washington port cities, north to British Columbia, and south to

San Francisco. Anti-Chinese riots then occurred in Tacoma and Seattle, which resulted in considerable property losses for Chinese residents and hasty evacuations.[3]

From the outset, the Chinese of the Pacific Northwest constituted a significant minority population, and they attracted and experienced some of the worst forms of legal and extralegal racism during the nineteenth century. Yet historical analysis of the legal issues involving the Chinese in the United States has been minimal.[4] Most treatments have dealt indirectly with such questions or have avoided them altogether. Only Milton Konvitz, in his *The Alien and the Asiatic in American Law*, has discussed the topic, but he concentrates on the federal level and ignores developments in the states and territories.[5]

What then of the courts of the Pacific Northwest? Were the Chinese afforded at least nominal legal equality? Could they go before a state or territorial court and obtain a fair hearing? To answer these questions, all decisions concerning Chinese litigants rendered by the territorial and state supreme courts of Oregon, Washington, Idaho, Montana, and Wyoming to 1902, when the third Chinese Exclusion Act permanently barred Chinese immigrants, have been reviewed. The following analysis discusses these cases under four general categories: civil cases appealed before passage of the first Chinese Exclusion Act (1882), criminal cases appealed before the passage of the same act, civil cases appealed between 1882 and 1902, and criminal cases appealed during the same period.[6]

In the Northwest prior to 1883, seven cases involving at least one Chinese litigant in a civil action reached state and territorial supreme courts.[7] In four of the seven civil cases, the highest courts ruled in favor of the Chinese party. Three of the four favorable decisions concerned such issues as child support, property rights obtained fraudulently, and misrepresentation of merchandise, and they all involved white litigants.[8] The fourth favorable decision dealt with a labor contract between Chinese and American Indian parties.

The Chinese-Indian dispute culminated in the 1871 decision of *Jack Gho v. Charley Julles* in Washington Territory. Gho, a Chinese, had been hired as a cook by Julles, a Snohomish who ran a logging camp. After Gho had performed his work as agreed, Julles refused to pay him. Gho then brought suit and won a lower court decision, which Julles appealed to the territorial supreme court. Territorial courts, Julles argued, had no jurisdiction over

Snohomish; in addition, he cited an 1847 congressional act that declared void all contracts made by Indians. The justices disagreed, finding that all persons, even Indians, could make binding agreements. The court looked more to the intent of Congress than to the letter of the law: "Does this law intend that the Indian, the moment he attempts to enter upon the pursuits that occupy the attention of our race, shall be stopped on the threshold, the door shut in his face? Is he to be walled up in barbarism? Is an insuperable obstacle to be thrust between him and all advance? . . . To forbid Indians to make executory contracts for money and goods only would be a derogation from natural right most hampering and injurious."[9]

It was a rarity when a western court sought to protect what Washington justices termed the "natural rights" of Native Americans, and in this instance such liberal reasoning benefited a Chinese plaintiff and many whites holding labor contracts with other Indians.

Not all pre-1883 civil cases resulted in favorable outcomes for Chinese litigants. Decisions reached in three instances by Northwest appellate tribunals favored over Chinese individuals such corporate interests as the First National Bank of Helena, the city of Portland, and the Seattle and Walla Walla Railroad.[10] The railroad case, in particular, represented a significant legal conflict for Chinese laborers.

The Seattle and Walla Walla Railroad, needing excavation and grading for its roadbed between Renton and Newcastle, negotiated a labor contract with L. D. Frank, who in turn made an agreement with three Chinese who promised to supply workers. The Chinese labor gangs toiled for several months, and when they received no wages, they sued the Seattle and Walla Walla Railroad. In a decision of far-reaching implications, the Washington Territorial Supreme Court reversed the lower court, which had held in favor of the Chinese laborers. In the opinion of the supreme court, only those Chinese specifically named in written contracts could collect (here, the three labor bosses only). The immediate result was that Chinese laborers could not be assured of their wages unless they signed agreements with the original procurer of their services. The long-term effect was more favorable since the decision helped inspire mechanics lien legislation and, more importantly for Chinese laborers, helped undermine the Chinese contract labor system.[11]

Just as with the majority of civil disputes involving Chinese, criminal cases decided in northwestern state and territorial supreme courts prior to

1883 indicated some effort by justices to protect Chinese defendants. Of the fifteen criminal appeals examined, nine resulted in reversals or affirmations favoring Chinese defendants. Appeals included convictions for rape, gambling, bribery, murder, and kidnapping.[12] Grounds for reversal usually were based upon gross violations of due process by local tribunals. In 1879 Tom, a Chinese, was indicted for allegedly raping a five-year-old Oregon girl, Ruby Sumption. At the circuit court level, two prospective jurors were seated even though they admitted having a "fixed opinion" about the guilt or innocence of the defendant. In addition, the testimony of the child was allowed into evidence even though she testified unsworn and was not subject to cross-examination. The Oregon Supreme Court ordered a new trial because the lower court's process of selecting jurors and taking testimony had violated constitutional guarantees.[13]

Blatant disregard for court procedure was also apparent in *Oregon v. Gitt Lee et al.* (1877), *Deer Lodge County v. At* (1878), and *Oregon v. Charley Lee Quong, Lee Jaw, and Lee Jong* (1879). In the first case the defendants had been found innocent by the lower court of unlawfully playing a game for money. The grand jury had not been presented with physical evidence or even the name of the game. The Oregon statute covering gambling required evidence showing either the type of game played—such as poker, vintun, or faro—or the device used—such as cards or dice. Even so, the district attorney appealed the innocent verdict to the Oregon Supreme Court, which curtly affirmed the lower court action because the indictment had not sufficiently described the offense.[14]

In *Deer Lodge County v. At*, it was G. W. Irwin, a Montana justice of the peace, who violated due process. While Irwin was interrogating Ung Hah, who had been arrested for murder, Lee Sue, a friend of the defendant, twice interrupted the proceedings to offer Irwin money for bail. The judge became so agitated that he ordered the sheriff to arrest Lee Sue for attempting to bribe an officer and immediately convened a hearing on the charge. The baffled Lee Sue made no defense, and Irwin ordered him to jail until a grand jury could issue an indictment. Following the indictment and Sue's release on bail, he refused to appear and a default judgment was rendered, although no complaint had been officially filed charging him with violating the law. The bail had been put up by a third Chinese named At, who now appealed to the Montana Territorial Supreme Court for dismissal of the charges against

Sue and the return of his bail money. The court agreed that Irwin had erred. Sue, declared the justices, had not waived "his statutory right to have a proper complaint containing a description of the offense with which he had been charged. Sue was arrested legally, and Irwin, as a justice of the peace, could take jurisdiction and proceed to judgment without issuing a warrant of arrest. But a written complaint against Sue, setting out his offense, was as necessary in his case as in any other."[15]

The supreme court of Oregon in the *Charley Lee Quong* case was also asked to scrutinize criminal trial procedures involving Chinese litigants. This dispute involved the murder of Chin Sue Ying, a recent Christian convert. Chin, the night before he was killed, had gone to a joss house, a building where Chinese cultural and religious activities were held, and smashed a Chinese "stink-pot" on the floor. A policeman was called, but Charley Lee Quong, the attendant, said he would wait until morning before swearing out a warrant. The next day Chin once again went to the joss house, and when he attempted to throw a piece of raw meat on a joss statue, he received two hatchet blows to the head and two pistol shots to the abdomen from Charley Lee Quong and two others.[16] At the ensuing trial the defendants were convicted of murder despite the testimony of two witnesses who stated in almost identical language that the deceased had attacked first, thus necessitating self-defense on the part of the accused. The prosecutor urged the judge to instruct the jury to disregard any Chinese testimony on the grounds that it was "prejudicial" or untrue. The judge refused, but he did tell the jury that the Chinese witnesses might be lying. The Oregon Supreme Court held that this instruction violated the defendants' right to a fair hearing and ordered a new trial.[17]

Two other decisions of northwestern supreme courts during this period resulted in favorable verdicts for Chinese, but they contained ominous implications. In *Oregon v. Moy Looke* (1879), the Chinese defendant was charged with kidnapping a Chinese woman, Wong Ho. During the trial, the legality of a marriage of Wong Ho to a Chinese national became crucial to the defense. Evidence concerning the customs of China was interpreted for the jury as a question of law by the judge. Upon conviction, Moy Looke appealed on the grounds that Chinese customs should be subject to cultural, not legal, interpretation. The Oregon Supreme Court reversed the lower court opinion, holding that as a "general rule . . . courts do not take judicial notice of the laws of a foreign country."[18] Moy Looke may have won, but now Oregon's frontier juries, noted for hostile attitudes toward Chinese customs, could interpret Chinese cultural values without judicial guidance.

A similar outcome emerged from a Montana dispute involving Chinese ownership of mining claims. The Montana territorial legislature in 1872 prohibited aliens from acquiring placer mine titles or profits and made alien claims subject to forfeiture to the territory. Fauk Lee challenged the validity of the statute by purchasing three thousand feet of placer-mining property. The district court found him guilty and confiscated his land; he appealed. In the landmark opinion of *Montana v. Lee* (1874), Justice Decius S. Wade, often called the "founder of Montana jurisprudence,"[19] focused upon two important issues: the rights of Chinese prior to the enactment of the forfeiture law and the power of the legislature to enact such legislation. Quoting liberally from such noted legal scholars as Coke, Blackstone, Marshall, and Kent, Wade observed that the Chinese had the power to own property against all the world except the sovereign "state," which he narrowly defined as Congress. Thus the Montana territorial legislature could neither prohibit Lee from owning property nor confiscate his property.[20] Justice Hiram Knowles, another outstanding figure in the early history of Montana, delivered a minority opinion that reflected the popular view. He believed sovereignty resided in both federal and territorial legislatures and that the denial of mining opportunities to the Chinese was a legitimate exercise of authority by the territorial legislature. "Time will fully demonstrate the benefits that would have accrued to this Territory had such legislation been sustained," he observed.[21] Although *Montana v. Lee* gave the Chinese defendant a significant victory over a hostile non-Asian community, it left the door ajar for the ouster of the Chinese from Montana's mines. By calling attention to the power of the federal government, the decision encouraged efforts to lobby Congress for a law barring alien ownership of real property. Such a proposal became law thirteen years later.

Though Chinese defendants prior to 1883 obtained favorable court decisions in such cases as *Lee* and *Moy Looke*, those decisions came grudgingly and rectified only flagrant violations. In other criminal decisions before 1883, appellate courts rejected Chinese efforts to assert their rights to due process of law. Tried and convicted of murdering John McGuinness, Ah Hop appealed to the Idaho Territorial Supreme Court, arguing that eight of the jurors at her trial had been summoned illegally, her counsel had not been permitted to give closing arguments, and the jury had not been instructed about the charges or her pleas. The Idaho court ruled in 1878 that she was raising "mere formalities" of the law, which did not warrant the overruling of the lower court decision.[22]

Like Ah Hop, Lee Ping Bow, who was found guilty of larceny and sentenced to two years' imprisonment in Oregon, failed to persuade the state supreme court to uphold his rights to due process. At his arraignment, the Chinese-speaking defendant had been refused an interpreter; at his trial his counsel had been absent when the verdict was announced and therefore unable to present necessary motions for appeal. However, the supreme court in 1881 reasoned that since Lee had appeared at all legal proceedings, he must have understood English, and since he understood English, absence of counsel did not constitute a reversible error.[23]

Courts arrived at such judgments by making considerations of due process secondary to certain broadly defined principles of common law. A graphic illustration of this practice occurred in 1876 in Montana Territory. The supreme court allowed the successful prosecution of Ye Wan for gambling to stand even though the Montana gambling statute did not cover the defendant's actions. Instead, the common law doctrine of criminal nuisance was construed as being applicable. Justice Decius Wade dissented, noting tersely that "it was a work of folly to make a Criminal Code, if the common law system of crimes remains in force."[24] Behind such reliance on common law was antipathy toward the Chinese, which became increasingly evident in the late 1870s. By the early 1880s some appellate courts did not even find it necessary to hide their prejudices behind common law. Symbolic of this change was the Oregon Supreme Court's hearing of the appeal that resulted from the retrial of the Chinese defendants in the Portland joss house murder. After the supreme court had reversed the initial conviction of the defendants, they had been retried separately. Ah Lee was the first to be reconvicted, and he appealed to the supreme court, alleging two lower court errors. He objected to the jury visiting the joss house without him or his counsel being present, but the court ruled he should have come along with the jury if he had wanted to be there. He also challenged the admission into evidence of Chin's dying declaration naming him as the killer on the grounds that Chin could not be believed because he was an "imperfect Christian" who did not believe in the existence of a Supreme Being. The court was not persuaded. Chin may have been "a worshiper of Joss, and the heathenish religion of his race," acknowledged the justices, but since he had been attending a Portland missionary school and since he had defaced the joss house, the common law rule—that the last words of a dying Christian were admissible testimony—prevailed.[25]

By 1883 appellate judges, such as those who decided the *Ah Lee* case, were becoming subject to the general anti-immigrant pressures of the late nineteenth century.[26] Their decisions reflected a changing US western society, which was forming strong attitudes of incomprehension or contempt for the Chinese and their culture. From 1883 to 1902, appellate courts heard twice as many civil disputes involving Chinese as in previous years, and most of the decisions had serious consequences for the Chinese community. Unlike before, a majority of the decisions—seventeen of twenty-nine—went against the Chinese and represented justice denied. Of the twelve favorable rulings, most dealt with mining claims, one of the more popular occupations of Chinese in the Northwest.[27]

Idaho Territorial Supreme Court justices defied these trends against Chinese when in 1893 they examined a mining dispute. A. C. McLean and his friends jumped a claim owned by James Witt and leased to Ah Kle and seven other Chinese miners; Witt, Kle, and the miners brought suit to regain the claim plus $7,000 damages. The Chinese lost in the lower court and appealed to Idaho's supreme court, which found in their favor. The defendants had argued that Chinese could not work or lease mining claims since an 1887 act of Congress had denied aliens the right to own claims. The court ruled that the legislation was not applicable since holding title and leasing were separate legal rights. Ten months later Ah Kle was again before the supreme court in a suit he brought against the sheriff of Idaho County. The law officer had refused to enforce the previous supreme court decision because the sheriff demanded an unusually high bond that the plaintiff could not afford. Angered at the sheriff's recalcitrance, the court ordered him to honor Ah Kle's claim.[28]

Most civil decisions after 1882, however, went against the Chinese and often reflected ethnocentrism if not racism.[29] The Montana Territorial Supreme Court, for example, upheld state legislation that required a $500 bond from any employer of Chinese labor.[30] Similarly, the Oregon Supreme

Court upheld lawyer J. W. Bennett, who had been sued by his Chinese client, Ah Foe. Bennett had encouraged Ah Foe to sell some valuable land for much less than its market value to another person who was secretly in partnership with Bennett. Ah Foe claimed he had been deceived because of his inability to understand English, but the court ruled against him on the grounds that he had been a cook for twenty years around English-speaking people and should have understood English even if he claimed he did not.[31]

Some of the civil opinions revealed distinctly anti-Chinese prejudices of appellate judges. A graphic example occurred in Oregon in a custody dispute over two Chinese children—Ah Won, age eight, and her sister, Ah Tie, age ten. The issue arose in 1889 when the Portland Women's North Pacific Presbyterian Board of Missions petitioned the court to transfer custody of the children from their uncle, Yum Chung, to the Presbyterian women. The petition noted that the children's parents were dead and they were then living with their stepmother, who kept a house of ill fame. Coming to the defense of the stepmother and Yum was Wong Chin Way, wealthy guardian of the estates of the children, who denied the allegations, accused the Presbyterians of trying to turn the children against Chinese ways, and promised to send the stepmother and children to China as soon as the father's estate was settled. When the lower court ordered the children placed in the custody of the Presbyterian women, Wong sought outside help and persuaded a ship captain, who was preparing to leave for Hong Kong, to take the children and deliver them to their relatives. The captain convinced the lower court judge to order the Presbyterians to give up the children, but rather than comply, the women appealed to the Oregon Supreme Court for a general review of all issues in the case.[32]

The court proceeded to ponder this classic example of cultural conflict in order to determine what was in the best interests of the children. It promised to render a decision not "influenced by fanatical zeal on the one side or by morbid sentimentality on the other."[33] Despite such wishes, the justices reversed the lower court with an opinion that revealed blatant anti-Chinese bias:

> The difficulty in such cases is to ascertain the truth. Chinamen such as we have among us can rarely be trusted in such matters, however bland and plausible they may appear. Those of the race who have come to this coast

have generally exhibited a total disregard of virtue, candor and integrity, and have shown such a propensity to cunning, deception and perfidy, that if they were to engage in an effort to accomplish an apparently meritorious object a strong suspicion would arise that there was some covert, sinister scheme at the bottom of it. In this case their purpose may be to send these children to their grandmother for the sole benefit of the children; but we have no means of ascertaining whether or not such is their real motive.[34]

So far as the court was concerned, sentimentality for these new Americans was misplaced and against the onrush of progress:

Our societies of today, whether in the church or out of it, are seldom engaged in any narrow sectarian schemes, but are endeavoring to elevate and improve the moral and physical condition of the lower strata of humanity.... Men and women who engage in such work,—who search in the dregs and scum of society, and find suffering and abused children, and relieve their wants and necessities, and train them in the path of rectitude, with a view to rendering them useful in the world, instead of being a burden and a nuisance,—are fit and proper to be the guardians of any child, whether of Christian or pagan extraction.[35]

Contemporaneous with such attacks upon Chinese social and cultural values were court efforts to restrain Asian economic interests. These came in cases involving agricultural disputes, railroad labor,[36] and especially mining. In 1883 the Montana Territorial Supreme Court agreed to resolve a question being sharply debated in the mining areas: can an alien hold title to a mining claim, which had been conveyed to him by an American, against an American citizen who later filed on the location and demanded possession? In *Tibbitts v. Ah Tong* the courts held that Congress in 1866 had opened mining lands to occupation and purchase by citizens and those intending to be citizens. Since Asians were aliens ineligible for citizenship, Ah Tong had to surrender his claim. But the court went further. It found the right to occupy contingent on the right to possess. In other words, Asians could not even work a mining claim because they had no potential to possess it. The practical effect of the decision was to overrule the earlier holding in *Montana v. Lee* and to ban Chinese in Montana from engaging in a major livelihood—placer mining.[37]

Civil suits in the Pacific Northwest after 1882 generally resulted in unfavorable verdicts for Chinese litigants, but even greater losses occurred as a result of criminal cases, which produced a rapid erosion of rights to due process. Of twenty-seven criminal decisions appealed, only eight led to reversals favorable for the Chinese, and some of these reversals came at the expense of basic rights.[38] In Oregon, two disputes decided by its supreme court were especially destructive for the Chinese. In *Oregon v. Mah Jim*, the supreme court reversed a lower court decision because Chinese witnesses had been allowed to offer testimony that convicted Mah Jim of murder. "Experience convinces everyone," declared the court,

> that the testimony of Chinese witnesses is very unreliable, and that they are apt to be actuated by motives that are not honest. The life of a human being should not be forfeited on that character of evidence without a full opportunity to sift it thoroughly.... The witnesses referred to may have been attempting to carry out a diabolical design—no one can tell what that class of persons may have in view. Their practices are very peculiar and mysterious, and the court, in no such case, should adopt a refined, technical rule as to the admission of evidence tending to show what their motives may be.[39]

Two years later, in 1888, the Oregon Supreme Court reaffirmed its earlier decision by voiding the murder conviction of a Chinese who had been found guilty on the basis of testimony of Chinese witnesses. "Juries should be loath," stated the court, "to convict a Chinaman of murder in the first degree upon Chinese testimony; not wholly on account of a tender regard for the life of the accused, but also from a respect and reverence for truth and justice."[40] The Oregon decisions produced new trials for the two Chinese defendants, but at a heavy price.

Those Chinese whose appeals were rejected lost out entirely as the courts made war on Chinese social and economic traditions. Of the twenty-seven criminal appellate decisions delivered after 1882, nineteen (or over 70 percent) went against Chinese defendants.[41] One such adverse decision that resulted in a major denial of due process occurred in Washington as a result of Seattle's efforts to outlaw Chinese lotteries. Chin Let had been acquitted at the circuit court level on the grounds that the Seattle ordinance had encroached on the police power of the state.[42] The supreme court disagreed, asserting that the Washington Constitution gave municipalities the authority to legislate on gambling. This decision went against Chin Let even though Seattle was not represented by lawyers. The court regretted "that counsel for the city have not seen fit to furnish us a brief or argument, or cite any authorities upon any of the questions noticed in this opinion," but this oversight proved no obstacle to the justices, who rationalized their position in a five-page opinion.[43]

The lottery case was representative of other disputes involving what the non-Chinese termed "Chinese crimes" against morality, but which in reality were assaults on Chinese cultural practices. Ten of the nineteen criminal cases going against Chinese defendants involved cultural crimes, especially opium smoking and challenges to laundry taxes. A typical example occurred in 1890 when Ah Lim was found guilty of violating an 1883 Washington statute against opium smoking.[44] He appealed to the Washington Supreme Court, asserting that the statute violated his constitutional right to life and liberty and deprived him of his means of enjoyment without due process of law.[45] The court was completely unsympathetic. "It is common to indulge in a great deal of loose talk about natural rights and liberties, as if these were terms of well-defined and unchangeable meaning," declared all but one of the justices. "There is no such thing as an absolute or unqualified right or liberty guaranteed to any member of society."[46] The lone dissenter may have faced the issue more squarely than the majority. Justice Elmon Scott observed that under the Washington statute "a single inhalation of opium, even by a person in the seclusion of his own house, away from the sight and without the knowledge of any other person, constitutes a criminal offense under this statute. And this regardless of the actual effect of the particular act upon the individual, whether beneficial or injurious."[47] He also took cognizance of the majority opinion's speculative notions of legislative intent. To Scott, this holding was a dangerous precedent that violated not natural but constitutional rights. "Individual desires," proclaimed the dissenter, "are too sacred to be ruthlessly violated where only acts are involved which purely appertain to the person, and which do not clearly result in an injury to society."[48]

Oregon in 1887 also outlawed both the smoking and possession of opium.

Convicted of illegal possession of the drug, Mon Luck appealed to the supreme court, which turned him down. The statute infringed on personal liberties, acknowledged the court, but this was permissible because opium was "an active poison." When the defendant asserted that opium was no more harmful than alcohol and merited a similar legal treatment, the court distinguished between these two narcotic substances:

> It is a matter of common knowledge that intoxicating liquors are produced principally for sale and consumption as a beverage, and so common has been their manufacture and use for this purpose that they are regarded by some courts as legitimate articles of property, the possession of which neither produces nor threatens any harm to the public. But the use of opium for any purpose other than as permitted in this act has no place in the common experience or habits of the people of this country, but is admitted by all to be an insidious and demoralizing vice, injurious alike to the health, morals, and welfare of the public.[49]

Judicial attitudes toward opium smoking clearly left no latitude for the Chinese. Any statute aimed at curbing the use of opium was permissible in the Northwest.

An even more blatant form of discrimination was the tax on laundries, a primary mode of occupation for many urban Chinese. The Montana legislature taxed three classes of laundries on a quarterly basis: steam laundry, fifteen dollars; laundry operated by one male, ten dollars; and laundry employing one or more persons, twenty-five dollars. Sam Loi challenged the constitutionality of this act by refusing to pay it. In his appeal to the Montana Supreme Court he relied on a twofold argument. First, he contended that the tax should be stricken because it was not a uniform tax as required by state law. The court reasoned that the levy was not a tax but a fee and constitutional provisions required uniformity for taxes only. Second, Loi claimed the law violated the Fourteenth Amendment of the US Constitution by discriminating against Americans on the basis of race. "The fact that Chinamen are engaged in the hand laundry business," reported the court in 1895, "is purely fortuitous. The law, in its terms, applies to all male laundrymen, of every condition and nationality."[50] Montana courts ignored California[51] and US Supreme Court decisions to the contrary. Nine years earlier, in *Yick Wo v. Hopkins*, the US

Supreme Court had reviewed the constitutionality of a San Francisco ordinance requiring a license for operating a laundry in a wooden building. The ordinance appeared to be fire protection legislation, but the Board of Supervisors, which held administrative power under the act, issued eighty licenses, seventy-nine to white owners, while denying licenses to some two hundred Chinese laundrymen. According to the US Supreme Court, the administration of the ordinance reflected a flagrant violation of the equal protection clause of the Fourteenth Amendment.[52]

Extreme violations of due process did not go unchecked. The Montana Supreme Court ruled that when the only prosecution witness in the grand larceny trial of a Chinese woman could not appear, her constitutional right to be confronted by her accuser had been violated.[53] The Washington Supreme Court found that even though a Chinese defendant's witness disobeyed a court order and stepped into the courtroom before being called to testify, he could not be prevented from testifying.[54] These decisions, however, were exceptions to the general trend of restricting Chinese civil liberties.

Statistically, two patterns can be identified in the disputes appealed to Pacific Northwest supreme courts between 1849 and 1902. Most cases decided prior to the Chinese Exclusion Act of 1882, whether criminal or civil, tended to favor Chinese litigants. From 1883 to 1902, however, the Chinese experienced a drastic turnabout in their success rates. They lost 70 percent of their appeals in criminal cases and 59 percent of their civil actions. Put another way, they achieved favorable verdicts in only 36 percent of all their appeals. (See table 7) Clearly Pacific Northwest supreme courts were joining in the wave of anti-Chinese sentiment following the Exclusion Act of 1882.

A further indication of this trend can be observed in table 8, which includes all criminal cases appealed to northwestern supreme courts.[55] Prior to 1883, 51 percent of the non-Chinese defendants and 60 percent of the Chinese defendants received favorable decisions. Between 1883 and 1902 the success rate for non-Chinese defendants fell ten percentage points while that for Chinese fell thirty percentage points. In every state and territory, a criminal defendant who was not Chinese had a better chance of vindication before a state or territorial supreme court than did a Chinese defendant.

The anti-Chinese juridical sentiment was doubtlessly aided by the collapse of the Reconstruction experiment. To the westerner, the end of Reconstruction

TABLE 7. Chinese Litigants before Pacific Northwest Supreme Courts, 1849–1902

	CASES DECIDED BEFORE 1883					
	Civil			Criminal		
State or Territory	For Chinese Litigants	Against Chinese Litigants	Total Civil Cases	For Chinese Defendants	Against Chinese Defendants	Total Criminal Cases
Idaho	1	0	1	1	2	3
Wyoming	1	0	1	0	0	0
Washington	1	1	2	0	0	0
Oregon	1	1	2	5	3	8
Montana	0	1	1	3	1	4
Total	4	3	7	9	6	15

	CASES DECIDED 1883–1902					
State or Territory	For Chinese Litigants	Against Chinese Litigants	Total Civil Cases	For Chinese Defendants	Against Chinese Defendants	Total Criminal Cases
Idaho	3	1	4	1	3	4
Wyoming	0	0	0	0	0	0
Washington	2	2	4	2	4	6
Oregon	5	10	15	4	9	13
Montana	2	4	6	1	3	4
Total	12	17	29	8	19	27

in the South may have made it easier to justify oppressing the Chinese—many had already been made the scapegoat for the severe depression in the West during the late 1870s, massive unemployment, the rise of labor unions, and anxiety over conquering a new technological world. In addition, late nineteenth-century America was preparing to follow Rudyard Kipling's call to take up the white man's burden and to remake "alien" cultures.

The increasingly restive hostility held by a suspicious majority toward a minority coincided with major political developments in much of the Northwest. Washington, Montana, Idaho, and Wyoming entered the Union between 1889 and 1890, and their evolution from territory to state necessitated

TABLE 8. Chinese and Non-Chinese Defendants before Northwestern Supreme Courts, 1849–1902

State or Territory	CRIMINAL CASES DECIDED BEFORE 1883			
	Decision Favoring Non-Chinese Defendant	Decision Favoring Government Prosecution	Decision Favoring Chinese Defendant	Decision Favoring Government Prosecution
Idaho	13 (38%)	21 (62%)	1 (33%)	2 (67%)
Wyoming	9 (56%)	7 (44%)	0	0
Washington	12 (80%)	3 (20%)	0	0
Oregon	34 (50%)	34 (50%)	5 (63%)	3 (37%)
Montana	12 (48%)	13 (52%)	3 (75%)	1 (25%)
Total	80 (51%)	78 (49%)	9 (60%)	6 (40%)

State or Territory	CRIMINAL CASES DECIDED 1883–1902			
	Decision Favoring Non-Chinese Defendant	Decision Favoring Government Prosecution	Decision Favoring Chinese Defendant	Decision Favoring Government Prosecution
Idaho	28 (29%)	68 (71%)	1 (25%)	3 (75%)
Wyoming	29 (60%)	19 (40%)	0	0
Washington	122 (38%)	198 (62%)	2 (33%)	4 (67%)
Oregon	97 (49%)	103 (51%)	4 (31%)	9 (69%)
Montana	78 (37%)	131 (63%)	1 (25%)	3 (75%)
Total	354 (41%)	519 (59%)	8 (30%)	19 (70%)

conventions, constitutions, elections, and significantly, a new system of appellate courts staffed by local rather than national personnel. The new western jurists watched the federal government adopt its first of several discriminatory policies toward the Chinese in 1882 and observed how the US Supreme Court undercut the Civil Rights Act of 1875. These developments doubtlessly provided the fledgling appellate courts with the political security and legal precedents essential to deny the Chinese those constitutional guarantees non-Asian Americans regarded as sacrosanct. In 1905 B. Frank Dake wrote in the *Albany Law Journal* a rare article concerning the status of the Chinese under American law. It concluded with an impassioned plea for justice for all Americans:

> The expulsion of the Moors by Spain, the expulsion of the Jews by every European nation but one, the revocation of the edict of Nantes, the expulsion of the Huguenots, the massacre of St. Bartholomew, the horrors of Ghetto life are some of the darker blots on the pages of history. The banishment and murder in recent years by a nation claiming to be a Christian people (Russia), of thousands of Jews, have been followed by swift and terrible retribution; and when the history of the dawn of the twentieth century shall be written, and we shall be judged by the standards by which we now judge other people and other times, shall it be said of us that, while claiming to be the greatest Christian country, proclaiming the principles of republican government and of universal freedom, to the pleas of the Chinaman for justice we have been deaf?[56]

These pleas, when taken to the appellate courts of the American Pacific Northwest during the late nineteenth century, met closed legal minds and considerable defective hearing.

Notes

Originally published as John R. Wunder, "The Chinese and the Courts in the Pacific Northwest: Justice Denied?," *Pacific Historical Review* 52 (May 1983): 191–211.

1. *Missoula and Cedar Creek Pioneer*, June 22, 1871.
2. Roger Daniels and Harry H. L. Kitano, *American Racism: Exploration of the Nature of Prejudice* (Englewood Cliffs, NJ: Prentice Hall, 1970), 35–45; US Dept. of Commerce, Bureau of the Census, *Ninth Census of the United States, 1870: Population* (Washington, DC, 1870), 1:8, 18; *Tenth Census of the United States, 1880: Population* (Washington, DC, 1880), 1:38–39; *Eleventh Census of the United States, 1890: Population* (Washington, DC, 1890), 1:468, 474.
3. Oregon Constitution, art. 15, sec. 8 (1857); Ore. Stat., chap. 35, 815–17 (1862); W. P. Wilcox, "Anti-Chinese Riots in Washington," *Washington Historical Quarterly* 20 (1929): 204–11. For a survey of Chinese experiences in the Pacific Northwest, see Larry D. Quinn, "'Chink Chink Chinaman': The Beginning of Nativism in Montana," *Pacific Northwest Quarterly* 58 (1967): 82–89; "The Japanese Problem in Oregon," *Oregon Law Review* 24 (1945): 208; Murray Morgan, *Skid Road: An Informal Portrait of Seattle* (New York, 1951), 63–102; Paul Crane

and T. A. Larson, "The Chinese Massacre," *Annals of Wyoming* 12 (1940): 47–55, 153–61; John R. Wunder, "Law and Chinese in Frontier Montana," *Montana, the Magazine of Western History* 30 (1981): 18–31; John R. Wunder, "The Courts and the Chinese in Frontier Idaho," *Idaho Yesterdays* 25 (1981): 23–32; M. Alfreda Elsensohn, *Idaho Chinese Lore* (Caldwell, ID: Caxton Printers, 1970); Jules A. Karlin, "The Anti-Chinese Outbreaks in Seattle, 1885–1886," *Pacific Northwest Quarterly* 39 (1948): 103–29; Jules A. Karlin, "The Anti-Chinese Outbreak in Tacoma, 1885," *Pacific Historical Review* 23 (1954): 271–283; and Robert E. Wynne, *Reaction to the Chinese in the Pacific Northwest and British Columbia, 1850–1910* (New York: Arno Press, 1978).

4. Historians have concentrated on social and economic issues within a federal or California framework. See B. Frank Dake, "The Chinaman before the Supreme Court," *Albany Law Journal* 67 (1905): 258–67; "Current Topics," *Central Law Journal* 17 (1883): 261; "Status of the Chinese in the United States," *Legal News* 1 (1878): 373–74; Alexander Saxton, *The Indispensable Enemy: Labor and the Anti-Chinese Movement in California* (Berkeley: University of California Press, 1971); Gunther Barth, *Bitter Strength: A History of the Chinese in the United States, 1850–1870* (Cambridge, MA: Harvard University Press, 1964); Cheng-Tsu Wu, ed., *"Chink": A Documentary History of Anti-Chinese Prejudice in America* (New York: New American Library, 1972); Leigh Dana Johnsen, "Equal Rights and the 'Heathen Chinese': Black Activism in San Francisco," *Western Historical Quarterly* 11 (1980): 57–68; Elmer C. Sandmeyer, *The Anti-Chinese Movement in California* (Urbana: University of Illinois Press, 1939); and Ping Chiu, *Chinese Labor in California, 1850–1880* (Madison: University of Wisconsin Press, 1963).

5. Milton R. Konvitz, *The Alien and the Asiatic in American Law* (Ithaca, NY: Cornell University Press, 1946). Other minorities have begun to receive some attention from legal scholars. Most provocative is A. E. Keir Nash, whose articles, among them "Fairness and Formalism in the Trials of Blacks in the State Supreme Courts of the Old South," *Virginia Law Review* 56 (1970): 64–100, have examined the judicial treatment of blacks between 1830 and 1860.

6. The first US restriction on Chinese immigration occurred in 1882, when Congress prohibited the entry of Chinese laborers for ten years. US Statutes at Large 23 (1882): 58–61. Six years later, the 1882 act was amended to prevent Chinese laborers who had arrived in the United States prior to 1882 from regaining entry if they left the United States. US Statutes at Large 25 (1888): 476–79. In 1892 the first exclusionary law was renewed, and in 1902 the ban was made permanent. US Statutes at Large 27 (1892): 25–26; 32 (1902): 176–77.

7. *Bridget Nine v. Lewis M. Starr*, 8 Ore 49 (1879); *First National Bank of Helena v. How et al.*, 1 Mont 604 (1872); *Hoy v. Smith*, 2 Wyo 459 (1878); *Jack Gho (a Chinaman) v. Charley Julles (an Indian)*, 1 Wash Terr 325 (1871); *Seattle and Walla Walla R. R. Co. v. Ah Kow et al.*, 2 Wash Terr 36 (1880); *City of Portland v. Lee Sam*, 7 Ore 397 (1879); *Wa Ching et al. v. Chris. Constantine*, 1 Idaho 266 (1869).

8. 8 Ore 49 (1879); 1 Idaho 266 (1869); 2 Wyo 459 (1878).
9. 2 Wash Terr 325, 327–28 (1871). On other occasions, the Chinese were considered Indians for bureaucratic or legal purposes. In 1877, when Roman Catholic priests desired to convert the Chinese in San Francisco, they found themselves without funds to set up a mission. To obtain the necessary financial support, they officially classified the Chinese as Native Americans, thereby giving them access to the Pius Fund, money put aside by Rome for the express purpose of educating Indians. James P. Gaffey, "Roman Catholic Efforts to Reach the Chinese in San Francisco, 1880–1925," paper presented at the annual meeting of the American Historical Association, Pacific Coast Branch, San Diego, August 17, 1976. Earlier in California, a statute prevented blacks, mulattos, and Indians from testifying in state courts for or against whites. When the question of whether the Chinese could so testify came before the California Supreme Court, it declared that because the Chinese came from Asia and Columbus thought he had discovered Asia, the Chinese were in fact American Indians and, therefore, no Chinese could testify in trials for or against white litigants. *People v. Hall*, 4 Cal 399 (1854).
10. 2 Wash Terr 36 (1880); 1 Mont 604 (1872); 7 Ore 397 (1879).
11. 2 Wash Terr 36, 40 (1880).
12. *Oregon v. Gitt Lee et al.*, 6 Ore 425 (1877); *Oregon v. Moy Looke*, 7 Ore 54 (1879); *Oregon v. Charley Lee* [indicted under the name of Charley Lee Quong], *Ah Lee* [indicted under the name of Lee Jaw], *and Lee Jong*, 7 Ore 237 (1879); *Oregon v. Ah Sam*, 7 Ore 477 (1879); *Oregon v. Tom, a Chinaman*, 8 Ore 177 (1879); *Idaho v. Ah Ho (Chinese Woman)*, 1 Idaho 691 (1878); *Montana v. Lee*, 2 Mont 124 (1874); *Deer Lodge County v. Alt*, 3 Mont 168 (1878); *Montana v. Ah Wah Yen*, 4 Mont 149 (1881).
13. 8 Ore 177–78 (1879).
14. 6 Ore 425 (1877).
15. 3 Mont 168, 169–71 (1878).
16. 7 Ore 237 (1879).
17. Ibid., 258.
18. 7 Ore 54, 56–58 (1879).
19. John D. W. Guice, *The Rocky Mountain Bench* (New Haven, CT, Yale University Press, 1972), 75.
20. 2 Mont 124, 130–38 (1874).
21. Ibid., 156.
22. *Idaho v. Ah Hop et al.*, 1 Idaho 698 (1878).
23. *Oregon v. Lee Ping Bow*, 10 Ore 27, 29–31 (1881).
24. *Montana v. Ye Wan*, 2 Mont 478, 481 (1876).
25. *Oregon v. Ah Lee*, 8 Ore 214, 218–19 (1880). Murder cases inevitably led to an examination of dying declarations, and courts treated them with considerable caution if Chinese were involved. See *Idaho v. Yee Wee*, 57 Idaho 188 (1900); and *Oregon v. Foot You*, 24 Ore 61 (1893).

26. *Oregon v. Ah Lee*, 8 Ore 214, 221 (1880).
27. *Ah How v. Jacob Furth et al.*, 13 Wash 550 (1891); *Don Yook v. Washington Mill Co.*, 16 Wash 459 (1897); *Ah Kle et al. v. McLean et al.*, 2 Idaho 812 (1891); *Ah Kle et al. v. McLean et al.*, 3 Idaho 538 (1893); *Edward Rooney v. George H. Tong et al.*, 4 Mont 596 (1883); *Ah Kle v. Gregory*, 3 Idaho 674 (1893); *Edward Rooney v. George H. Tong et al.*, 4 Mont 597 (1883); *Chung Yow v. Hop Chong et al.*, 11 Ore 220 (1884); *Ah Lep v. Gong Choy and Gong Wing*, 13 Ore 204 (1886); *Ah Lep v. Gong Choy et al.*, 13 Ore 429 (1886); *Oh Chow v. B. Brockway*, 21 Ore 440 (1891); *Marx v. Moy Ham*, 31 Ore 579 (1897).
28. *Ah Kle et al. v. McLean et al.*, 3 Idaho 538, 540, 544 (1893); *Ah Kle v. Gregory*, 3 Idaho 674, 675–76 (1893); Wunder, "The Courts and the Chinese in Frontier Idaho," 30–32.
29. *Riborado et al. v. Quang Pang Mining Co.*, 2 Idaho 131 (1885); *Tibbitts v. Ah Tong*, 4 Mont 536 (1883); *Power et al. v. Gum*, 6 Mont 5 (1886); *Gum v. Murray et al.*, 6 Mont 5 (1886) and 6 Mont 10 (1886); *Montana v. Owsley et al.*, 17 Mont 94 (1895); *Woo Dan v. Seattle Electric Railway and Power Co.*, 5 Wash 466 (1893); *Sam Chong v. C. W. Fowler et al.*, 18 Wash 694 (1898); *Henry Weiner v. Lee Ching et al.*, 12 Ore 276 (1884); *Victor Guille v. Wong Fook*, 13 Ore 577 (1886); *Chee Gong and Fong Long Dick v. L. B. Stearns*, 16 Ore 219 (1888); *In re North Pacific Presbyterian Board of Missions v. Ah Won and Ah Tie*, 18 Ore 339 (1890); *Yick Lee v. William Dunbar*, 20 Ore 416 (1891); *Ming Yue v. Coos Bay Railroad Co.*, 24 Ore 392 (1893); *Ah Doon v. Smith*, 25 Ore 89 (1893); *Alexander v. Ling*, 31 Ore 222 (1897); *Ah Foe v. Bennett*, 35 Ore 231 (1899); *Pot Lick v. Mason*, 37 Ore 629 (1900).
30. 17 Mont 94 (1895).
31. 35 Ore 231, 235 (1899).
32. 18 Ore 339, 340–42 (1890). Similarly, in *Tape v. Hurley*, 66 Cal 473 (1885), the California Supreme Court ruled that Chinese must be allowed to enter public schools under existing California law. A teacher could not prevent a Chinese child from attending classes because the child was Chinese. However, the court invited the California legislature to make changes by classifying Chinese students as vicious or filthy. See also Charles M. Wollenberg, *All Deliberate Speed: Segregation in California Schools, 1855–1975* (Berkeley: University of California Press, 1977); and Irving G. Hendrick, *The Education of Non-whites in California* (San Francisco: R and E Research Associates, 1977).
33. 18 Ore 339, 346.
34. Ibid., 348.
35. Ibid., 349.
36. *Victor Guille v. Wong Fook*, 13 Ore 577 (1886); *Ming Yue v. Coos Bay Railroad Co.*, 24 Ore 392 (1893).
37. 4 Mont 536, 540–41 (1883). See also Konvitz, *The Alien and the Asiatic in American Law*, 212–18, on the right of aliens to share in natural resources.
38. *People v. Ah Too*, 2 Idaho 47 (1884); *Montana v. Lee*, 13 Mont 248 (1893); *Oregon v. Mah Jim*, 13 Ore 235 (1886); *Oregon v. Ching Ling*, 16 Ore 419 (1888); *Oregon v.*

Chee Gong and Fong Long Dick, 16 Ore 534 (1888); *Washington v. Hui and Sam Lee*, 3 Wash Terr 396 (1888); *Washington v. Lee Doon*, 7 Wash 308 (1893).

39. 13 Ore 235, 236–37 (1886).
40. 16 Ore 419, 425 (1888).
41. *Idaho v. Kuok Wah Choi*, 2 Idaho 85 (1885); *Idaho v. Yee Wee*, 7 Idaho 188 (1900); *Idaho v. Quong*, 8 Idaho 191 (1902); *Ah Lim v. Washington*, 1 Wash 156 (1890); *Washington v. Gin Pon*, 16 Wash 425 (1897); *Seattle v. Chin Let*, 19 Wash 38 (1898); *Montana v. Ah Jim*, 9 Mont 167 (1890); *Sam Toi v. French*, 17 Mont 54 (1895); *Montana v. Camp Sing*, 18 Mont 128 (1896); *Oregon v. Tom Louey and Loo Wan*, 11 Ore 326 (1884); *Jennie Wong v. Astoria*, 13 Ore 538 (1886); *Oregon v. Ah Sam*, 14 Ore 347 (1887); *Oregon v. Chee Gong*, 17 Ore 635 (1889); *Oregon v. Chew Muck You*, 20 Ore 215 (1890); *Ex parte Ah Hoy*, 23 Ore 89 (1892); *Oregon v. Foot You*, 24 Ore 61 (1893); *Ex parte Mon Luck*, 29 Ore 421 (1896); *Oregon v. Wong Gee*, 35 Ore 276 (1899).
42. 19 Wash 38 (1898).
43. Ibid., 43.
44. Wash. Terr. Statutes, chap. 2073, sec. 30 (1883).
45. 1 Wash 156, 158 (1890).
46. Ibid., 165.
47. Ibid., 167.
48. Ibid., 173.
49. 29 Ore 421, 427–28 (1896). See also 14 Ore 347 (1887).
50. 17 Mont 54, 60 (1895). See also 18 Mont 128 (1896) for further refinements of this concept.
51. For laundry legislation and subsequent court interpretations in California, see *Ex parte Moynier*, 65 Cal 33 (1884); and *In re White*, 67 Cal 102 (1885).
52. *Yick Wo v. Hopkins*, 188 US 356 (1886). The Yick Wo ruling was eroded and isolated by the court in 1915 in *Truax v. Raich*, 239 US 33 (1915).
53. *Montana v. Lee*, 13 Mont 248, 249–50 (1893).
54. *Washington v. Lee Doon*, 7 Wash 308, 313 (1893).
55. Information for criminal cases decided before 1883 was derived from *Idaho Reports*, vols. 1–2; *Wyoming Reports*, vols. 1–2; *Washington Territory Reports*, vols. 1–2; *Oregon Reports*, vols. 1–10; and *Montana Reports*, vols. 1–4.

    Information for criminal cases decided from 1883 to 1902 was derived from *Idaho Reports*, vols. 2–8; *Wyoming Reports*, vols. 3–11; *Washington Territory Reports*, vols. 2–3; *Washington Reports*, vols. 1–30; *Oregon Reports*, vols. 10–42; and *Montana Reports*, vols. 5–27.
56. Dake, "Chinaman before Supreme Court," 267.

CHAPTER 7

The Courts and the Chinese in Frontier Idaho

ON MARCH 25, 1865, the *North Idaho Radiator* reported on an anti-Chinese meeting held the previous night at the Nez Perce County Courthouse in Lewiston. A well-known California clergyman, A. W. Sweeney, had come to the mountain interior to spread his message of hate. The Chinese, according to the minister, had been very bad for California, and Idaho should make every effort to keep them out. In his home state, the Chinese presence had been destructive of the interests of American miners and merchants; white miners were forced to relocate, and the Chinese dealt with fellow Chinese businessmen. Sweeney argued that prosperity in California was temporary; long-term economic growth required the expulsion of the Chinese. He urged Idahoans to ask the Chinese to leave or force them out. Sweeney was not in favor of taking the law into one's own hands except in special circumstances— and for him the Chinese migration to Idaho constituted one of those circumstances.[1]

W. W. Thayer, a Lewiston resident who was called upon to respond, objected to Sweeney's ideas and proposed methods; he was surprised to hear a clergyman advocate mob rule. Thayer believed that California was not suffering economically but had entered a period of lengthy prosperity. And he believed that US treaty obligations overruled any attempt to force out the Chinese. After all, the Chinese coming to Idaho represented the continuing tradition of America opening its borders to the emigrants of all countries.[2]

The newspaper noted that the speakers made "sharp thrusts" at each other; the meeting adjourned with sides chosen and strong feelings expressed. But the newspaper also predicted that organized violence was not likely to be used against Idaho's Chinese.[3]

The first Chinese to come to frontier Idaho probably arrived in 1864 at the Oro Fino gold fields. They were brought in from California on contract to alleviate a shortage of labor. The high point of Chinese population in Idaho came in 1870, when 4,274 Chinese were discovered by the census. Subsequent countings reflected a decline in Idaho Chinese; in 1880, 3,379 Chinese resided in Idaho; in 1890, 2,007; and in 1900, 1,467. The bulk of the Chinese population throughout the last third of the nineteenth century lived in southern Idaho's Boise County. Although these numbers appear to be small, the Chinese constituted 28.5 percent of Idaho's entire population in 1870. This percentage decreased to 11.6 percent in 1880 and 2.4 percent in 1890, reflecting the out-migration of Chinese and in-migration of non-Chinese.[4]

Fortunately for Idaho's Chinese, the predictions of the *North Idaho Radiator* proved correct. No regionally organized anti-Chinese groups emerged in Idaho, unlike its neighbor states. Still, there was anti-Asian hostility that took several forms. Sporadic violence, including murders, occurred in rural Idaho. As many as one hundred Chinese may have been killed—most during 1885–86, a time of much greater anti-Chinese violence throughout the West.[5]

Other actions came as lawful challenges to the status of the Chinese. As in other western states, the Chinese were forced to endure legal harassment in Idaho, and these matters eventually came before the highest Idaho court. But the territorial supreme court of Idaho refused to imitate the anti-Chinese hysteria sweeping Oregon, Washington, and Montana.[6] Instead, it sought to balance judiciously the interests of Idaho's Chinese and non-Chinese populations.

The initial major test of Chinese rights came before the Idaho Territorial Supreme Court during the 1869–70 term. Two cases, one civil and one criminal, were decided.[7] The first, in 1869, concerned several Boise County Chinese who sued one Christopher Constantine for money owed them. The Chinese plaintiffs had amended their complaint, but when the defendant had objected, the district court had found against the Chinese. The plaintiffs appealed to Idaho's highest court, which heard the procedural arguments and ruled for the Chinese. Most significantly, the court held that Idaho's rules were copied from California, and since California had allowed such amendments, so would Idaho.[8] In other words, California decisions would have a great influence upon future Idaho judicial interpretations.

The next year the supreme court reinforced this new rule in the criminal case of *People v. Ah Choy*. Here the defendant had appealed a murder conviction. He argued that the indictment against him was defective because it did not allege "a deliberate and premeditated" killing and that the district court had wrongly refused to hear his evidence concerning his reasons for fleeing the murder scene.[9]

The supreme court had no sympathy for Ah Choy. It ruled as a matter of law that Idaho statutes were copies of California's and that therefore the court had to look to California case law for guidance. In *People v. Lloyd*,[10] the California court had found that degrees of murder did not need to be specifically stated in indictments, so in Idaho they would not be necessary either. The Idaho court also noted that since the defendant had admitted striking a blow on the dead person, evidence of reasons for flight was not necessary to determine guilt or innocence. Ah Chow was executed.[11]

During the same term of the Idaho Territorial Supreme Court, one of its justices was called upon to rule at the district court level on what may have been the most important Chinese litigation of the nineteenth century. This controversial legal question centered on several Idaho statutes directly relating to the Chinese.

In the 1864 session of the Idaho territorial legislature, a bill was passed placing a head tax of four dollars per month on all Chinese who engaged in mining. The tax was raised during the next legislative session to five dollars per month, and a provision was added requiring a keeper of a Chinese gambling house or brothel to obtain an operating license at fifty dollars per month.[12]

There is evidence of Chinese resistance to the head tax. Joseph H. Boyd, deputy sheriff of Shoshone County, estimated he collected the tax from only 20 percent of the approximately nine hundred Chinese miners operating around Pierce City.[13] But Boise's Chinese decided to take more direct action, challenging the constitutionality of the laws in Idaho's courts. In August 1869, Ah Bow sought a permanent injunction against Frank P. Britten, preventing him from collecting Chinese taxes.[14]

The case was heard before the district court of Justice David Noggle.[15] The

Boise Capital Chronicle reported the arguments presented before Justice Noggle. Many leading citizens of Boise took part in the proceedings, and the *Capital Chronicle* made its own position quite clear in its recapitulation of the trial.[16] Former Idaho Territorial Supreme Court justice John Rogers McBride, for the plaintiffs, opened arguments by discussing the lax national immigration laws.[17] The *Chronicle* twisted McBride's remarks to suggest that there was so little control that "Feejeeians [sic], Hawaiians, Greenlanders, Chinese, and perhaps Gorillas with a little more training" might become citizens.

Attorney S. P. Scanniker for the defense countered McBride's opening salvo by reminding the court that "a decent woman could not walk to [through] the two 'China rows' in Boise City [without fear]" and decrying "a civilization of Joss Houses and the well-known chastity of Chinese 'ladies.'"

At this point J. W. Huston, the new US attorney, tried to defend the Chinese by noting that they were imitators of Americans and learned prostitution from American moral examples. His argumentation did not sit well with the newspaper.[18]

Justice Noggle seemed most concerned about the enforcement provisions behind the tax act. He noted that a sheriff could seize all Chinese property if the Chinese could not pay the tax on immediate demand, and within one hour after a verbal announcement the property could be sold at a public auction. Noggle found this an abusive process and noted, "These Territorial laws seem to be a branch of California's legal history, and of a pernicious system of legislation that certainly is not creditable to American statesmen." Noggle believed that the purpose of the law was to discourage future Chinese migration to Idaho, thus violating the spirit of US-China treaties and the uniform tax provisions of the US Constitution. Noggle concluded, "I have considered the claims of the plaintiff in this case thus hoping thereby to direct the attention to these laws which may speedily result in a correction of the evil by the proper power."[19]

Noggle then in *Marbury v. Madison* fashion proceeded to deny the Chinese their request for an injunction against the Ada County sheriff. The plaintiffs had asked for an order from a court of equity. But Noggle's court was a court of law, hearing only cases alleging wrongdoing under the common law or laws of the territory. Such could not be proven by Ah Bow; even if he could, the remedy of the injunction was not available to him.[20]

The message was clear to Idaho's Chinese. Even with legal fairness and a sympathetic judge on their side, unless the political machinery was somehow altered, Chinese civil rights could easily be eroded. The *Capital Chronicle* commented on what would prove to be a landmark Idaho opinion: "The Chinese miners were greatly disappointed in the result of the tax suit, and have been made to face the music strictly in accordance with the stringent provisions of the severe statute law against them. The decision of Chief Justice Noggle must make both lawmakers and the council for the Chinamen feel a little 'all overish'—like a two-edged sword; it cuts both ways with a polished blade and keen edge."[21] No further court determination was sought.

The Idaho Territorial Supreme Court next dealt with Chinese litigants in 1878. Two criminal cases were heard that term, one concerning murder and the other prostitution.[22] On January 12, 1877, the Idaho territorial legislature passed a statute giving Boise's mayor and council the power to regulate prostitution. Although the city officials passed no ordinances, Ah Ho was arrested and found guilty in Boise magistrate court of living in a bawdy house. In a two-to-one decision, the Idaho Territorial Supreme Court, although completely ignoring Ah Ho's attorney's arguments, reversed the lower court and found for the Chinese defendant. The majority reasoned that the power to regulate prostitution had been delegated to a lower legislative body; with the absence of statutory law in conjunction with the silence of the common law on this subject, no offense could possibly have been committed.[23]

In the other cases heard by Idaho's highest court in 1878, Ah Hop—aided by Yung Sing, Ah Pong, Hong Chu, and Ah Doe—had been found guilty of murdering John McGuinness. They appealed, alleging four procedural irregularities. They claimed that no arraignment of the defendants appeared in the record, more than one offense was charged in the indictment, jury selection was irregular, and their counsel was not allowed the final closing argument to the jury—each a grievous error in its own right, allowing a reversal.[24] The district attorney, George Ainslie, countered by presenting no less than twenty-seven California cases on these same legal points, all in his favor,[25] and this case law was found persuasive by a unanimous court. While clearly seeking to give defendants their day in court, the tribunal did not view latter-day objections kindly. In upholding the convictions, the court noted,

> A defendant in a criminal case is entitled to have all the formalities of

the law complied with, and if anything is omitted, he is entitled to have it corrected; but if he does not insist upon any of those matters which are merely formal and do not affect his substantial rights at the proper time, he will be deemed to have waived them—he cannot be permitted to take the chance of a verdict in his favor, and then failing in this, be given another trial, because of an informality which might have been avoided if it had not been passed [in] silence at the first trial.[26]

By 1883, when Congress passed the first of several restrictions on Chinese immigration, the Idaho Territorial Supreme Court had heard four cases concerning Chinese litigants. Half of these disputes were resolved in favor of Chinese litigants, and it did not appear that Chinese were denied fundamental rights by Idaho's highest tribunal. From 1883 to 1902, when federal statutes permanently barred all Chinese immigration to the United States, the Idaho Supreme Court heard eight cases involving Chinese litigants, four criminal and four civil.[27] Of the four criminal cases, only one resulted in a reversal favoring the Chinese defendant.

In 1884, the Ada County District Court convicted Ah Too of murdering Ah You in daylight before a number of witnesses. Ah Too admitted the bullet came from his revolver but argued that it was an accidental shooting; Ah You, in a dying declaration, accused Ah Too of murder. After the conviction, Ah Too appealed to the Idaho Territorial Supreme Court, composed of Chief Justice John T. Morgan and Justices Norman Buck and Henry E. Prickett.[28] The defendant's attorneys, Fremont Wood and G. W. Adams, argued that new evidence had been found that would show the killing to be a misadventure—in other words, an excusable homicide—and that the district court judge had erred when he instructed the jury not to consider the lack of proven motive. Indeed, the court record showed a rambling, irrelevant instruction by the trial judge. The district attorney, T. D. Cahalan, merely countered by stating that the new evidence was not sufficient to change the verdict.[29] The court found for Ah Too and ordered a new trial. In a unanimous opinion written by Justice Buck, the arguments brought forward by Wood and Adams were accepted as legitimate grounds for reversal.[30] It was not a surprising verdict from a man who was known for his fairness, respect for Chinese culture, and regional and Republican loyalties.[31]

The other three post-1882 criminal cases—*State v. Quong* (1902), *State v.*

Yee Wee (1900), and *People v. Kuok Wah Choi* (1885)—resulted in lost appeals for Chinese litigants. The *Quong* decision involved a battery conviction in Boise city police court appealed to the Idaho Supreme Court, where the defendant argued that testimony of the police magistrate about bruises on the complainant one day after the alleged altercation should not have been admitted, nor should the defendant have been denied a jury trial. The high court had no sympathy for the defendant's contentions.[32]

Similarly, in *People v. Kuok Wah Choi* a criminal procedural question was raised on appeal to the Idaho Territorial Supreme Court. The defendant had been found guilty of murder in Alturas County District Court, but the judge had forced Kuok Wah Choi's attorney to use all of his peremptory challenges before all twelve jurors were selected. Because two Idaho statutes conflicted over this matter, the supreme court decided in a unanimous opinion written by Chief Justice Morgan that the district court judge's rule would prevail. To Morgan the better law prevented any possible corrupt influences commonly confronting jurors. This the highest Idaho court found in the face of California precedents that were carefully distinguished.[33]

The most significant Chinese criminal dispute in Idaho history was decided by the state's highest tribunal in 1900—*State v. Yee Wee*. This case involved a murder, dying declaration, confession, and conspiracy, and it did not end until it reached the Idaho Board of Pardons.

On the night of May 3, 1899, Wee Wah was shot while he was in Sam Wah's store, which served as a gathering place for Hailey's Chinese community, as a general store, gambling hall, and joss house. The local physician, Dr. N. J. Brown, treated Wee Wah for his wound with pine tar and opium, but the patient contracted blood poisoning and died on May 19. Sixteen days before Wee Wah died, he spoke in broken English, accusing Yee Wee of shooting him. Numerous witnesses came forward to corroborate the accusation.[34]

Yee Wee was arrested and placed on trial for murder in the court of prominent local Democrat Charles O. Stockslager.[35] The jury trial began on June 29, with Lyttleton Price defending and R. M. Angel prosecuting. The defendant was thirty years old and born in China; he had lived in the United States for twenty-one years and in Hailey for two years. Wee Wah was his uncle's son, and Yee Wee had lived in a cabin with the deceased the previous winter. The defendant worked as a cook at Baxter's Hotel in Ketchum and also for the Red Cloud Mining Company, which was owned by his attorney.[36]

The prosecution called sixteen witnesses, including ten Chinese (who placed the defendant with a gun in Sam Wah's store at the time of the shooting) and six whites. Asked to confirm Chinese veracity were the local physician, dentist, sheriff, and newspaper publisher and Hailey founding father. Among the issues raised were the dying declaration of Wee Wah; a note written by the defendant in custody that was translated by Charlie Shung, a local restaurant owner, for the state as a confession; and testimony that the defendant owed money to a man in Pocatello who asked the defendant to carry out a contract murder on the deceased.[37]

The defense called but one new witness—the defendant. Yee Wee testified that he was present at the murder scene but that he had tried to stop an unknown assailant when the gun discharged. He also wrote that he was unaware of any contract out on his cousin. Unfortunately for the defendant, the jury did not believe him, and they found Yee Wee guilty of first-degree murder.[38]

Price immediately appealed to the Idaho Supreme Court, alleging three significant grounds for reversal—issues that many state courts had spent years refining. First, the appellant's attorney argued that the dying declaration was defective because no direct quote was ever made, Wee Wah was not in extremis at the time of the declaration some sixteen days before his death, and no mention was made of the deceased's commitment to Christianity. Price neglected to consult California precedents on this matter. Second, Price argued that malice aforethought, a necessary ingredient in first-degree murder, was not proven because the gun was never actually through testimony placed in Yee Wee's hands and "the prosecution rests its case upon the character of testimony from Chinese witnesses."[39] No doubt Price hoped the Idaho court would follow the lead of neighboring states that had barred or lessened the value of Chinese testimony.[40] And third, the appellant's attorney tried to show that the confession note was mistranslated and that a conspiracy did exist—to frame the defendant.

The state of Idaho was represented by Attorney General Samuel H. Hays. In his respondent brief, Hays offered no legal citations and treated the allegations of Price as trivialities.[41] Evidently the Idaho Supreme Court was not moved by the defendant's arguments any more than Hays was. The court in a unanimous opinion affirmed the conviction.

Answering Price, the justices ruled that "dying declarations" are legitimate even if one only thinks one is dying. This was a rather liberal evidential construction, but to cushion this point of law, the court noted, "It might well be argued that the admission of the evidence showing this dying declaration was unnecessary, and there was sufficient evidence to convict the accused without it."[42] The court also dismissed the argument that lack of proof of malice and false confession were possible errors. Regarding malice, the court found ample evidence placing the defendant, gun, and motive at the murder. In fact, the court seemed so anxious to put this legalism to rest that it somewhat irrationally concluded that Yee Wee tried to find who did the shooting and "such acts on the part of the defendant tended to prove his guilt."[43] On the matter of the confession, the court reminded counsel that new translations were inadmissible and that the proper place for a hearing might be the Board of Pardons.[44] *State v. Yee Wee* effectively considered major questions of criminal procedure for Idaho and did not make determinations on the basis of race.

Lyttleton Price did not leave his client. He continued his fight for Yee Wee, this time before the Idaho Board of Pardons. The center of his appeal was the false confession. Price offered translations from the Chinese embassy in Washington, DC, and Chinese scholars from Spokane and Portland that countered the criminal-trial testimony. The board, meeting in November 1900, decided that Yee Wee's sentence should be commuted to life imprisonment at hard labor.[45]

Criminal disputes in Idaho did not result in significant losses of civil liberties for Chinese. Although three of four Chinese lost their appeals, the Idaho Supreme Court chose not to place unfair restrictions upon Idaho's Chinese residents.

Conversely, four civil cases decided from 1883 to 1902 resulted in three victories for Chinese litigants. These cases concerned two issues—Chinese economic rights to mine in Idaho and the desire of a Chinese man to be licensed as a physician.

The latter question reached the Idaho Supreme Court in 1900 from the dispute of *Ah Fong v. McCalla et al.* (as the State Board of Medical Examiners). The plaintiff applied for a license to practice as a physician and surgeon, but the Board of Medical Examiners refused to grant one in spite of the fact that Ah Fong had held a license from 1887 to 1897. The board, operating under an 1899 law, required US citizenship and graduation from a recognized college for licensure.⁴⁶ This statute was directly aimed at curtailing Chinese doctors and indirectly designed to discourage Chinese immigration. Similar Idaho laws applied to attorneys, dentists, liquor sellers, and optometrists. Other western states such as Montana and Wyoming put similar restrictions on their physicians.⁴⁷

Ah Fong appealed to the Ada County District Court, which denied a hearing; he then appealed to Idaho's highest tribunal. The supreme court ruled that the record was "a jumbled mass of papers" and that the district court must hear the case. It did not decide whether the 1899 statute imposed ex post facto conditions on Ah Fong. Ah Fong would receive "his day in court."⁴⁸

The other civil cases all involved disputes over mining claims. A Chinese mining concern, Quang Pan Mining Company, lost a suit for damages to a ditch and property of Diego Riborado and his neighbors. The Chinese company was working old diggings that were washed out and abandoned, and its workers piled the dumpings on the plaintiffs' property. The Idaho Supreme Court in a unanimous opinion written by Justice Buck found applicable mining district rules that in this instance required the defendant to place its refuse on its own property.⁴⁹

The most important Chinese civil case before Idaho's courts involved the fundamental rights of Chinese to lease and work mining claims. Unlike courts in many other western states, the Idaho Supreme Court went out of its way to protect a principal occupation of Idaho's Chinese. The cases involved James Witt, Ah Kle, and seven other Chinese mining partners; A. C. McLean and three other non-Chinese mining associates; and the Idaho County sheriff. James Witt, US citizen, arrived in Pierce City in the spring of 1862. He bought out many miners in the Elk City Mining District and distinguished his claim by the construction of excellent ditch networks. He stayed in the area until 1882, probably "the last big mine owner in this section."⁵⁰ Witt believed the rush of the Chinese, whom he considered superior placer miners, completely changed the nature of the mining district for the better.⁵¹

On July 8, 1882, Witt leased sixteen claims on Buffalo Hill in the Elk City Mining District to Ah Kle and seven other Chinese for twenty-five years. They operated the mine from this date until October 18, 1889, when A. C. McLean and three other whites entered the property and forcibly ejected Ah

Kle and the other Chinese leaseholders. The Chinese filed a complaint and took McLean and his friends to court.[52]

The district court judge, Willis Sweet, was not impressed by the claims of the Chinese; he was perhaps more concerned with the congressional race he would shortly enter and win and his fights to retain the university in Moscow and to keep North Idaho from being annexed to Washington.[53] The defendants argued that the Chinese had no legal capacity to sue because they were not citizens and because the placer ground once was on public lands.[54] Judge Sweet accepted the first of these arguments and went further. He took judicial notice of the Chinese and extended his ruling to all noncitizens:

> Before passing to an investigation of the legal points involved, it is but just to state that the plaintiffs are treated not as Chinamen, but as foreigners. Much stress seems to have been placed on the treaty between the United States and China, and the duty of this court is to observe the rights of plaintiffs thereunder. It all amounts simply to this: That by the terms of the treaty mentioned, a Chinaman is entitled to the same rights and privileges under our laws guaranteed to any other foreigner, no more, no less. This disposes of all the talk made by counsel on both sides, the one in disparagement of the Chinaman and the other in eulogy of him and his rights under the treaty.[55]

Sweet then cited the Montana case of *Tibbitts v. Ah Tong*, in which the Montana court ruled Chinese could not lease mining property, as precisely the same case as that before his bench.[56] Upon reviewing other mining decisions by Idaho, Oregon, Montana, and California courts, Sweet excluded counter California determinations and opted for a new path in Idaho law.[57]

Ah Kle decided to appeal this decision to the Idaho Supreme Court. A first appeal in 1891 was stricken without prejudice because of a defective district court transcript. The high court obviously wanted to hear the case without any detracting errors, and it would receive its chance.[58]

In January 1893, the Chinese miners once again brought their suit before the Idaho Supreme Court. Their attorneys, James W. Poe and James W. Reid, argued that only one question was presented—did US law prohibit leasing of mining claims by noncitizen Chinese? To them it did not. An 1887 US statute prohibited future aliens from owning or holding real estate, but the lease was signed in 1882. To bar this lease allowed an unconstitutional ex post facto application.[59]

The supreme court proved sympathetic to the plaintiff's position. To allow Judge Sweet's interpretation to remain law constituted a fundamental attack on property ownership. The court reasoned, "The Chinamen plaintiffs were the tenants of Witt at the time of the alleged ouster by defendants. Their possession was his possession. An ouster of the tenants by one claiming adverse to the landlord is an ouster of the landlord."[60] The court was also uneasy with a departure from California precedents. It specifically rejected the decisions of Oregon and Montana courts.[61]

Later that same year the Idaho Supreme Court found its determination in the *Ah Kle* case being subverted by lower officials. The sheriff of Idaho County refused to allow the Chinese to enforce a writ of attachment against other new occupants of their rightfully leased claims. The sheriff demanded an indemnity that the Chinese could not afford. The supreme court ordered the sheriff to honor his legal commitments.[62]

Clearly, in civil cases decided from 1883 to 1902, the Idaho Supreme Court refused to treat Chinese as racially or culturally inferior persons. More often than not, the court defended the Asian minority against hostile non-Asian majority attacks, even in the sensitive area of mining-claim disputes.

The Idaho Supreme Court did not succumb to the anti-Chinese pressures present throughout the West. When other state courts adopted scurrilous, racist invectives and twisted legal doctrines beyond rational construction against Chinese litigants,[63] Idaho's court of last resort refused to follow their lead. When anti-Chinese violence spilled forth in Idaho's rural outposts, when local courts sought to encourage such activity, and when Idaho's legislature passed discriminatory legislation aimed specifically at the Chinese, the Idaho Supreme Court maintained a balanced view in attempting to protect the rights of an unpopular minority.

Why did Idaho's supreme court not legitimize the anti-Chinese feeling present within and surrounding Idaho? Certainly Idaho was not immune from minority persecution. It experienced brutal anti–Native American, anti-Mormon, antilabor, and anti-Chinese hysterias. But the higher court resisted the opportunity to legally approve Chinese persecution.

Several factors may have contributed to this unique western legal development. Perhaps most significant was the high court's dogged reliance upon California precedents. California had in fact experienced anti-Chinese hysteria in its legal opinions in the 1850s and early 1860s, but contemporary jurisprudence had modified and sometimes reversed these early transgressions. Rather than break from California as did Idaho's neighbors, the supreme court seldom strayed from its legal guidance.

Another reason for this legal behavior may in part be the nature of Idaho itself. Topographically, economically, and environmentally, the territory and then state was splintered.[64] Diversity characterized politics and protected against the possibility of narrow political and racial ideologies prevailing. A related characteristic of Idaho was slow settlement, especially after initial mining rushes. To business interests, the Chinese represented a positive economic contribution and less of an organized labor threat.

But the weakness of political and economic internal institutions also carried over to Chinese settlements. There seemed to be little Chinese organization outside of Boise. Direct challenges to law were infrequent. and, as in the important *Ah Bow* case, they often stopped short of the Idaho Supreme Court, accepting hostile lower court decisions. The lack of a politically attuned Chinese community combining the resources of those Chinese of Hailey and Pierce City, Pocatello and Silver City, or Florence and Lewiston meant fewer chances for Idaho Supreme Court vindication.[65]

Nevertheless, the court was not afraid to enforce its determinations or to tackle important issues relevant to Idaho's Chinese. And to its credit, the Idaho Supreme Court upheld a tradition of fundamental fairness and remained a bastion of justice for the Chinese of frontier Idaho.

Notes

Originally published as John R. Wunder, "The Courts and the Chinese in Frontier Idaho," *Idaho Yesterdays* 25 (Spring 1981): 23–32.

1. *North Idaho Radiator* (Lewiston), March 25, 1865. Unrest in Lewiston and the Oro Fino Mining District was noted earlier in the *Oregonian* (Portland), February 6, 1865; *North Idaho Radiator*, February 4, 1865; and *Golden Age* (Lewiston), March 12, 1864.
2. *North Idaho Radiator*, March 25, 1865.
3. Ibid.
4. US Department of Commerce, *Ninth Census of the United States, 1870*:

Population (Washington, DC, 1870), 1:8, 18; US Department of Commerce, *Tenth Census of the United States, 1880: Population* (Washington, DC, 1880), 1:38–39; US Department of Commerce, *Eleventh Census of the United States, 1890: Population* (Washington, DC, 1890), 1:468, 474. See also Rose Hum Lee, *The Growth and Decline of Chinese Communities in the Rocky Mountain Region* (New York: Arno Press, 1978), 77–79, 81.

5. Merrill D. Beal and Merle W. Wells, *History of Idaho* (New York: Lewis Historical Publishing, 1959), 1:577–80; M. Alfreda Elsensohn, *Idaho Chinese Lore* (Caldwell, ID: Caxton Printers, 1970). See also Stan Steiner, *Fusang: The Chinese Who Built America* (New York: Harper & Row, 1979), for a popular, general treatment of Chinese American history.

6. For example, see *In re North Pacific Presbyterian Board of Missions v. Ah Won and Ah Tie*, 18 Ore 339 (1890); *Woo Dan v. Seattle Electric Railway and Power Company*, 5 Wash 466 (1893); *Tibbitts v. Ah Tong*, 4 Mont 536 (1883). See also John R. Wunder, "Law and Chinese in Frontier Montana," *Montana, the Magazine of Western History* 30 (Summer, 1981): 18–31; and Robert Edward Wynne, *Reaction to the Chinese in the Pacific Northwest and British Columbia, 1850 to 1910* (New York: Arno Press, 1978).

7. *Wa Ching et al. v. Chris. Constantine*, 1 Idaho 266 (1869); *People v. Ah Choy*, 1 Idaho 317 (1870).

8. *Wa Ching et al. v. Chris. Constantine*, 1 Idaho 266 at 267–68. See also *Natoma Water and Mining Co. v. Clarkin*, 14 Cal 544 (1860).

9. *People v. Ah Choy*, 1 Idaho 317.

10. *People v. Lloyd*, 9 Cal 54 (1857).

11. *People v. Ah Choy*, 1 Idaho 317 at 321.

12. Idaho Territorial Statutes, 3rd session, chapter 31, 174–76 (1864); 4th session, amended (1866).

13. Joseph H. Boyd, *Reminiscences of Joseph H. Boyd* (Seattle: University of Washington Press, 1924), quoted in Elsensohn, *Idaho Chinese Lore*, 26–27.

14. *Ah Bow v. Britten*, Ada County, Idaho, District Court (1869), proceedings recorded in *Capital Chronicle* (Boise), August 18, September 1, 1869. This case is referred to in Beal and Wells, *History of Idaho*, 1:578, although incorrectly interpreted through reliance on the reporting of the *Idaho World* (Idaho City).

15. For a complete list of Idaho Territory's supreme court justices, see Earl S. Pomeroy, *The Territories and the United States, 1861–1890* (Philadelphia: University of Pennsylvania Press, 1947; reprint, Seattle: University of Washington Press, 1969), 186–88.

16. *Capital Chronicle*, August 18, 1869.

17. Beal and Wells, *History of Idaho*, 1:333–34, 337, 381.

18. *Capital Chronicle*, August 18, 1869. See also Thomas Donaldson, *Idaho of Yesterday* (Caldwell, ID: Caxton Printers, 1941), 207–8, for a discussion of the Scanniker and Burmester law firm.

19. *Capital Chronicle*, September 1, 1869.
20. Ibid.
21. Ibid.
22. *People v. Ah Hop et al.*, 1 Idaho 698 (1878); *People v. Ah Ho (a Chinese woman)*, 1 Idaho 691 (1878).
23. *People v. Ah Ho*, 1 Idaho 691 at 692; appellant's brief, filed January 11, 1878, Idaho State Archives, Boise.
24. *People v. Ah Hop et al.*, 1 Idaho 698 at 699–700.
25. Respondent's brief, *People v. Ah Hop et al.*, filed January 14, 1878, Idaho State Archives.
26. *People v. Ah Hop et al.*, 1 Idaho 698 at 702.
27. The criminal cases included *People v. Ah Too*, 2 Idaho 47 (1884); *People v. Kuok Wah Choi*, 2 Idaho 85 (1885); *State v. Yee Wee*, 7 Idaho 188 (1900); and *State v. Quong*, 8 Idaho 191 (1902). The civil cases included *Riborado et al. v. Quang Pang Mining Co.*, 2 Idaho 131 (1885); *Ah Kle et al. v. McLean et al.*, 2 Idaho 812 (1891) and 3 Idaho 528 (1893); *Ah Kle v. Gregory* (Sheriff), 3 Idaho 674 (1893); and *Ah Fong v. McCalla et al.* (as State Board of Medical Examiners), 7 Idaho 20 (1900).
28. *People v. Ah Too*, 2 Idaho 47.
29. Appellant's brief, *People v. Ah Too*, filed January 29, 1884, Idaho State Archives; respondent's brief, *People v. Ah Too*, filed January 31, 1884, Idaho State Archives.
30. *People v. Ah Too*, 2 Idaho 47 at 49–50.
31. Beal and Wells, *History of Idaho*, 1:602; Elsensohn, *Idaho Chinese Lore*, 16.
32. *State v. Quong*, 8 Idaho 191 at 193–95.
33. *People v. Kuok Wah Choi*, 2 Idaho 85 at 88.
34. Blaine County District Court trial transcript, *State v. Yee Wee*, June 29, 1899, 15, 17, Idaho State Archives.
35. Beal and Wells, *History of Idaho*, 2:93, 207.
36. District Court trial transcript, *State v. Yee Wee*, 120–27.
37. Ibid., confession testimony, 90–91.
38. Ibid., 120–31 (gap in transcript).
39. Appellant's brief, *State v. Yee Wee*, filed May 4, 1900, 2–7, 8, Idaho State Archives.
40. See *People v. Hall*, 4 Cal 399 (1854); *Speer v. See Yup Co.*, 13 Cal 73 (1859); *State v. Mah Jim*, 13 Ore 235 (1886); *State v. Ching Ling*, 16 Ore 419 (1888).
41. Respondent's brief, *State v. Yee Wee*, filed May 14, 1900, 3–4, Idaho State Archives.
42. *State v. Yee Wee*, 7 Idaho 188 at 191.
43. Ibid. at 192.
44. Ibid. at 192–93.
45. Application to the Idaho Board of Pardons from Lyttleton Price, *State v. Yee Wee*, filed September 23, 1900, Idaho State Archives; Minutes of the Idaho Board of Pardons, November 24, 1900, Idaho State Archives.

46. *Ah Fong v. McCalla et al.* (as the State Board of Medical Examiners).
47. Milton R. Konvitz, *The Alien and the Asiatic in American Law* (Ithaca, NY: Cornell University Press, 1946), 187–88, 192, 205, 208, 210.
48. Appellant's brief, *Ah Fong v. McCalla et al.*, filed January 2, 1900, Idaho State Archives; Respondent's brief, *Ah Fong v. McCalla et al.*, filed January 17, 1900, Idaho State Archives; *Ah Fong v. McCalla et al.*, 7 Idaho 20 at 22.
49. *Riborado et al. v. Quang Pang Mining Co.*, 2 Idaho 131 at 133–35. See John Fahey, *Ballyhoo Bonanza: Charles Sweeny and the Idaho Mines* (Seattle: University of Washington Press, 1971), for a specific treatment of Idaho mining history.
50. Elsensohn, *Idaho Chinese Lore*, 34.
51. Ibid., 34–39.
52. Idaho County District Court trial transcript, *Ah Kle et al. v. McLean et al.*, October 9, 1890, 2–4, Idaho State Archives.
53. Beal and Wells, *History of Idaho*, 1:587–90, 602–3, 605, 2:73.
54. Trial transcript, *Ah Kle et al. v. McLean et al.*, 6, 14–15.
55. Ibid., 18.
56. *Tibbitts v. Ah Tong*, 4 Mont 536. See also *Territory of Montana v. Lee*, 2 Mont 124 (1874); and Wunder, "Law and Chinese in Frontier Montana," 23–30.
57. Eventually Idaho did attempt to restrict landownership. Idaho Statutes, chap. 313, sec. 58 (1905), 148–49: "sales of state lands shall only be made to citizens of the United States and to those who shall have declared their intentions to become such."
58. *Ah Kle et al. v. McLean et al.*, 2 Idaho 812.
59. Appellants' brief, *Ah Kle et al. v. McLean et al.*, filed January 11, 1893, Idaho State Archives.
60. *Ah Kle et al. v. McLean et al.*, 3 Idaho 538 at 544.
61. Ibid.
62. *Ah Kle v. Gregory* (Sheriff), 3 Idaho 674 at 675–76.
63. For example, see *State of Oregon v. Chee Gong and Fong Long Dick*, 16 Ore 534 (1888); *Territory of Washington v. Hui and Sam Lee*, 3 Wash Terr 396 (1888); and *State ex rel Sam Toi v. French* (County Treasurer), 17 Mont 54 (1895).
64. F. Ross Peterson, *Idaho: A Bicentennial History* (New York: W. W. Norton, 1976), 3–19, 158–81.
65. Jung Pang Lo, "Chinese Reform in Idaho," *Idaho Yesterdays* 5 (Spring, 1961): 20–21; Betty Derig, "The Chinese of Silver City," *Idaho Yesterdays* 2 (Winter 1958–59): 2–5. See *Owyhee Avalanche* (Ruby City, Idaho Territory), August 25 and September 29, 1866, for reporting on the insular features of the local joss house and Chinese internal violence.

CHAPTER 8

Law and Chinese in Frontier Montana

DIVERSITY CHARACTERIZED MONTANA'S early population. The mining boom attracted settlers from all over the nation and several foreign countries. The majority were Christian and Caucasian, but a substantial minority were neither; they were Chinese, and in 1870 they constituted nearly 10 percent of Montana's population. As was the case in other parts of the American West, the Chinese were a distinctive minority, easily recognized and rarely understood. To many westerners their customs seemed odd, their food was unusual, their dress was different. Most of all, westerners were frightened by Chinese religious beliefs and what was perceived to be a clannishness that kept Chinese life veiled from view. These differences singled the Chinese out for abuse, from name-calling and obstruction of their legal rights to anti-Chinese laws and even violence.

There was little the Chinese in Montana could do to protect themselves from a pervasive anti-Chinese feeling that blocked them economically and labeled them as "uncivilized," "idolatrous and filthy," and much worse. Their only protection was the law. Believing that an appeal to reasonable men and the heritage of common law might make a difference, Chinese victims of abuse and discrimination brought their complaints before Montana's courts. There the cases would be argued on their merits, the Chinese hoped, and court decisions would eventually answer the essential question: could the Chinese minority live within a majority society with full rights and liberties?

At first the legal institutions in Montana faced their task squarely and blunted the force of anti-Chinese public opinion. From the late 1860s until the first passage of a federal statute limiting Chinese immigration in 1882, Montana's courts listened to Chinese complaints, recognized their seriousness, and judged them equitably. But it was not long before this judicial monitoring broke down and the Chinese lost in the courts. After the mid-1880s, Montana's justices seemed to reflect popular attitudes toward the Chinese. The surpreme court became anti-Chinese, too.

Chinese came to Montana from California, Colorado, Nevada, and other mining areas in the West, as well as from China. They had the reputation of working harder than whites and for lower wages, of working old mine tailings with success, and of working closely together to maximize their efforts. For some Montanans the Chinese constituted an economic threat, as a little-known incident in Helena during the winter of 1866 demonstrates. Many Chinese in Helena had opened laundry shops and previously established washerwomen complained.

On January 27 the *Montana Radiator*, a month-old Helena newspaper published by T. J. Favorite, featured a notice signed by "A Committee of Ladies." It referred to certain "Mongolian hordes" who were preventing these Helena women from making a living washing clothes.[1]

The women desired the community to boycott all Chinese residents engaged in the laundry business, and they secured the support of the local press. T. J. Favorite was so captivated by the episode that it moved him to commemorate the event in poetry:

> Chinamen, Chinamen, beware of the day,
> When the women shall meet thee in battle array!
>
> Ye hopeless professors of salsoda and soap,
> Beware of the fates that await ye,
> No hangman's committee with ladder and rope,
> But the ladies are coming to *bate* ye.
>
> Ye almond-eyed leather faced murthering heathens
> Ye opium and musk stinking varmints,
> We will not object to your livin' and breathin'

> But beware of the washing of garments.
>
> To stay or to go ye can do as ye choose
> To us it don't make any odds
> So long as ye keep your hands off of the clothes
> And keep out of the lather and suds.²

Favorite noted that the would-be laundresses had obtained his personal support "against the almond-eyed citizens of the John persuasion," and he called upon "every true American [to] be on the alert" for the start of the ban.³

The next week the *Radiator* softened its rhetoric, recording that no news had been heard from "along the lines (clothes lines)." Favorite's poem had evidently stirred someone to compose verse vindicating the Chinese of Helena, but he refused to publish it because he still favored the "ladies' position."⁴

Two weeks later, on February 17, several Chinese citizens, forced to air their position through a paid notice, expressed their feelings about the laundry hysteria.

> GOOD CHINAMEN
> This is to certify that we, the undersigned, are good Chinamen and have lived in California and other parts of the United States, and that we have at all times been willing to abide by all the laws of the United States, and the States and Territories in which we have lived. And are now willing to report ourselves as good law abiding citizens of Montana Territory, and ask but that protection that the liberal and good government of this country permits us to enjoy. We pay all our taxes and assessments, and only ask that the good people of Montana may let us earn an honest living by the sweat of our brow.
> YE SING
> HOB HEE
> YE HOB and others⁵

In the publisher's column on the next page, Favorite made light of the eloquence of Ye Sing and his fellow Chinese. Favorite appended that "AHIU SINWERTH," clearly an attempt at phonetic humor, had delivered the ad to the *Radiator* office. The deliverer was described as "an agent of his countrymen ... who have been threatened of late with the vengeance of the ladies engaged in the laundry business."[6]

As these events in Helena disclose, Chinese residents in Montana Territory had difficulties with non-Chinese settlers. Attitudes had formed early, and they conveyed a strong disdain for Chinese personally, their culture, and their economic pursuits.

Whites perceived Chinese individuals as dishonest, perverse, and ungodly. The *Tri-Weekly Republican* reported in July 1866 that Chinese residing in Australia had been making spurious gold imitations from copper and silver. The implication for Montanans was obvious: be cautious of Chinese mining practices.[7] The *Missoula and Cedar Creek Pioneer* declared that Chinese women in general prostituted themselves at the instigation of their brothers and enjoyed disseminating venereal disease.[8] And the *Virginia City Tri-Weekly Democrat* denounced the Chinese residents as barbarians and heathens.[9] Indeed, most Montanans rarely recognized Chinese as individual human beings. References such as "Melican Man," "John Chinaman," or "Chink Chink Chinaman" perpetrated and observed group racial prejudices.

Non-Chinese Montanans also attacked Chinese customs and habits. Wherever the Chinese New Year was celebrated, newspapers labeled the holiday as mysterious or unexplainable.[10] They accused the Chinese of living "upon less than the refuse from the table of a civilized man," in an obvious reference not only to economic suffering but also "uncivilized" beggary.[11]

Anti-cultural propaganda and individual insult eventually solidified into group prejudice. That prejudice, as one historian notes, grew as the number of Chinese in Montana grew. Concern over the Chinese, confusion about their customs, and related fears soon turned to hatred and even violence when the Chinese seemed to be an economic threat. But even before their numbers increased, anti-Chinese attitudes abounded in Montana.[12]

Although census data for non-Caucasians tended to underestimate actual counts, the 1870 census identified 1,949 Chinese in Montana, representing nearly 10 percent of the total Montana population. By 1880 there were 1,765 Chinese in Montana, and that number increased to 2,532 in 1890. Even though there were more Chinese in Montana at the end of the frontier era, their percentage of the population in the territory decreased to 5 percent in 1880 and 1.9 percent in 1890. But these percentages were still much larger than the proportion of Chinese in the United States, which from 1870 to 1890 remained static at 0.2 percent.[13]

The Chinese came to Montana during the 1860s and 1870s because of mining discoveries and also employment by railroad and supply companies. Their reception varied from acceptance, at least as laborers, to outright hostility. By the mid-1880s, when the anti-Chinese movement swept across the trans-Mississippi West, the Chinese working and living in rural regions such as Montana Territory simply did not feel safe. Many fled to urban centers. At the same time, Congress passed and the president signed the first Chinese Exclusion Act (1882), prohibiting Chinese labor immigration for ten years. Eventually, in 1902, all Chinese were barred from coming to the United States for temporary settlement purposes.[14]

To counter this irrational and insulting reception, the Chinese in Montana, as in other western states and territories, turned to American law for relief and protection. As Ye Sing had written in 1866, the Chinese of Montana had no intention of removing themselves, because they considered themselves under the guardianship of righteousness and lawful sensibility. For Montanans the question was simple and direct: would the Chinese be afforded legal equality and a fair hearing?

An examination of all cases heard before the highest court in Montana from 1864 to 1902 that concerned Chinese litigants and issues primarily related to the well-being of the Chinese reveals a trend concerning the treatment of the Chinese under American law. Prior to 1883, the first year of the passage of national legislation limiting Chinese migration to the United States, five decisions were rendered by the Montana Territorial Supreme Court dealing with Chinese-related disputes. Three of those decisions favored Chinese litigants. After 1883, however, this trend reversed. Ten cases were heard, and seven resulted in unfavorable opinions for Chinese Montanans.

Of the five decisions made before 1883, three criminal cases resulted in pro-Chinese determinations.[15] In one of those cases, G. W. Irwin, lawyer and justice of the peace from Deer Lodge County, unlawfully attempted to imprison a Chinese resident known as At who had entered a recognizance, or bail bond, for Lee Sue. The controversy began in Irwin's court during a preliminary examination of Ung Hah, who was charged with having committed a murder. Lee Sue, who thought he was posting Ung Hah's bail, offered the magistrate money. Irwin interpreted the offer as a bribe and ordered Lee Sue arrested. Now confused and frightened, Sue, according to Irwin, confessed to the bribery charge and was jailed to await trial before the district court. Then At paid a bail bond for the defendant, but when the grand jury met Sue failed to appear and the court ordered the bond forfeited.[16]

Refusing to pay the bond, At argued that the failure of the justice of the peace to file a written complaint annulled the bondholder's liability. Losing at the district court level on the basis of a decision by Justice Hiram Knowles, Deer Lodge County appealed to the full territorial court. Justice Henry Blake, writing a unanimous opinion, upheld his colleague's lower court action, thereby guaranteeing a Chinese defendant in any court action the right to be informed of charges against him in writing. This procedure was statutorily required by the territorial legislature, and it applied to *all* litigants.[17]

In a second criminal case Ah Wah and Ah Yen sat in the Madison County jail during March 1881, charged with first-degree murder. The regular grand jury convened and failed to return an indictment. However, the court insisted upon calling a second grand jury, which met and dutifully returned a true bill. Tried and convicted of murder in the first degree, Ah Wah and Ah Yen appealed the conviction to the Montana Supreme Court.[18]

Henry Blake, former Montana Supreme Court justice, and James E. Callaway, former Montana territorial secretary, argued for the Chinese defendants. They alleged no less than fourteen significant procedural violations, including the use of the "extra" grand jury. The court accepted only one of their objections, but it was sufficient. In a unanimous opinion delivered by Chief Justice Decius S. Wade, the court overruled the trial court decision because only eleven jurors reached a final determination. During the trial one of the jurors, Michael A. Halfield, was excused and not replaced, but the prosecution and trial judge ignored the situation and proceeded to a verdict anyway.[19]

The lower court's conduct appalled Wade. Calling this trial for a capital offense a "mere arbitration," the chief justice railed against tampering with what he termed the defendants' fundamental liberties. Quoting from a New York case, Wade placed Montana Territory directly on the jurisprudential side of guaranteeing litigants, Chinese or non-Chinese, certain inalienable rights: "The state, the public, have an interest in the preservation of the liberties and the lives of the citizens, and will not allow them to be taken away 'without due process of law' (Const. art. I. Sec. 6), when forfeited, as they may be, as a punishment for crime."[20]

As significant as the Ah Wah and Ah Yen case was to Chinese residents of Montana, resolution of a dispute in 1874 had even more profound effects upon the Chinese. The Montana Territorial Legislature passed a law providing for the forfeiture to the territory of placer mines held by aliens. No alien could acquire any possessory interest in a mining claim and profit from it. The law applied retroactively and charged district attorneys with prosecuting those violating the law.[21]

Clearly this statute struck out at Chinese Montanans. Most gained their livelihoods from mining claims, many of them previously abandoned. To allow the law to stand would severely curtail Chinese economic development. In what might have been a case of collusion designed to test the constitutionality of the statute, Henry Blake, district attorney for Deer Lodge County and previously retained by Chinese litigants, brought an action against Fauk Lee, a citizen of China who had purchased from S. Stevens three thousand feet of placer-mining ground in direct violation of the law. In district court, Lee lost and then appealed to the Montana Territorial Supreme Court.[22]

Blake did not file a written argument. Instead J. C. Robinson, district attorney for another district, submitted the territory's position. Robinson very briefly argued that the statute in question complemented existing federal laws and common law. Fauk Lee's representatives, however, raised more substantive issues. They contended that because the territory lacked sovereignty it could not acquire title to mining lands, that the act violated the Burlingame Treaty, which gave citizens of China the rights of a most favored nation, and that "legislatures cannot enact that one person can hold by complying with the law, and another shall not. Distinctions on account of race or color are 'ante bellum' fossils."[23]

The justices on the Montana Territorial Supreme Court in 1874 hearing the *Lee* case included Decius Spear Wade, chief justice and the "founder of Montana jurisprudence"; Hiram P. Knowles, founder of the Montana Bar Association and coauthor with Wade of one of the first and most extensive codifications of Montana law; and Francis G. Servis, an Ohioan who served but two years on the bench in Montana.[24] Each judge wrote an individual opinion, Wade finding for the Chinese defendant with Servis concurring and Knowles dissenting. The opinions together represented the most comprehensive legal treatment of Chinese rights and responsibilities ever authored by a Montana court and perhaps by any group of sitting western frontier jurists.

Decius Wade's opinion immediately recognized the fundamental issue as whether or not the Montana statute was constitutional. His test was threefold. Wade examined the rights of aliens in Montana Territory prior to the enactment of the statute to see if any fundamental rights had been abrogated. Then he considered whether the territorial legislature had had the power to enact such a law. Finally he determined whether the Organic Act creating Montana Territory permitted the act in question.[25]

Liberally citing such historic British legalists as Coke and Blackstone, the chief justice answered the first question by concluding that aliens hold the same rights as citizens in the absence of legislation enacted by the "state" in the exercise of its sovereign power. "Only the sovereign power of the State or government can demand forfeiture of an alien's property, and this authority [comes] from the right of self-preservation which inheres in every government, giving it the power of self-preservation."[26]

That led him to ponder the second question in terms of who holds sovereignty in the US territorial system. After defining sovereignty as the right to make and enforce laws without modification, Wade concluded that sovereignty, indeed pure sovereignty, was not vested in the Montana Territorial Legislature. Giving a territory an organic act or any other special status was not a delegation of any sovereign power by Congress. Therefore, the territory had no sovereign power, making it impossible for the court to sustain a statute demanding property forfeiture from aliens. Wade then went further. He wrote that the territory had no ability to hold mineral lands belonging to the United States and that "the Territory is not the party of interest and is officiously meddling with what does not concern it."[27]

The third question would not seem to need discussion, but the chief justice also found that the statute in question was in violation of section 6 of the Montana Territory Organic Act, prohibiting any law from interfering with the federal government's ability to dispose of the public domain.

Justice Servis agreed with Wade's arguments and also contended that states did not have the power to appropriate the public domain, and therefore territories certainly could not. Even more significantly, he found the act to have violated section 1 of the Fourteenth Amendment to the US Constitution, specifically the equal protection of the laws.[28]

The dissent of Justice Knowles directly challenged the majority opinion. Knowles argued that once the United States divested itself of public domain, it no longer had any interest in it. Therefore, the forfeiture to the territory would not conflict with federal rights. Knowles also found that Montana Territory retained certain amounts of residual sovereignty, citing jurists Story, Kent, Taney, and Blackstone. He then speculated, "The majority [Wade and Servis] of the court have based their judgment upon the ground mainly that the legislative power does not extend as far as to provide for such forfeiture. I have contended that it does, and that it is a rightful subject of legislation. And I believe that time will fully demonstrate the benefits that would have accrued to this Territory had such legislation been sustained."[29]

Knowles would not have to wait too long for the *Lee* precedent to be eroded. Nine years later another case, *Tibbitts* v. *Ah Tong* (1883), revised significant portions of *Lee*. And although the *Lee* case reaffirmed the rights of Chinese Montanans to continue to own mining property, one of their major economic activities, there was still room for anti-Chinese Montanans to maneuver against entrepreneurial Chinese. The legislature could prevent Chinese from working claims, and it could urge the national government to restrict Chinese real property ownership.

Hiram Knowles wrote all the majority opinions of the only Montana Territorial Supreme Court decisions finding against Chinese litigants before 1883. In a dispute over ownership of the quartz-crushing equipment of the Cole Sanders Mining Company, the court found in favor of the First National Bank of Helena rather than Chinese defendant How. How had been defrauded by the bank, which had knowingly sold him property to which the title was disputed, but the justices felt How should have had reason to know of the risk and thereby disallowed the fraud claim as a valid defense.[30]

The other case centered around the usage of the common law to prevent Chinese gambling. At the lower court level, Ye Wan was indicted and acquitted of the crime of creating a common law nuisance. The territory appealed to the supreme court of Montana Territory. Before the higher body, Ye Wan claimed there was no such legalism in Montana Territory as a common law nuisance because the statute defining nuisances stated it supplanted common law forms. However, Knowles, with Justice Henry Blake, found another Montana statute to apply. It stated that "all offenses recognized by the common law as crimes, and not here enumerated, shall be punished." This law was declared to be overriding, and the territory's prosecution was vindicated.[31]

Justice Wade dissented. He thought a legal injustice had been perpetrated, and he worried that the common law doctrine of criminal nuisance might be applied to harass Montana's Chinese. Wade noted, "It was a work of folly to make a Criminal Code; if the common law system of crimes remains in force, and that it should so remain, seems clear to my mind, was not the intention of the legislature."[32]

The *Ye Wan* and *How* cases were forerunners of the Montana judicial assault upon Chinese legal rights that would occur after the first Chinese Exclusion Act of 1882. From 1883 to 1902, a significant shift occurred in the jurisprudential treatment of Montana's Chinese. No longer could Chinese litigants expect to obtain judicial fairness from Montana's territorial and new state courts. Of ten decisions made by Montana's highest court, seven held against Chinese litigants.[33] Four of the ten involved criminal disputes, three of which went against Chinese litigants.

The one case ruling in favor of the Chinese defendant, *State* v. *Lee* (1893), required the Montana Supreme Court to restate a previously guaranteed fundamental right. The defendant had been charged with grand larceny and convicted in the district court of Missoula County on the sole basis of the testimonies of John Nelson and J. M. Evans. The prosecution witness, Charles Peterson, was in Australia so the state asked Nelson, a friend of Peterson, and local magistrate Evans to verify the alleged facts. In overruling the previous decision, a unanimous supreme court reaffirmed the right of all defendants to face their accusers. Counsel for the state, Attorney General Henri J. Haskell and his assistant Ella K. Knowles, made no appearance and presented no brief—it was obviously a lost cause.[34]

Other criminal cases decided were not as clear-cut. On December 3, 1889, Ah Jim was arrested and information was filed by the county attorney of Lewis and Clark County charging him with commission of a first-degree murder. Ah Jim filed a motion to throw out the indictment because under

Montana law only justices of the peace or grand juries could issue formal criminal charges. This was appealed to the supreme court of Montana, the state being represented by Haskell.

In a curious opinion by Chief Justice Henry Blake, the court cited many authorities, including Blackstone, that verified the defendant's position, but then it considered the entire Montana Criminal Code as a common entity and observed that the charge itself did not deprive Ah Jim of his liberty without due process. The court noted that just because the county attorney was not the proper authority to file the charges, the state should not be deterred from a successful prosecution. It sent the case back to the grand jury without prejudice, but now with instructions for the information to be signed by the correct legal entity. Such liberal attention to criminal procedure did not characterize most Montana criminal disputes.[35]

The last two Chinese criminal cases, *State ex rel. Sam Toi v. French* (1895) and *State v. Camp Sing* (1896) concerned the constitutionality of a laundry tax passed by the Montana legislature. This statute, aimed at a primary economic practice of the Chinese, taxed owners of steam laundries fifteen dollars; one-male laundries, ten dollars; and laundries employing one or more persons, twenty-five dollars—all per quarter.[36] To test the law, Sam Toi, owner of a hand laundry that employed other males, demanded a ten-dollar license. Lewis and Clark treasurer Eugene S. French refused to authorize one and forced Toi to obtain a writ of mandamus to compel issuance of the license. This action brought in state authorities and Attorney General Haskell.[37]

The dispute was taken to the Montana Supreme Court, where Toi challenged the statute as discriminatory, violating uniform taxation principles and the equal protection clause of the Fourteenth Amendment. A nativistic court, finding in favor of the county treasurer, testily noted that Sam Toi was not a US citizen and that "the fact that Chinamen are engaged in the hand-laundry business is purely fortuitous. The law, in its terms, applies to all male laundrymen, of every condition and nationality. If the equality and uniformity provisions of the constitution do not apply to the license fee under consideration, the subjects of the Emperor of China are certainly in no different or better condition to make complaint than the subjects of any other foreign power who may be residing within this state, or even the citizens of the United States themselves."[38]

The court had refused to confront the constitutionality of the laundry tax in the *Sam Toi* case. One year later Camp Sing deliberately operated a hand laundry for six months without a license and was fined fifty dollars plus seventeen dollars in costs. He appealed this decision to the Montana Supreme Court and directly challenged the constitutionality of the law.

An unusual husband-and-wife legal team—Attorney General Henri Haskell and Ella Knowles Haskell—represented the state. Prior to their marriage, they had been political opponents. In 1892 Republican Haskell, Glendive attorney and ten-year Montana resident, defeated Populist Knowles by only five thousand votes. Knowles, a graduate of Bates College in Maine, had become the first woman to be admitted to the Montana bar in 1889. Unfortunately for the Chinese, her feminist and Populist propensities did not carry over into civil liberties. Instead, her mining property interests seemed to become overriding. The Haskells, combining their legal talents for a brief period, became successful prosecutors of Chinese litigants at Montana's highest judicial level.[39]

Forced to confront the constitutionality of the laundry tax, the court held that the tax was not a tax but a fee and therefore it could avoid uniformity and equality restrictions. In addition, the justices took judicial notice of the financial loss that would occur to the state should the statute be adjudged unconstitutional.[40] The *Camp Sing* case represented an end of Chinese attempts to fight Montana's efforts to curtail Chinese business development. After 1896 the Montana legislature was free to pass further discriminatory economic regulations distinctly directed toward the Chinese.

Montana civil cases involving Chinese litigants from 1883 to 1902 followed the same trend as criminal cases. Of the six civil disputes, two resulted in positive decisions for Chinese litigants. A merchant, Gum, lost a dispute and won another before the Montana Supreme Court, each decision involving a contractual disagreement and each case centering on procedural questions.[41]

Other actions dealt directly with the Chinese presence in Montana mining. In two 1883 cases concerning a title dispute to a mine, George Tong and Edward Rooney swapped procedural legal victories only to return the question to the lower courts.[42]

The crucial case defining Chinese rights in mining also occurred in 1883 in *Tibbitts v. Ah Tong*. In 1880 James McDonald and his partners sold claims in the Pioneer Mining District to Ah Tong and several other Chinese. Almost one year later plaintiff Tibbitts, along with several friends, located on the same claims and then he went to court to force a determination of the rightful owner.[43]

Losing at the lower court level, Tibbitts appealed to the Montana Territorial Supreme Court, where he found a receptive audience. Chief Justice Decius Wade, apparently joined by Justice Everton J. Conger, although the record is not clear, authored the majority opinion, which defined the dispute in terms of one fundamental question. Could an alien, especially one of Chinese descent, take and hold title to a mining claim, against a US citizen?

Wade held that under common law Ah Tong won, but common law did not apply because it had been superseded by the US statute opening mineral lands for occupation. This law allowed citizens the right to absolute title to mineral lands. To Wade, the fact that Ah Tong had purchased the land from a citizen made no difference. He reasoned that whoever possesses a mining claim "must be capable of becoming a purchaser from the government, for such possession is part of the purchase."[44]

With this rather odd legal opinion, Wade denied most Chinese in Montana from owning mining claims, and he set up a unique legal doctrine whereby the federal government retained a residual legal interest in all mineral lands. Although he noted that "these views are not supported by authority," this admittance did not deter him from making new law.[45]

An even more difficult problem for Wade was rationalizing his 1874 opinion in *Territory v. Lee* with his sudden reversal in the *Tibbitts* case. Clearly the *Lee* precedent, which had allowed Chinese aliens to purchase placer-mining property, had been rendered useless. Wade, however, marshaled his legal semantics for the task. The *Lee* case, Wade argued, concerned a territorial law, not an act of Congress. He went even further: "The question as to the right of an alien to purchase from a citizen who owned the possessory title to a mining claim was not in the case [*Territory v. Lee*]."[46] This statement simply was not true.

Justice William J. Galbraith dissented. The effect of this decision, quipped Galbraith, was to prevent absolute title from passing in much of Montana's lands, which in turn challenged basic real property law. He sarcastically suggested, "We cannot understand that there could be language expressing in stronger terms that mining claims, such as that in question, are property."[47]

Galbraith's dissent could do nothing, however, to remove the onus placed upon the Chinese of Montana. Their ability to participate in a significant economic activity was severely limited. Mining-claim ownership after 1883 was beyond the fundamental rights of Chinese Montanans.

Not content with simply denying the Chinese the right to own mining property, the Montana legislature in 1891 attempted to force them from the mines by writing and approving a circuitous law. Under section 171 of a Montana revenue act, all employers were required to submit a list of their employees to county assessors, who in turn would charge a poll tax on each employee. This statute was directly aimed at Chinese laborers, who could ill afford the "head tax."[48]

Challenging the statute were three businessmen from Silver Bow County, John Cowan, William Owsley, and James A. Talbott. They refused to submit a list and were fined $500. They appealed to the Montana Supreme Court, which was persuaded to rule against the defendants by Attorney General Haskell. Most of the arguments centered around procedural questions that the court dismissed with twentieth-century acumen: "These technical and nice distinctions are, however, now rapidly ceasing to be of interest except as [a] matter of legal history."[49] It ignored the substantive issues raised by the poll tax and turned back the Butte entrepreneurs' challenge.

Chinese legal rights in Montana had been significantly altered since 1882. Especially under attack were laundry and mining activities, the major employment opportunities sustaining the Chinese community. Without jobs and business opportunities, the only recourse for the Chinese was the Montana Supreme Court, whose decisions consistently limited Chinese economic participation and encouraged Chinese migration from Montana. Prior to 1883, such attacks against the Chinese seemed to be legally obscured. The vitriolic statements and actions made by anti-Chinese extremists were not sustained in Montana courts, but sometime after the first federal exclusion act judicial opinion shifted in Montana. Nowhere is this more obvious than in the comparison of Justice Decius Wade's decisions in *Territory v. Lee* (1874) and in *Tibbitts v. Ah Tong* (1883).

Comparing conviction rates in criminal cases of non-Chinese defendants to Chinese defendants provides more evidence of the shift in legal opinions. The Montana Supreme Court before 1883 decided twenty-five criminal cases with non-Chinese defendants; thirteen cases resulted in decisions favoring the government prosecution (52 percent). Only two criminal cases involving Chinese defendants were heard; the court favored the prosecution once (50 percent). From 1883 to 1902 criminal cases more frequently favored government prosecution. In 209 cases concerning non-Chinese defendants, the government won 131 (63 percent). Four criminal cases included Chinese defendants, three of which were won by the prosecution (75 percent). There was a movement in Montana courts favoring government prosecution, and this movement was even more pronounced against Chinese litigants.

Why had this significant change in Montana jurisprudence occurred? Several explanations can be offered. Perhaps foremost was the inevitable transfer of anti-Chinese attitudes held by the majority of citizens into statutory law and then sanctioned by judicial interpretation. Montana moved from territory to state in the 1880s and this democratic process required conventions, constitutions, elections, and the installation of local rather than national personnel in the judiciary and executive departments. These new officials were more susceptible to local demands for anti-Chinese legal action.

During the 1889 Montana Constitutional Convention, delegate Allan R. Joy, Republican attorney from Livingston and six-year Montana resident, offered Proposition 7.

> Section 1. No corporation now existing or hereafter formed under the laws of this state, shall, after the adoption of this constitution, employ directly or indirectly in any capacity, any Chinese or Mongolian. The legislature shall pass such laws as may be necessary to enforce this proposition.
>
> Section 2. No Chinese shall be employed on any state, county, municipal or other public work within this state, except as punishment for crime.
>
> Section 3. The legislature shall discourage by all means within its power the immigration to this state of all foreigners ineligible to become citizens of the United States. All contracts for Chinese of coolie labor to be performed in this state shall be void. All companies or corporations whether found in this country or any foreign country for the importation of such labor, shall be punished by such fines and penalties as the legislature shall prescribe. The legislature shall delegate all necessary power to the incorporated cities or towns in this state, for the removal of Chinese

without the limits of such cities, and every other location within prescribed portions of those limits.[50]

Hearing no objection, Proposition 7 was assigned to the Labor Committee, chaired by Peter Breen, Jefferson County Democrat and labor leader. On July 20, Breen reported to the Committee of the Whole that the Labor Committee had defeated all but the last sentence of the resolution and they urged that that section be sent to the Committee on City, County and Town Organizations.[51] This was approved, but two days later the Committee of the Whole took up the entire Joy resolution; it was defeated by an unrecorded majority of the delegates present.[52] Although the completed Montana Constitution did not contain any such explicit anti-Chinese planks, public debate opened the door to future legislative and judicial action.

Other national pressures may have also contributed to the changes in Chinese legal perceptions by Montanans. The end of Reconstruction signaled the destruction of black legal rights in the South and, predicted Henry George, would legitimatize the anti-Chinese movement in the West.[53] On June 16, 1866, the *Montana Radiator* reported in adjacent columns two separate stories. One recorded the highlights of a Memphis race riot and the fears of white southerners, the other noted the invidious invasion of the Chinese to the mines of the Boise Basin in Idaho. The comparison would have been obvious to any reader.[54] In the next decade, when economic panics and depression rocked the West, unemployment increased and racist feelings solidified against the hard-working Chinese, who supplied cheap labor. And then in 1882 the federal government began enforcement of the first of several discriminatory statutes against the Chinese. All of these happenings contributed to a legalistic rationale encouraging western jurists to compose fundamental alterations in the civil rights and liberties of the Chinese. By 1902 the doors to economic opportunity and cultural equality for Chinese Montanans had been closed with appropriate legal fanfare.

Notes

Originally published as John R. Wunder, "Law and Chinese in Frontier Montana," *Montana, the Magazine of Western History* 30 (Summer 1981): 18–31.

1. *Montana Radiator* (Helena, Montana Territory), January 24, 1866.

2. Ibid.
3. Ibid.
4. Ibid., February 3, 1866.
5. Ibid., February 17, 1866.
6. Ibid.
7. *Tri-Weekly Republican* (Helena, Montana Territory), July 26, 1866.
8. *Missoula and Cedar Creek Pioneer* (Missoula, Montana Territory), June 22, 1871.
9. *Montana Tri-Weekly Democrat* (Virginia City, Montana Territory), February 13, 1869.
10. Ibid.; *Montana Radiator*, January 24, 1866.
11. *Missoula and Cedar Creek Pioneer*, June 22, 1871.
12. Larry D. Quinn, "'Chink Chink Chinaman': The Beginning of Nativism in Montana," *Pacific Northwest Quarterly* 58 (1967): 83.
13. US Department of Commerce, Bureau of the Census, *Ninth Census of the United States, 1870: Population*, 1:18; US Department of Commerce, Bureau of the Census, *Tenth Census of the United States, 1880: Population*, 1:38–39; US Department of Commerce, Bureau of the Census, *Eleventh Census of the United States, 1890: Population*, 1:468, 474.
14. "An Act to execute certain treaty stipulations relating to Chinese," US Statutes at Large, 22 (1882): 58–61; "An Act to prohibit the coming into and regulate the residence within the United States, its territories, and all territory under its jurisdictions, and the District of Columbia, of Chinese and persons of Chinese descent," US Statutes at Large, 32 (1902): 176–77.
15. *First National Bank of Helena v. How et al.*, 1 Mont 604 (1872); *Territory of Montana v. Lee*, 2 Mont 124 (1874); *Deer Lodge County v. At*, 3 Mont 168 (1878); *Territory of Montana v. Ah Wah and Ah Yen*, 4 Mont 149 (1881); *Territory of Montana v. Ye Wan*, 2 Mont 478 (1876).
16. *Deer Lodge County v. At*, 3 Mont 168 at 169 (1878).
17. Ibid., 168 at 169–71.
18. *Territory of Montana v. Ah Wah and Ah Yen*, 4 Mont 149 (1881).
19. Ibid.
20. Ibid., 149 at 169.
21. "An Act to provide for the forfeiture to the Territory of placer mines held by aliens," Mont. Terr. Statutes (1872).
22. *Territory of Montana v. Lee*, 2 Mont 124 (1874).
23. Ibid., 124 at 125–26.
24. John D. W. Guice, *The Rocky Mountain Bench* (New Haven, CT: Yale University Press, 1972), 72–75; Earl S. Pomeroy, *The Territories and the United States, 1861–1890* (Seattle: University of Washington Press, 1970), 140; Clark Spence, *Territorial Politics and Government in Montana, 1864–1889* (Urbana: University of Illinois Press, 1975), 127, 132, 141–42, 236–38, 241, 244, 253, 304.

25. *Territory of Montana v. Lee*, 2 Mont 124 (1874).
26. Ibid., 124 at 129.
27. Ibid., 124 at 136.
28. Ibid., 124 at 139–44.
29. Ibid., 124 at 156.
30. *First National Bank of Helena v. How et al.*, 1 Mont 604 (1872).
31. *Territory of Montana v. Ye Wan*, 2 Mont 478 at 479 (1876).
32. Ibid., 478 at 481.
33. *Tibbitts v. Ah Tong*, 4 Mont 536 (1883); *Rooney v. Tong et al.*, 4 Mont 596 and 597 (1883); *State v. Ah Jim*, 9 Mont 167 (1890); *State v. Lee*, 13 Mont 248 (1893); *Power et al. v. Gum*, 6 Mont 5 (1886); *State ex rel. Sam Toi v. French* (County Treasurer), 17 Mont 54 (1895); *State v. Owsley et al.*, 17 Mont 94 (1895); *State v. Camp Sing*, 18 Mont 128 (1896); *Gum v. Murray et al.*, 6 Mont 10 (1886).
34. *State v. Lee*, 13 Mont 248 (1893).
35. *State v. Ah Jim*, 9 Mont 167 (1890).
36. Act of December 13, 1867, Mont. Terr. Statutes; Act of January 15, 1869, Mont. Terr. Statutes. Clark Spence, in *Territorial Politics and Government in Montana, 1864–1889*, notes that "legislation pertaining to the civil rights of minorities, especially the Chinese . . . reflected . . . the basic racism of territorial residents" (199–200).
37. *State ex rel. Sam Toi v. French* (County Treasurer), 17 Mont 54 (1895).
38. Ibid., 54 at 60.
39. *Helena (MT) Herald*, May 23, 1895; *Anaconda (MT) Standard*, January 28, 1911.
40. *State v. Camp Sing*, 18 Mont 128 at 137 (1896).
41. *Power et al. v. Gum*, 6 Mont 5 (1886); *Gum v. Murray et al.*, 6 Mont 10 (1886).
42. *Rooney v. Tong et al.*, 4 Mont 496 and 497 (1883).
43. *Tibbitts v. Ah Tong*, 4 Mont 536 (1883).
44. Ibid., 536 at 539; US Revised Statutes, sec. 2319, p. 427 (1866).
45. *Tibbitts v. Ah Tong*, 4 Mont 536 at 540 (1883).
46. Ibid., 536 at 541.
47. Ibid., 536 at 547.
48. *State v. Owsley et al.*, 17 Mont 94 (1895).
49. Ibid., 94 at 97.
50. *Proceedings and Debates of the Constitutional Convention Held in the City of Helena, Montana, July 4, 1889–August 17, 1889*, 60–61.
51. Ibid., 176–77.
52. Ibid., 214–15.
53. Alexander Saxton, *The Indispensable Enemy: Labor and the Anti-Chinese Movement in California* (Berkeley: University of California Press, 1971), 104–5.
54. *Montana Radiator*, June 16, 1866.

Southwest

CHAPTER 9

Law and the Chinese on the Southwest Frontier, 1850s–1902

The Chinese are the least desired immigrants who have ever sought the United States. They came in with the famous Burlingame Treaty, which angled for the celestial empire, but caught the almond-eyed Mongolian with his pig-tail, his heathenism, his filthy habits, his thrift and careful accumulation of savings to be sent back to the flowery kingdom .... No degree of inhibitions excludes him. The most we can do is to insist that he is a heathen, a devourer of soup made from the fragrant juice of the rat, filthy, disagreeable, and undesirable generally, an incumbrance that we do not know how to get rid of, but whose tribe we have determined shall not increase in this part of the world.[1]

THESE WERE THE words with which a number of the readers of the *Tombstone Epitaph* could sympathize in 1882. Such words, however, were not confined to isolated southern Arizona. Anti-Chinese sentiment could be found throughout the Southwest in the nineteenth century, and it would eventually be subsumed in the law.

The first Chinese journeyed to the Southwest in the 1850s seeking economic opportunities, primarily in the mines and on the railroads. They also functioned in service capacities, ran general stores, laundries, and restaurants, and raised and sold vegetables, fruit stuffs, and meat for local consumption.[2] By 1880, while Chinese constituted only 0.2 percent of the US population, 9 percent of all Nevadans were Chinese and one in every twenty-five Arizonans was Chinese. Chinese constituted 1 percent of all persons living in the Southwest according to the 1880 US Census.[3]

The reception of the Chinese in the Southwest was generally hostile. Individual non-Chinese attacked Chinese with some frequency. In Deming, New Mexico Territory, when two Chinese attempted to claim a town lot, E. A. Kidder opposed them. According to the *Deming Headlight*, "When on Monday last two hop joint Celestials attempted to make a location[,] he [Kidder] enforced with a club a vigorous protest." Kidder prevailed, and the paper urged someone to buy the property soon.[4] Bisbee, Arizona, had a reputation for being especially inhospitable to Chinese. No Chinese were allowed to stay overnight.[5] The situation was so bad in Flagstaff that Deputy Sheriff James L. Black took out an ad in the local newspaper: "NOTICE: All boys that have been in the habit of throwing stones and clubs at Chinamen will take notice that hereafter they will be promptly arrested for any unnecessary assault on Chinamen."[6]

Eventually, organized efforts to expel the Chinese occurred in the Southwest. A strong anti-Chinese movement began in Nevada in Carson City in 1860. In 1876 two Chinese were killed in Eureka, and others were forced to leave. This anti-Chinese extralegal action continued into the twentieth century at Tonapah, where a white mob murdered Chong Bing Long during an attempt to force all Chinese to leave the town.[7]

Many communities formed anti-Chinese cells that worked to develop an uncomfortable climate. In Tucson a petition was drafted arguing that the Chinese should be forced to a "Chinatown." "The present condition," its signers proclaimed, "is a disgrace and outrage to our city. There are 60 Chinese stores in Tucson which are dirty, carry cheap goods, and in most of which they smoke opium."[8] Silver City, New Mexico, also experienced much agitation. Citizens met and debated on taking forms of direct action.[9] In Graham County, Arizona Territory, in 1884 three Chinese men were lynched by a mob.[10] The largest mob action occurred in Denver in 1880, which resulted in the beating to death of a Chinese laundryman.[11]

Given the nature of this hostile reaction, the Chinese in the Southwest sought legal protection in American law through American courts and legislatures. In the Southwest this took many forms, and the Chinese quickly found that their legal situation somewhat mirrored their initial societal problems. One way to examine the issues central to the Chinese and non-Chinese on the Southwest frontier is to analyze the cases decided by territorial and state supreme courts in Utah, Colorado, Arizona, Nevada, and New Mexico. Four categories will be used to facilitate the analysis: (1) civil cases appealed before passage of the first Chinese Exclusion Act (1882); (2) criminal cases appealed before passage of the act; (3) civil cases appealed from 1883 to 1902; and (4) criminal cases appealed from 1883 to 1902.[12]

Southwest Civil Cases before the First Chinese Exclusion Act

Only two civil cases involving Chinese litigants before state and territorial supreme courts were decided in the Southwest before 1883.[13] The paucity of Chinese litigation stems from several factors. Foremost, few Chinese migrated to four of the five Southwest areas. The combined Chinese population in Arizona, New Mexico, Colorado, and Utah in 1870 and 1880 did not match the numbers of Chinese in Nevada or other areas of the West. Those Chinese who came first to the Southwest were not in control of their own economic destiny. Time and stability were required before a merchant class could develop. In 1881, for example, there were twenty-five Chinese businesses listed for all of Arizona Territory, the most being located in Tucson— four restaurants, one drugstore, and two Chinese mercantile owners.[14] There were only three Chinese businesses in Phoenix. By 1898 in Phoenix the Chinese business community numbered twenty-two separate establishments.[15]

Most of the Chinese in the Southwest prior to 1883 were living in Nevada. Here a significant civil case involving a Chinese defendant evolved, *Hagerman v. Tong Lee*.[16] Tong Lee made a contract with P. N. Marker to cut wood. It appears Marker was to supply wood to Tong Lee, who in turn sold wood to other customers, including J. C. Hagerman. Hagerman paid Tong Lee a sum in excess of $600 for cut wood, but Tong Lee did not supply it because Marker had not supplied him. Thus, Hagerman claimed a breach of contract and sued Tong Lee in Nevada district court.[17]

At the district court level, the judge appointed a referee to make a determination. The referee ordered P. N. Marker & Co. to pay $669.11 "in satisfaction of the judgment recovered by the respondent Hagerman, against the defendant, Tong Lee." If the Markers, P. N. and John, refused to pay, they would be held in contempt and sent to the Washoe County jail. P. N. Marker appealed this decision to the Nevada Supreme Court.[18]

The issue before Nevada's highest court was procedurally limited to the powers of a court-appointed referee, but there were significant economic ramifications to this case. Business activities in a frontier community were dependent upon the kind of contractual relationships these litigants had developed, and the referee's decision placed a chilling effect upon third parties, in this case, the Markers. Moreover, the factual situation involved the timber-supply business, a business that could ill afford legal interruption. The scarcity of wood was a fact of life for Nevadans, let alone for the mining and railroad industries.[19]

In a decision by Chief Justice Thomas P. Hawley, the Nevada Supreme Court reversed the referee's decision and ordered further proceedings if they were necessary. The court decided that an order reaching to a third party over an uncompleted contract could not stand. It found that the referee had the power to issue an order and to hold defendants in contempt, but that no court could demand a sum due a creditor from a third party unless it was clear that the third party owed the debtor. In this case P. N. Marker & Co. had not completed the contract with Tong Lee, and the Markers implied that they intended to complete the contract. Thus, Tong Lee was liable, and Hagerman would need to go back to court.[20] There is no evidence that Hagerman returned to the legal system. Presumably Tong Lee supplied the wood or the funds requested.

In the other civil case decided by Southwest frontier supreme courts, the Chinese litigant fared better. W. G. Phifer and Thomas H. Simonton were in partnership in the city transfer business. While in partnership, Phifer and Simonton contracted with Lehow (Lee How) to supply them with $2,000 worth of merchant goods. The materials were provided by Lehow, but the city transfer company did not pay. Before Lehow could sue, William H. Pierce bought out Phifer's share of the company.[21]

Lehow sued Simonton and Phifer in Arapahoe County probate court. Here the court decided in favor of the defendants, adopting the common law rule that "a stranger to the consideration [the buy-out contract of Pierce and Phifer] cannot enforce the contract by an action thereon in his own name, though he be avowedly the party intended to be benefited."[22]

On appeal to the Colorado state supreme court, Lehow alleged fraud may have been committed and that American court precedents precluded the new partnership from preventing his recovery. The court decided for Lehow.

It did not believe a fraud had been committed but adopted the rule of fourteen other states that had dispensed with the common law in this third-party action. Colorado's court reasoned that to deny Lehow would be to cause a grave injustice needlessly.[23]

Thus, in the two civil cases decided by Southwest supreme courts prior to 1883, Chinese litigants were treated fairly. Both situations considered complex contractual matters in which third-party good-faith purchases were involved. The courts chose to establish a commercial atmosphere free from procedural restriction, and their opinions were noticeably free of any inflammatory remarks directed at Chinese litigants or business practices.[24]

Southwest Criminal Cases before the First Chinese Exclusion Act (1882)

Prior to 1883, Southwest appellate courts heard seventeen criminal cases involving Chinese defendants.[25] Of the seventeen, fourteen cases affirmed convictions while only three cases were reversed ordering new trials for Chinese defendants.[26] Crimes of violence, unlawful taking of property, and use of opium were of primary concern to law enforcement officials. All of the criminal cases appealed were in Nevada.

In the fall of 1871, Ah Fung arrived in Reno with a trunk full of his belongings. He met Ah Tom, a friend of several years, and asked him if he could leave his trunk at Ah Tom's cabin while he went to San Francisco. No one lived at Ah Tom's except his relatives, Ah Ping, Ah Mok, and Ah Loy. They saw the contents of the trunk—a watch, a chain, a pistol, and over $500 worth of coins—when Ah Fung returned to take twenty dollars out to pay for his trip. Later, when Ah Fung went with Ah Tom to move his trunk from the cabin, the trunk and its contents were missing.[27]

Evidently Ah Fung suspected all four cabin inhabitants, including Ah Tom. Ah Fung went to San Francisco and demanded satisfaction before a Chinese meeting where he confronted Ah Tom. Ah Tom stated that he had not stolen the contents of the trunk, but that his three relatives had.

After this event the Washoe County district court convened and convicted Ah Tom and his three relatives of grand larceny. At the trial, evidence from the tong proceeding was admitted, and the defendants objected. In addition, Ah Fung told how after he had returned to Reno, Ah Ping and Ah

Loy admitted to taking the trunk and gambling the contents away. They had offered to pay him one hundred dollars to drop the charges.[28]

On appeal the Nevada Supreme Court overruled the trial court and ordered a new trial. Justice Thomas Hawley wrote that the tong proceeding testimony should not have been admitted because "admission of this testimony was calculated to mislead the jury to the prejudice of the defendants."[29] Thus a confession by a Chinese defendant before his peers was not acceptable in a non-Chinese court setting. Although this case was decided in favor of the Chinese defendants, it restricted the role the Chinese as a community might have in criminal dispute resolution.

The other two criminal cases decided in favor of Chinese defendants were primarily concerned with misinterpreted legal language. In *State of Nevada v. On Gee How*, the state supreme court ruled that a statute suppressing the smoking of opium was constructed so as to prevent opium dens from operating.[30] Therefore, any indictment had to focus on the frequenting of "a place of resort" rather than simply any room or building.[31] Similarly, in *State of Nevada v. Ah Tong* the defendant had been convicted of murdering Ah Wy in Carson City but was discharged because the trial judge charged the jury in an offensive way. After explaining the definition of murder, the judge lectured the jury: "Such is the law which you, the jurors, are called upon to vindicate, and such is the charge against the defendant."[32] He went on to state that no jury can err in making its decision. Nevada's state supreme court was not inclined to let such instructions stand.

In the opium and murder cases, Nevada's highest court participated in a common nineteenth-century legal ritual. It felt constrained to rectify mistaken legal language. This incidentally benefitted Chinese defendants, and in the *Ah Tong* case there appeared some dicta to suggest the trial was somewhat hostile to the Chinese defendant. Other western courts took note, and lawyers in Utah tried to use the *Ah Tong* precedent to argue in favor of John Lee and other defendants in a Mountain Meadows Massacre case. Utah's supreme court would not accept the *Ah Tong* decision.[33]

Although some Chinese involved in criminal disputes received positive treatment before pre-1883 Southwest appellate courts, most did not. Those who lost were primarily involved in cases concerning opium use, violent crimes against persons, and crimes against property.

Unlike On Gee How, Chinese who raised questions regarding Nevada's attack on opium usually lost. In 1880 Ah Sam challenged the constitutionality of Nevada's Opium Act. The act had been amended to include prohibitions against places where opium was frequently smoked. Nevada's supreme court upheld the constitutionality of the act. The court reasoned that Nevada had the police power necessary to justify the need for the law and that the law itself, while prohibiting the sale or use of opium and the maintenance of a place where the sale or use of opium occurs, did not embrace more than one subject. The court argued that the act did not oppress opium dens generally, but specifically; this position, however, seemed to beg the defendant's assertions.[34]

Immediately following *Ah Sam* was *State of Nevada v. Ah Chew*.[35] Having failed to dislodge Nevada's anti-opium legislation, the Chinese defendant charged discrimination based upon the Fourteenth Amendment. Chinese in Nevada were not serving on juries. E. R. Garber and Alexander Wilson argued for Ah Chew that under the US Constitution "civil rights of a Mongolian or yellow person are identical with those of an African, or black person, and are protected by the constitutional amendments and the acts of Congress in relation thereto in precisely the same manner as the rights of an African."[36] The Nevada Supreme Court was not convinced. It was of the opinion that the Constitution as amended following the Civil War must be narrowly construed. The justices believed that it applied almost exclusively to blacks. Justice Hawley wrote, "The language used necessarily extends some of the provisions to all persons of every race and color; but their general purpose is so clearly in favor of the African race, that it would require a very strong case to make them applicable to any other."[37] The court went on to note that Chinese, like women, were not qualified "electors" to serve on juries.[38]

Two more cases decided that same term cited *Ah Chew* as controlling.[39] The Nevada Supreme Court clearly hoped it had put all issues concerning opium to rest. Nevertheless, one exclusion needed to be clarified. The opium act allowed physicians to distribute legal portions of opium. Ching Gang was arrested and convicted, and he claimed he was a physician. The court ruled he must prove he was a certified physician under Nevada rules, rules that all but openly denied the Chinese a physician's status.[40] The door was closed.

It appeared that Chinese were often involved in crimes of violence. Many non-Chinese complained that this was a natural predisposition of the Chinese, and it was justification alone for their removal. Courts logically became the focus of the debate, and Nevada's courts before 1883 heard a significant number of criminal cases involving Chinese.

The Nevada Supreme Court appeared to embrace the anti-Chinese attitudes prevalent in the general population. In *State of Nevada v. Ah Mook*, the defendant was tried and convicted of second-degree murder.[41] Ah Mook had shot Ah Long while the latter was in custody for having wounded Ah Mook's brother. Ah Long was being carried into jail at the time he was killed by Ah Mook. At the trial the judge neglected to tell the jury that a manslaughter verdict could be found if the crime was committed in a moment of passion. A divided Nevada Supreme Court affirmed the decision of the district court even though it strongly criticized the trial court judge. Justice Hawley submitted a lengthy dissent.[42]

An unusual rehearing was granted whereupon the attorneys for Ah Mook directly attacked the court. They accused the justices of arriving at a decision "upon no hypothesis except that it was the result of hatred for Chinamen, with the fear of newspaper censure, together with the bold and glaring misstatements of the law by the court below."[43] Justice William H. Beatty responded testily. He charged the attorneys with being too sympathetic to the Chinese. Such a trait "in cases of this character may always be expected to cloud their judgment to a greater or less extent."[44] No minds were changed except that a prejudice had clearly surfaced.

Two years later another, similar situation resulted in the execution of the defendant Ah Chuey. At his trial white witnesses testified that Ah Chuey was in Reno near a Chinese washhouse that burned. A body was found in it that could not be identified. The owner of the washhouse, Ah Tong, never surfaced after the fire. The defendant claimed he was Sam Good, not Ah Chuey. He also was forced to reveal a tattoo on his arm that was identified by a questionable witness as a mark found on Ah Chuey.[45]

The defendant appealed the conviction on the basis that he had been compelled to testify against himself, a violation of the Nevada Constitution, and that there was no identifiable corpus delicti. The court ruled that unless torture or the rack had been used, the testimony was acceptable, and it found reason to believe the dead person was the washhouse owner.[46] Justice Orville R. Leonard vigorously dissented. In a twenty-two-page dissent Leonard remonstrated the majority. There was overwhelming doubt as to the identity of the defendant and the body. Moreover, Leonard found the tattoo showing to violate Nevada's constitution and the common law.⁴⁷ He wrote, "I think the error is as great as it would have been had the court compelled the defendant to admit that he was Ah Chuey."⁴⁸

Thus, by 1883, Chinese defendants in violence-to-person cases were in trouble. Southwest appellate courts were willing to overlook what seemed to be significant legal issues in order to affirm convictions. The same was also true in cases appealed that concerned crimes to property (grand larceny, burglary, and robbery).⁴⁹ The message was clear to lower courts: appeals would be sustained for questionable procedures in cases involving Chinese defendants.⁵⁰

Perhaps the most notorious case decided occurred in 1875. Ah Bau and Ah You were convicted of attempting to break out of jail, and Nevada's supreme court affirmed the decision. This was in the face of evidence showing neither defendant was charged with a crime. Both had just been acquitted of a kidnapping charge. The justice of the peace had not wanted to discharge the defendants, and he had ordered them to stay in the custody of the sheriff. For the court, the fact that a charge was contemplated was sufficient to warrant temporary incarceration of Ah Bau and Ah You.⁵¹ Such was the state of civil liberties in the Southwest for Chinese at the time of the passage of the first Chinese Exclusion Act in 1882.

Southwest Civil Cases after the Passage of the First Chinese Exclusion Act

Eleven civil cases involving Chinese litigants were decided in Southwest appellate courts from 1883 to 1902. They included four from Arizona, four from Colorado, two from Nevada, and one from New Mexico.⁵² Three of the eleven involved Chinese suing Chinese. Of the eight cases concerning a Chinese versus a non-Chinese litigant, four were decided in favor of the Chinese party.⁵³

The Ethel Mine in Eureka County, Nevada, was the subject of a legal dispute in 1895. Ah Tone owned and worked the mine, and he had as his agent M. McGarry. Ah Tone gave McGarry ore to sell. McGarry sold it for $2,077.20 but reimbursed Ah Tone for only $1,384.80, and Ah Tone took McGarry to court.

At the trial McGarry claimed he owned or was leased a portion of the mine. He had given one-third of his interest to a man named McCaffery and two-thirds to his lawyer, Frank X. Murphy. They in turn conveyed these interests to McGarry's wife. The judge, however, found no evidence existed of this ownership, and the jury agreed that Ah Tone should be given $692.40. On appeal to the Nevada Supreme Court, McGarry argued he was a multiple agent and entitled to the money, but Nevada's highest court did not agree. In this instance Chinese mining interests were protected.[54]

Chinese also fought successfully to own nonmining lands in Nevada.[55] In 1884 Nevada attorney general W. H. Davenport attempted to deny Fook Ling the right to own property. Davenport argued the Chinese were not persons within the meaning of the Nevada Constitution. Indeed, as in California's *People v. Hall* (1854), Nevada's highest legal official hoped to have Chinese classified as Indians under Nevada law.[56] Nevada's supreme court was not convinced and determined that Chinese were foreigners entitled to own Nevada's lands.[57] Clearly, by the late nineteenth century some Southwest appellate courts were not willing to give in to attempts to strip the Chinese of their real property rights.

The Chinese also used the civil courts to settle internal community disputes, although usually on rare occasions. More often than not, a filing settled a dispute. For example, in Grant County, New Mexico Territory, Chang Hung sued Mok Che Ling in district court. One day later the defendant announced that the plaintiff would not appear. The court dismissed the case, charging the defendant court costs but authorizing him to collect from Chang Hung.[58]

In Arizona Territory an internal Chinese civil action was heard by the territorial supreme court. Ah You was cleaning out an irrigation ditch when he was attacked and mauled to death by a vicious boar. His widow and children brought a wrongful death action against Don Yan, who may or may not have had a financial interest in the hog. Don Yan was accused of negligence because he had kept a known-to-be-dangerous animal. At the trial level, the widow won. The defendant appealed based upon what he termed a misinterpretation of the Arizona Territory's wrongful death statute.[59]

Under Arizona Territory law a person could sue another for the cost of injuries leading to a death if negligence was caused by a proprietor of a vehicle or his agent or if "the death of any person is caused by the wrongful act, negligence, unskillfulness, or default of another."[60] Thus Don Yan, possibly not the owner of the hog, might not be liable, nor would the owner be liable for his agent. The court noted Arizona's statute copied Texas's wrongful death act verbatim and that Texas's supreme court had made the same narrow determination. Thus the decision was reversed, and Ah You's relatives lost on appeal.[61] In this particular dispute, Chinese litigants became central to the formation of an important interpretation of Arizona law. Given the economic status of most Chinese, the result was not necessarily a positive one for Chinese Arizonans.

Chinese litigants lost out in two other important cases during this era. In Colorado a Mr. Kennedy rented a store to the Sing Wah Company. When the rent of $141 was not paid, Kennedy sued Look Ding, the only person identified with the Sing Wah Company. The jury rendered a verdict in favor of Kennedy, and Look Ding appealed, arguing that the company, not an individual, should have been sued.[62]

The Colorado state court of appeals heard the case and seemed sympathetic to Look Ding. It noted, "The testimony on the question of fact was contradictory. It was found against appellant, on very meager and unsatisfactory evidence of former statements of appellant [Look Ding] that might have been misunderstood."[63] Nevertheless, the court refused to change the verdict. It reasoned, "juries are made judges of the veracity of witnesses,"[64] and in this instance discredited the evidence. In Colorado, white juries had great latitude to discount Chinese testimony.

Similarly, when Roe Chung attempted to fight New Mexico's physician regulations, he lost. New Mexico Territory passed a statute that fined doctors who practiced medicine without certification. A justice of the peace, H. H. Ribble, assumed jurisdiction and fined Roe Chung. The Chinese defendant challenged the constitutionality of the act, but the New Mexico Territory Supreme Court found all arguments without merit.[65]

Certainly civil actions appealed from 1883 to 1902 in Southwest courts gave mixed messages to Chinese litigants. Some jurisdictions protected the Chinese, especially in basic property rights. Yet others quickly abrogated responsibilities to lower courts, which allowed for discrimination to occur without sanction.

Southwest Criminal Cases after the Passage of the First Chinese Exclusion Act

Criminal cases appealed in Southwest courts from 1883 to 1902 also met with a mixed reception for Chinese defendants.[66] This contrasts with the imbalance against Chinese defendants prior to the passage of the first Chinese Exclusion Act in 1882. The turnaround was in part due to Nevada's supreme court adopting more favorable precedents from California courts for Chinese defendants. After 1902, Southwest courts would reverse the balanced trend of two decades primarily because of their strict holdings in immigration and deportation cases.[67]

Of the ten criminal cases heard by Southwest supreme courts involving Chinese defendants, half resulted in favorable verdicts for the Chinese. These included murder, assault with intent to kill, attempted rape, and grand larceny cases along with an important immigration ruling.

Four of the favorable decisions for Chinese defendants occurred in Nevada. In 1895 Ah Kee and several other Chinese were arrested by the sheriff of Humboldt County for the crime of grand larceny, but upon a hearing the warrant was judged insufficient. The justice of the peace, however, thought Ah Kee and his friends were guilty, and he ordered them held. Three weeks later they were still detained. The state supreme court was not impressed by this illegal incarceration and ordered the Chinese defendants set free.[68] In a sense this case was a natural result of the *Ah Bau and Ah You* case decided twenty years earlier. The court in effect overruled *Ah Bau and Ah You* without mentioning its previous indiscretion.[69]

The Nevada Supreme Court also reversed the murder conviction of Wong Fun and the assault with intent to kill conviction of Ong Gee. In the former case Wong Fun was convicted of the first-degree murder of Hing Lee by an admittedly prejudiced jury on the basis of second-degree murder evidence and an incompetent judicial instruction. This conviction was overturned.[70] In the latter case, Ong Gee and Ah Kung were convicted of attempting to kill Ah See after a gambling dispute. Supposedly Ah Kung fired the pistol, but, for reasons unknown, Ong Gee was brought before a delirious Ah See, who identified him as his assailant. Later, Ah See recanted this statement, noting that Ong Gee was merely present at the gambling hall and fled after the shooting by Ah Kung.[71] The Nevada Supreme Court reversed the conviction and showed an uncharacteristic degree of toleration. Regarding Ong Gee's attempt to flee, Justice Leonard excused him, noting, "He might have been afraid of the other Chinamen who accompanied the Sheriff. He might have thought they came to do something else beside causing his arrest for the crime of which he was charged. He may have thought the sheriff came to arrest him for the commission of some other crime of which he felt guilty."[72] Whatever the case, the verdict had not been sustained by the facts.

In a different case the Nevada Supreme Court found itself having to make new law. Charley Lung was convicted of attempted rape. He had given a woman cantharides, or Spanish fly, in a cup of coffee with the intent of having intercourse with her. From the facts of the case it was determined that Charley Lung never went any further than placing the Spanish fly in the coffee. He did not "offer or attempt to have the connection with her, by force or otherwise."[73] Yet he had been convicted of attempted rape. The Nevada court extensively reviewed case law from numerous jurisdictions and concluded that Spanish fly, although it caused nausea and irritation of the genital organs, could not render a woman helpless; therefore, she could not be raped without force. Furthermore, the court found that some form of physical preparation had to occur for an attempted rape conviction to be upheld. Charley Lung was allowed to go free.[74]

New law of even greater magnitude was created by Arizona Territory's supreme court. In the first of many immigration cases involving Chinese defendants, the court decided that US statutes did not allow for appeals to state courts from hearings conducted by immigration commissioners.[75] Lee Ching Goon was arrested and brought before Commissioner Frank Dysart. US Attorney Robert E. Morrison wanted Lee Ching Goon deported, but Dysart was of the opinion that the defendant was a "Chinese person of a privileged class,"[76] thereby entitling him to stay in the United States. The 1882 Chinese Exclusion Act did not apply. Morrison took the case to the Arizona Territory district court, and the judge ruled he had no jurisdiction. The high court agreed, stating that the commissioner had original and final jurisdiction.[77] This was a rather unusual opinion in view of most courts' normal predisposition toward expanding jurisdiction and was particularly so in Arizona, with its popular anti-Chinese feeling.

Although the Chinese were protected on some issues, they were not as fortunate with others. Chinese defendants in Southwest appellate courts from 1883 to 1902 lost on five separate occasions. These involved two murders, a habeas corpus proceeding, a burglary, and selling alcohol to Indians.

Charley Dan lost his appeal in Nevada because the court refused to accept his argument that when he broke into the vacant house owned by Joseph

Olcovich he was not burglarizing a "dwelling."[78] Likewise, Chung Hong lost his application for a writ of habeas corpus in the Arizona Territory.[79]

More complex cases were heard in New Mexico Territory. Yee Dan was convicted for the murder of Yee Yot Who. He bludgeoned the latter on the head with an iron pipe before being controlled. Yee Yot Who was then taken to a hospital, where a physician performed a trepanning on him. He died shortly thereafter. Yee Dan claimed that at this trial the interpreter was incompetent and that the deceased man died not because of his attack but because of a faulty operation. New Mexico Territory's supreme court would accept none of this. It summarily dismissed the interpreter argument, allowing great latitude, and while it agreed with the defendant that the doctors were negligent, it found the jury had to determine the cause of death. They believed it to be Yee Dan.[80]

Similarly, Yee Shun lost on his appeal of a murder conviction. He was charged with the killing of Jim Lee, a proprietor of a laundry in East Las Vegas. He based his appeal on the oath Chinese witnesses were required to take before testifying, in which they had to discuss their religion within a Christian framework. The New Mexico Territory Supreme Court found nothing wrong with this oath, and the case became the controlling legal opinion on this matter throughout the trans-Mississippi West.[81]

As significant perhaps was *United States v. Chung Sing*.[82] Here the defendant was convicted of disposing of ardent spirits to Native Americans, a federal offense. At his trial Chung Sing wished to call a white witness, J. B. McNeil, to testify on his behalf. The trial judge refused to allow it. Arizona's appellate court agreed. The justices believed that all persons before the law were clothed in a presumption of innocence. They wrote, "It is a cardinal point, to be ever kept in view, and if followed, it is hardly possible for the stings of passion, prejudice, and suspicion to furnish a victim for judicial condemnation."[83] Passion, prejudice, and suspicion certainly describe many non-Chinese attitudes toward the Chinese. Arizona's justices chose not to confront the real world of the Gilded Age West.

Thus, in the two decades following the passage of the first Chinese Exclusion Act, Southwest appellate courts proved to be cautious in their treatment of Chinese litigants. Blatant procedural irregularities were reversed, but numerous loopholes were opened so that anti-Chinese prejudice could flourish in the lower courts. One impact would be even less reliance upon the court systems of the states and territories of the Southwest.

TABLE 9. Chinese Litigants before Southwest Supreme Courts, 1849–1902

CASES DECIDED BEFORE 1883

State or Territory	Civil			Criminal		
	For Chinese Litigants	Against Chinese Litigants	Total Civil Cases	For Chinese Defendants	Against Chinese Defendants	Total Criminal Cases
Arizona	0	0	0	0	0	0
Colorado	1	0	1	0	0	0
Nevada	0	1	1	3	14	17
New Mexico	0	0	0	0	0	0
Utah	0	0	0	0	0	0
Total	1	1	2	3	14	17

CASES DECIDED 1883–1902

State or Territory	Civil			Criminal		
	For Chinese Litigants	Against Chinese Litigants	Total Civil Cases	For Chinese Defendants	Against Chinese Defendants	Total Criminal Cases
Arizona	1 1/2*	2 1/2*	4	1	2	3
Colorado	2	2	4	0	0	0
Nevada	2	0	2	4	1	5
New Mexico	0	1	1	0	2	2
Utah	0	0	0	0	0	0
Total	5.5	5.5	11	5	5	10

* Includes Chinese vs. Chinese civil disputes (computed as half for and half against Chinese litigants).

Throughout the last half of the nineteenth century, Chinese came to settle in the Southwest portion of the United States. They met with limited economic success and some of the worst forms of racial bigotry. The interpretation of law proved to be of minimal help in Chinese attempts to assure themselves fundamental forms of fairness. Of forty cases heard before the highest regional courts, over twenty-five were decided against Chinese litigants—more than 63 percent. Setbacks, along with some advances, occurred in both civil and criminal law. Nevertheless, as regards the Chinese, law in the Southwest was not color-blind.

Notes

Originally published as John R. Wunder, "Law and the Chinese on the Southwest Frontier, 1850s–1902," *Western Legal History* 2 (Summer/Fall, 1989): 139–58.

1. "That Little Man from China," *Tombstone (AZ Terr.) Epitaph*, February 13, 1882.
2. See Roscoe G. Willson, "Chinese Had Rough Time," *Arizona Magazine*, in the *Arizona Republican* (Phoenix), May 17, 1964; Lawrence M. Fong, "Sojourners and Settlers: The Chinese Experience in Arizona," *Journal of Arizona History* 21 (Autumn 1980): 227–56; Heather S. Hatch, "The Chinese in the Southwest: A Photographic Record," *Journal of Arizona History* 21 (1980): 257–74; Gary P. BeDunnah, *A History of the Chinese in Nevada, 1855–1904* (San Francisco: R and E Research Associates, 1973); Gregg Lee Carter, "Social Demography of the Chinese in Nevada: 1872–1880," *Nevada Historical Society Quarterly* 18 (1975): 73–90; Loren B. Chan, "The Chinese in Nevada: An Historical Survey, 1856–1970," *Nevada Historical Quarterly* 25 (1982): 266–314; George Kraus, "Chinese Laborers and the Construction of the Central Pacific," *Utah Historical Quarterly* 37 (1969): 41–57; Donald R. Abbe, *Austin and the Reese River Mining District* (Reno: University of Nevada Press, 1985), 59–60.
3. US Dept. of Commerce, Bureau of the Census, *Ninth Census of the United States, 1870: Population* (Washington, DC, 1870): 1:8, 18; US Dept. of Commerce, Bureau of the Census, *Tenth Census of the United States, 1880: Population* (Washington, DC, 1880): 1:38–39; US Dept. of Commerce, Bureau of the Census, *Eleventh Census of the United States, 1890: Population* (Washington, DC, 1890): 1:468, 474. To compare these figures with those for the Northwest, see John R. Wunder, "The Chinese and the Courts in the Pacific Northwest: Justice Denied?," *Pacific Historical Review* 52 (1983): 192 [hereinafter cited as Wunder, "Chinese and the Courts"].
4. *Deming (NM Terr.) Headlight*, September 28, 1888.
5. Annie M. Cox, "History of Bisbee, 1877 to 1937" (MA thesis, University of Arizona, 1938), 25–26.
6. *Flagstaff Champion*, October 5, 1889.
7. L. Chan, "Chinese in Nevada," 312n1.
8. Petition quoted in Claudette Simpson, "The Chinese: Early Arizonans Gave These Hard Working Orientals a Rough Time," *Prescott (AZ) Westward*, February 7, 1975, 3–4.
9. *Silver City (NM Terr.) Enterprise*, November 27, December 11, 25, 1885; January 1, 15, 22, 1885.
10. Ibid., April 11, 1884.

11. Roy T. Wortman, "Denver's Anti-Chinese Riot, 1880," in *Anti-Chinese Violence in North America*, ed. Roger Daniels (New York: Arno Press, 1978), 275–91.
12. The same model is used in Wunder, "Chinese and the Courts," 194n3. See also 194n6. Chinese Exclusion Acts: 22 Stat. 58–61 (1882); 25 Stat. 476–79 (1888); 27 Stat. 25–26 (1892); 32 Stat. 176–77 (1902).
13. *Hagerman v. Tong Lee*, 12 Nev 331 (1887); *Lehow v. Simonton et al.*, 3 Colo 346 (1877).
14. *Arizona Business Directory and Gazetteer* (San Francisco, 1881), 125, 129, 141, 143, 157, 161, 164–65, 176, 178, 181, 183, 189–91, 193, 196, 202, 230, in Arizona Historical Foundation Room, Arizona State University Library, Tempe.
15. Ibid., 154, 230; *City Directory of Phoenix, Arizona* (Phoenix, 1898), 11, 14, 59, 67, 93, 99–101, 106, 109, 111, 117–18, 120, 143, in Arizona Historical Foundation Room, Arizona State University Library, Tempe.
16. *Hagerman v. Tong Lee*, 12 Nev 331 (1877).
17. Ibid.
18. Ibid., 333.
19. See Gordon Bakken, *The Development of Law on the Rocky Mountain Frontier: Civil Law and Society, 1850–1912* (Westport, CT: Greenwood Press, 1983).
20. *Hagerman v. Tong Lee*, 12 Nev 334–37 (1877).
21. *Lehow v. Simonton et al.*, 3 Colo 346 (1877).
22. Ibid., 348.
23. Ibid., 348–49.
24. This balanced treatment of the Chinese in the public sector prior to 1883 compares similarly to the actions of appellate courts of the Northwest during the same era. See Wunder, "Chinese and the Courts," 194–95n3.
25. *State of Nevada v. Ah Tong*, 7 Nev 148 (1871); *State of Nevada v. Ah Tom et al.*, 8 Nev 213 (1873); *State of Nevada v. On Gee How*, 15 Nev 184 (1880); *State of Nevada v. Ah Loi*, 5 Nev 99 (1869); *State of Nevada v. Ah Sam and Ah See*, 7 Nev 127 (1871); *State of Nevada v. Ah Chuey*, 14 Nev 79 (1879); *State of Nevada v. Charley Hing*, 16 Nev 307 (1881); *State of Nevada v. Ah Sam*, 15 Nev 27 (1880); *State of Nevada ex rel. Ah Chew v. Richard Rising*, 15 Nev 164 (1880); *State of Nevada v. Ah Chew*, 16 Nev 50 (1881); *State of Nevada v. Ching Gang*, 16 Nev 62 (1881); *State of Nevada v. Ah Gonn*, 16 Nev 61 (1881); *Ex parte Ah Bau and Ah You*, 10 Nev 264 (1875); *State of Nevada v. Ah Mook*, 12 Nev 369 (1877); *State of Nevada v. Chin Wah*, 12 Nev 118 (1877); *State of Nevada v. Ah Hung*, 11 Nev 28 (1876); *State of Nevada v. I. En*, 10 Nev 277 (1875).
26. This is a decidedly different ratio of affirmations to reversals compared to Northwest criminal cases of the same era: in the Southwest 3:14, in the Northwest 9:6. Wunder, "Chinese and the Courts," 209n3.
27. *State of Nevada v. Ah Tom et al.*, 8 Nev 214 (1873).
28. Ibid.
29. Ibid., 217.

30. *State of Nevada v. On Gee How*, 15 Nev 184 (1880); 1879 Nev Stat. 121. The state of Washington took a similar stance. See *State of Washington v. Ah Lim*, 1 Wash 156 (1890); Wunder, "Chinese and the Courts," 205–6n3.
31. *State of Nevada v. On Gee How*, 15 Nev 187 (1880).
32. *State of Nevada v. Ah Tong*, 7 Nev 150 (1871).
33. *The People v. John D. Lee et al.*, 2 Utah 443 (1876).
34. *State of Nevada v. Ah Sam*, 15 Nev 27–31 (1880).
35. *State of Nevada v. Ah Chew*, 16 Nev 50 (1881).
36. Ibid., 51.
37. Ibid., 58. California also adopted this reasoning in cases concerning Chinese testimony against whites and blacks. See *People v. Washington*, 36 Cal 568 (1869); and *People v. Brady*, 40 Cal 198 (1870). See also J. A. C. Grant, "Testimonial Exclusion because of Race: A Chapter in the History of Intolerance in California," *UCLA Law Review* 17 (1969): 192–201; and John R. Wunder, "Chinese in Trouble: Criminal Law and Race on the Trans-Mississippi West Frontier," *Western Historical Quarterly* 17 (January 1986): 25–41.
38. *State of Nevada v. Ah Chew*, 16 Nev 59 (1881).
39. *State of Nevada v. Ah Gonn*, 16 Nev 61 (1881); *State of Nevada v. Ching Gang*, 16 Nev 62 (1881). Idaho also used this mechanism, and it became a focus of litigation. John R. Wunder, "The Courts and the Chinese in Frontier Idaho," *Idaho Yesterdays* 25 (Spring 1981): 23–32.
40. *State of Nevada v. Ching Gang*, 16 Nev 62–63 (1881); 1875 Nev Stat. 47.
41. *State of Nevada v. Ah Mook*, 12 Nev 369 (1877).
42. Ibid., 369–92.
43. Ibid., 384.
44. Ibid.
45. *State of Nevada v. Ah Chuey alias Sam Good*, 14 Nev 79 (1879).
46. Ibid., 81–93.
47. Ibid., 93–115; Nevada Constitution, sec. 8, 18.
48. *State of Nevada v. Ah Chuey alias Sam Good*, 14 Nev 115 (1879).
49. *State of Nevada v. Chin Wah (Chinaman)*, 12 Nev 118 (1877); *State of Nevada ex rel. Ah Chew v. Richard Rising*, 15 Nev 164 (1880); *State of Nevada v. Ah Sam and Ah See*, 7 Nev 127 (1871); and *State of Nevada v. Ah Loi*, 5 Nev 99 (1869).
50. See also *State of Nevada v. Ah Hung*, 11 Nev 428 (1876); and *State of Nevada v. Charley Hing*, 16 Nev 307 (1881). In the latter case a juror claimed he opposed capital punishment. He was removed, and this action was sustained by the high court.
51. *Ex parte Ah Bau and Ah You*, 10 Nev 264 (1875).
52. *Wong Fat et al. v. Woo Park et al.*, 8 Ariz 110 (1902); *Ah You v. Don Yan*, 3 Ariz 443 (1892); *Don Yan v. Ah You*, 4 Ariz 109 (1893); *Look Ding v. Kennedy*, 7 Colo App 72 (1895); *Denver & Rio Grande Railway Co. v. Tong*, 11 Colo 539 (1888); *Lee v. Justice Mining Company*, 2 Colo App 112 (1892); *Lee et al. v. Stahl*, 9 Colo 208

(1886); *In re Roe Chung*, 49 Pac 952 (1897); *Wang How et al. v. William Dee*, 3 Ariz 314 (1891); *State of Nevada ex rel. Fook Ling v. C. S. Preble*, 18 Nev 251 (1884); *Ah Tone v. McGarry* 22 Nev 310 (1895).

53. Cases decided in Southwest courts from 1883 to 1902 are fewer and more jurisprudentially balanced than in the Northwest for the same period. The ratio of cases in the Southwest was 5½ pro-Chinese to 5½ anti-Chinese (cases with two Chinese litigants were designated ½ each); in the Northwest the ratio was 12 pro-Chinese to 17 anti-Chinese. Wunder, "Chinese and the Courts," 209n3.
54. *Ah Tone v. McGarry*, 22 Nev 310 (1895).
55. *State of Nevada ex rel. Fook Ling v. C. S. Preble*, 18 Nev 251 (1884).
56. *People v. Hall*, 4 Cal 399 (1854).
57. *State of Nevada ex rel. Fook Ling v. C. S. Preble*, 18 Nev 253 (1884).
58. *Chang Hung v. Mok Che Ling*, no. 1040, and *Chang Hung v. Sam Ling alias Mok Che Ling*, no. 1018, Grant County District Court Records, Record Book No. 7a, 1883–1885, New Mexico State Records Center, Santa Fe.
59. *Don Yan v. Ah You*, 4 Ariz 109 (1893).
60. Ibid., 111.
61. Ibid., 112; *Hendrick v. Walton*, 69 Tex 193 (1892).
62. *Look Ding v. Kennedy*, 7 Colo App 72 (1895).
63. Ibid., 73.
64. Ibid. Other appellate courts in the West went even further than Colorado in allowing juror discrimination against the Chinese. See *In re North Pacific Presbyterian Board of Missions v. Ah Won and Ah Tie*, 18 Ore 339 (1890); *People v. Ah Too*, 2 Idaho 47 (1884); *Speer v. See Yup Company*, 13 Cal 73 (1859).
65. *In re Roe Chung*, 49 Pac 952 (1897).
66. *United States v. Lee Ching Goon*, 7 Ariz 2 (1900); *State of Nevada v. Wong Fun*, 22 Nev 336 (1895); *State of Nevada v. Charley Lung*, 21 Nev 208 (1891); *Ex parte Ah Kee et al.*, 22 Nev 374 (1895); *State of Nevada v. Ah Kung and Ong Gee*, 17 Nev 361 (1883); *In the Matter of Chung Hong*, 3 Ariz 246 (1890); *United States v. Chung Sing*, 4 Ariz 217 (1894); *Territory v. Yee Dan*, 37 P. 1101 (1894); *State of Nevada v. Charley Dan*, 18 Nev 345 (1884). Again, this ratio in the Southwest is more positive for Chinese litigants. From 1883 to 1902 in the Southwest, the ratio is five pro-Chinese to five anti-Chinese decisions; in the Northwest, it is eight pro-Chinese to nineteen anti-Chinese decisions. Wunder, "Chinese and the Courts," 209n3.
67. See *United States v. Gin Hing*, 4 Ariz 416 (1904); *United States v. Wong Lee Foo*, 108 Pac. 488 (1910); *Jung Good Jow v. United States*, 108 Pac 490 (1910); *Lee Kim Fong v. United States*, 108 Pac 237 (1910); *United States v. Quong Chee*, 89 Pac 525 (1907); *Quong Yu v. Territory*, 100 Pac 462 (1909).
68. *Ex parte Ah Kee et al.*, 22 Nev 374 (1895).
69. *Ex parte Ah Bau and Ah You*, 10 Nev 264 (1875).
70. *State of Nevada v. Wong Fun*, 22 Nev 336 (1895).

71. *State of Nevada v. Ah Kung and Ong Gee*, 17 Nev 361 (1883).
72. Ibid., 364.
73. *State of Nevada v. Charley Lung*, 21 Nev 216 (1891).
74. Ibid., 217.
75. *United States v. Lee Ching Goon*, 7 Ariz 2 (1900).
76. Ibid., 3.
77. Ibid., 4.
78. *State of Nevada v. Charley Dan*, 18 Nev 345 (1884).
79. *In the matter of Chung Hong*, 3 Ariz 246 (1890).
80. *Territory v. Yee Dan*, 37 Pac 1101 (1894).
81. *Territory v. Yee Shun*, 3 NM 100 (1884). For an extensive discussion of this case and its broader implications, see Wunder, "Chinese in Trouble," 25n37, 29–32, 41; and John R. Wunder, "*Territory of New Mexico v. Yee Shun*: A Turning Point in Chinese Legal Relationships in the Trans-Mississippi West," *New Mexico Historical Review* 65 (July 1990): 305–18.
82. *United States v. Chung Sing*, 4 Ariz 217 (1894).
83. Ibid., 219.

CHAPTER 10

Territory of New Mexico v. Yee Shun

A Turning Point in Chinese Legal Relationships in the Trans-Mississippi West

THE LEGAL RELATIONSHIPS of the Chinese in the American West during the post–Civil War era included numerous complex issues to be resolved. These issues went to the heart of basic human rights—the right to own property, the right to work in certain jobs, and the right to participate in the American constitutional system. One of these latter rights—the ability of the Chinese to testify in court—was resolved eventually in part by a landmark case: *Territory of New Mexico v. Yee Shun* (1882).[1]

The *Yee Shun* precedent, articulated by the New Mexico Territory Supreme Court, decided whether non-Christian Chinese could take an oath to testify in court. The court held that Chinese were allowed to testify but only after they were subjected to racial, cultural, and religious probing. Nevertheless, a legal breakthrough had occurred. Throughout the trans-Mississippi West religious belief could no longer prevent Chinese witnesses from testifying in most jurisdictions.[2]

Before the *Yee Shun* precedent, only Colorado, Iowa, Nebraska, Nevada, Oregon, and Texas had protected the Chinese right to take an oath before a court. These protections occurred in state constitutions but had not been tested in court. Special oath ceremonies were required in California and in Arkansas, but Chinese testimony was not allowed if the litigant denied the being of a God.[3] After *Yee Shun*, most states and territories accepted the New Mexico decision as law.[4]

Given the importance of this case to the developing relationship of law and race in the nineteenth-century American West, it is crucial to understand the forces that led to this particular decision. In short, what follows is a legal biographical essay designed to trace the "lifespan" of *Territory of New Mexico v. Yee Shun*.[5]

On February 24, 1882, Yee Shun got off a train at the depot in Las Vegas, New Mexico Territory, and walked to John Lee's laundry. New Mexico Territory in the 1880s was in its formative years. Twelve counties were divided into three judicial districts for administrative law purposes. Las Vegas, in San Miguel County, and Santa Fe composed one of the judicial districts. The first railroad to enter New Mexico, the Atchison, Topeka and Santa Fe, reached Las Vegas along the Old Santa Fe Trail through Raton Pass. More than one thousand miles of railroad track already had been laid in the territory, connecting it to Colorado, Texas, and Arizona Territory. Santa Fe was the largest city in the territory, with 6,185 residents in 1890. The population of Las Vegas was nearly 2,000, making it one of the ten largest towns in the territory.[6]

Las Vegas grew as a city of dualities. Old Town constituted the more established, affluent section; New Town included East Las Vegas and a merchant area around the depot. By 1882 Chinese residents had begun to concentrate in New Town. The first Chinese had arrived in Las Vegas five years earlier to work on the railroad and conduct service businesses such as laundries and restaurants. By 1890 a Chinatown had developed in the 300 and 400 blocks of Grand Avenue. Six Chinese laundries separated by restaurants and boardinghouses dotted the street. John Lee's laundry was located at 411½ Grand Avenue. To the east was an upholstery shop and to the west was a large building of furnished rooms. Across the street was an intersection with Sixth Street. One block north was Railroad Avenue and the Atchison, Topeka and Santa Fe Railroad depot.[7] On the evening of February 24, 1882, a murder occurred in John Lee's laundry for which Yee Shun would be charged.

The Chinese constituted 1 percent of all persons living in the Southwest by 1880. Mining, railroad, and service business opportunities attracted most Chinese to the region. Chinese communities developed in numerous New Mexican towns, most notably in Silver City, Albuquerque, Raton, and Las Vegas. Although the Chinese tended to contribute economically to the betterment of most communities, their reception had not been pleasant. In

Deming, when two Chinese tried to claim a lot, E. A. Kidder prevented it with violence. According to the *Deming Headlight*, "when on Monday last two hop joint Celestials attempted to make a location, he [Kidder] enforced with a club a vigorous protest." The Chinese opted not to locate on the lot, and the paper called for a more desirable citizen to buy the property so the incident would not be repeated.[8]

Rumored Silver City and Raton disturbances caused the governor of New Mexico Territory to request federal troops. None were forthcoming, although anti-Chinese cells were active in Silver City. At the Blackhawk mine, violence broke out. Thirty-two white miners threatened bodily harm to mine manager Platt McDonald's Chinese cook. Only the intervention of McDonald's wife reportedly prevented bloodshed. The men were fired, the company wood yard was set afire, and the cook left. In the mid-1880s the West seemed consumed with anti-Chinese hysteria, and New Mexico was not immune.[9]

Into this racially tense arena came Yee Shun. Born in China, he emigrated to the United States shortly before 1882. Like most young Chinese, Yee Shun was a laborer. Prison records describe him as five feet, three and one-half inches tall, with black hair, black eyes, and a light yellow-brown complexion. Yee Shun was twenty years old when he arrived in Las Vegas on the evening of February 24, 1882, the night of the murder.[10]

The killing occurred at John Lee's laundry on Grand Avenue. Inside the two-part building were two Chinese—the owner, who was lying down in a corner smoking opium, and his ironer, known as Jo Chinaman. Coming to visit around 7:00 p.m. were Ah Locke and Sam Lee. They had come to buy out John Lee, offering to purchase his laundry, house, and lot. John Lee set $1,700 as the asking price. They said that was too much, so Lee came down to $1,400.[11]

Yee Shun arrived about a half hour later. He said he was looking for a friend, Gum Ting. Yee Shun had been working in Silver Cliff, Colorado, but was in the process of relocating. He thought he would come to Las Vegas to work in a hotel laundry, but he had decided to go on to Albuquerque instead. Thus, he wanted to ask his friend to forward any mail he might receive. Yee Shun asked the four men if anyone knew Gum Ting. John Lee said he did and that after he finished smoking, he would take Yee Shun to Gum Ting's home. He offered Yee Shun a seat.[12]

At this point Jim Lee (also known as Sam Ling Wing and as Frank) came into the room from a back room and sat on a soapbox near the stove. Suddenly two shots rang out from a .44-caliber Bulldog pistol. Jim Lee slumped to the floor in the middle doorway. In the midst of the smoke and fire, the four Chinese capable of fleeing did so. Yee Shun was first out the front door, followed closely by Ah Locke and Sam Lee. Jo Chinaman ran out the back door. John Lee, dead or dying, was in no condition to escape.[13]

Jo Chinaman went to tell the butcher—a Mr. Baker—next door to the incident, then he informed Jim Lee's brother, before returning to the scene of the murder. Ah Locke and Sam Lee ran to Sam Lee's laundry on Eighth Street, where they stayed the night. In testimony, Ah Locke said they were all extremely frightened. When asked "Ever hear pistol shots before?" Ah Locke replied, "In this town I saw lots of pistol shooting before."[14]

Having only just arrived in Las Vegas, Yee Shun ran toward the railroad tracks and livery stables before walking on to Sixth Street, toward the scene of the murder. D. B. Borden, who had been strolling with his wife, Jennie, and saw the commotion, demanded that Yee Shun stop and explain his behavior. Yee Shun told him he was afraid and had panicked. Borden then turned Yee Shun over to Marshal H. J. Franklin, who put him under arrest. After spending a half hour at the jail, Franklin and Yee Shun returned to John Lee's laundry, where Dr. Russell Bailey was conducting an inquest. Jim Lee was Dr. Bailey's laundryman. Bailey cut the bullet out of Jim Lee's body and gave it to Franklin. Jo Chinaman was then asked under oath to identify Yee Shun as the killer, but he refused.[15]

Nevertheless, Yee Shun was arraigned on March 10, 1882, before LeBaron Bradford Prince, chief justice of the New Mexico Territory Supreme Court, and charged with murder. John Lee was later added to the indictment. Both pleaded not guilty, and Sidney Barnes, attorney for John Lee, successfully moved for two separate trials. Change of venue requests were denied, but a postponement was granted to the fall term. Yee Shun's attorney, T. A. Green, would have time to prepare a defense.[16]

The murder trial of Yee Shun began on August 16, 1882, with a new judge, Chief Justice Samuel B. Axtell, presiding. A jury of twelve was chosen. They included Blas Martinez, Manuel Tagaija, Runaldo Archibeque, Alsolinario Almanzar, Jose Leon Martinez, Hijinio Garcia, Marcos Tagoya, Ysidro Torres, Manuel Jimenes, Manuel Urioste, Juan Chavez, and Juan E. Sena. All were Mexican American residents of Las Vegas. Attorneys present included

T. A. Green for the defendant and Attorney General William Breeden for the territory. When actual testimony began on August 17, the prosecution sought to place Yee Shun in John Lee's laundry at the time of the murder with the murder weapon and to identify him as the killer. Breeden called six witnesses to establish his case.[17]

The first witness sworn was D. B. Borden. He and his wife had been out for an evening walk and were heading for their residence on Lincoln Avenue when they heard two shots and saw a man with a pistol run out of John Lee's laundry. Borden followed the man across the street and through a vacant lot, then lost him, only to see the man again walking toward him near Dr. Bailey's office on Sixth Avenue in front of the Martinez Dry Goods Store. Borden stopped the man and had him arrested by Marshal Franklin. Borden admitted the man he stopped had no weapon on him, but Borden looked around Dr. Bailey's lot and found a pistol that had been fired recently. The man arrested was Yee Shun, but Borden could not swear that the defendant was the man he had seen leaving the laundry.[18]

San Miguel deputy sheriff Marshal H. J. Franklin then identified Yee Shun as the man arrested. Franklin also testified that Borden had found the .44-caliber Bulldog pistol with two chambers discharged and given it to him. Franklin had given the gun to Justice of the Peace William Steele at the coroner's inquest. When Franklin heard the shots, he ran to the laundry and then turned up Sixth Avenue to make the arrest. According to Franklin, Yee Shun had understood English and he had spoken in English. William Steele was called to testify next and presented the pistol as well as the bullet Dr. Bailey had taken from Jim Lee's body.[19]

The prosecution then turned to R. P. Hesser, who claimed to be an eyewitness. Hesser had arrived in Las Vegas from Kansas City on February 22. He said he was going to Kate Nelson's restaurant when he heard a shot, then saw Yee Shun with a pistol. Under cross-examination Hesser seemed rather vague.

> Green: Can you name, or did you know any of the men you saw there at the wash-house?
> Hesser: I cannot name them.
> Green: Did you know any of them?
> Hesser: No, sir, not by name.

> Green: State whether they were Americans, Chinamen, or what kind of men they were?
> Hesser: They were Americans.
> Green: How many Chinamen did you see?
> Hesser: At the time of the shooting, or [in the laundry] afterwards?
> Green: I am asking you, at the time you got there.
> Hesser: I saw one or two.
> Green: State whether or not you were the first man that got there?
> Hesser: I don't know.[20]

Judge Axtell intervened to get Hesser to clarify his statements identifying the defendant. Green took exception to the court's interruption, arguing that Hesser was a drifter—a sign painter and a coal miner from Pennsylvania and Iowa. Green asked Hesser why he needed to be subpoenaed to testify. Hesser said he did not like trials. Pressing further, Green finally asked, "Have you a special prejudice against Chinamen?" Hesser tried to deny the accusation: "No sir, not a bit. Notice they get my washing when it is dirty." After another series of sharp exchanges, Green submitted a question in writing to Judge Axtell. "I want to ask this witness whether or not he is not a fancy house runner or pimp as they are called. I am told he is." Judge Axtell disallowed the question. Nevertheless, Hesser's testimony was littered with inaccuracies and had not proven persuasive.[21]

The key witness for the prosecution, Jo Chinaman, came next. Chinaman was a twenty-six-year-old ironer employed by John Lee, who had been present when the murder was committed. Chinaman had been in Las Vegas for one year, having migrated from Shasta, California, where he had been a gold miner. Jo Chinaman was sworn at the beginning of his testimony, and it was this portion of the trial that proved to make new law. Through an interpreter, the attorneys quizzed Chinaman.

> Green: I will ask you if you believe in Chinese worship: their Chinese Joss houses, do you believe in Chinese Joss?
> Jo: I live in a Chinese house.
> Green: I will ask you if you believe in the Chinese joss house where they worship, where they have their religious services? Do you ever go with Chinamen in this country where they worship? Do you understand what a God is?

Jo: I don't know what it is? Yes, I believe the Chinese religion.
Green: Have you ever changed from Chinese to Christian religion since you came to this country?
Jo: I am a Chinaman, and believe in the Chinese religion.
Green: Was you ever a witness in court before?
Jo: Yes.
Green: Do you know anything about the obligations of an oath under the Christian religions?
Jo: I don't know it.[22]

Breeden then sought to soften the blow to allow Jo Chinaman to testify.

Breeden: Ask him what he is to do, or what his duty is in telling his story as a witness? If he knows what his duty is as to telling the truth?
Jo: I can tell the truth in this case.
Breeden: Do you know that you are sworn here so that you are to tell the truth?
Jo: Yes.

Judge Axtell allowed Jo Chinaman to be sworn for testimony. Green offered a strong objection.

Attorney General Breeden proceeded to take Chinaman through the events leading toward the murder. In the process Chinaman identified Yee Shun specifically as the killer. But Chinaman also laid the groundwork for what an alert attorney might have used for perjury. Green did not recognize the inconsistencies. At one point Chinaman testified that Yee Shun said nothing at all and shot Jim Lee when he came in the door. Later, under cross-examination, Chinaman said Yee Shun "just went in, and just talk with one person; put his hand in his pants pocket, drew a pistol and shot." Chinaman also testified that only four persons were in the laundry at the time of the murder, instead of six. Two others had come by earlier to try to force John Lee to sell out. Chinaman said they argued that there were too many laundries in town. He suggested a shakedown was happening.[23]

Under severe cross-examination the defense began to build its case for a tong murder. Green established that Jo Chinaman left town after the murder. He was given thirty dollars to go to Pueblo, Colorado. If he stayed in Las Vegas, Green suggested, Chinaman would have been killed. Chinaman was a member of the Hip Wo Company, the same as Jim Lee and one of the two trial interpreters, it was later discovered. Green also noted how Tam Kay Tung, owner of two laundries, was assisting the prosecution and that he had helped Jo Chinaman. Chinaman then became uncooperative as a witness.[24]

The prosecution next called Dr. Russell Bailey, who verified the gunshot wounds to the deceased, and recalled Borden and Franklin to go over the discovery of the pistol.[25] The prosecution then rested. Jo Chinaman's testimony was crucial. Only Chinaman had identified Yee Shun as the murderer.

T. A. Green pinned Yee Shun's defense on the testimony of the defendant and two other eyewitnesses, Ah Locke and Sam Lee. Locke stated Yee Shun was unarmed, that the defendant had not fired a shot, and that the shots came from the back. Lee verified Locke's testimony. On cross-examination, Lee admitted he belonged to the Kong Chow Company and that Yee Shun was a member of the Sam Yup Company.[26] Breeden tried to establish an unsavory motive in Locke's testimony by forcing him to admit that he used the name John Lee. Breeden then asked Locke,

> Breeden: What is your religion?
> Ah Locke: American, and Chinese too.
> Breeden: Have a mixed religion, do you?
> Ah Locke: Yes, sir.
> Breeden: When did you get the American religion?
> Ah Locke: In Denver.
> Breeden: Didn't you learn it for this case so as to come in and testify about it?
> Ah Locke: At the church in Denver.
> Breeden: In the church you went to in Denver, did you hear the American religion?
> Ah Locke: Yes, sir.
> Breeden: What is the American religion?
> Ah Locke: American believes that good men are sent to Heaven and bad-men to Hell.
> Breeden: What is the Chinese religion?
> Ah Locke: The Chinese religion is to always do good.
> Breeden: Haven't you been going to Sunday school here a little, getting ready for this trial? Haven't you been to Sunday school at all?
> Ah Locke: No, sir.[27]

Clearly, the attorney general was worried about an appeal based upon oath-taking objections.

Yee Shun took the stand next, but before he testified for very long, the court interrupted and allowed the prosecution to call Jennie Borden to tell her account. Evidently, she had been unavailable at the beginning of the trial. This tactic upset the momentum for the defense, and then the defendant's attorney may have made a crucial error in his cross-examination of Mrs. Borden.

> Green: I will get you to state whether or not you were present with your husband when he pursued someone that ran from the washhouse?
> J. Borden: Yes, sir.
> Green: I will get you to state whether or not it was light enough to distinguish a man as to whether it was a Mexican or American?
> J. Borden: Not unless I met them face to face.[28]

The all-Hispanic jury no doubt listened intently to this new racial element interjected into the trial. Yee Shun returned to the stand and denied shooting Jim Lee, but the damage had been done and the defense never recovered. Green called J. C. Minner, whom he mistakenly believed could impeach the previous testimony of Hesser. This tactic backfired when Minner could not verify that Hesser ran a "fancy house," although Franklin said Hesser had a bad reputation. The defense rested.[29]

The jury could not help but be confused. A murder had occurred, but there was conflicting testimony over who had weapons, who was present, who had seen the murder, and who had fired the shots. The identity of the witnesses and the accuracy of the interpreters also were doubtful. There also was a question of whether the fundamental legal basis upon which testimony could be heard was satisfied, and it was this latter issue that proved to be the basis of Yee Shun's appeal. Despite the uncertainties, the jury found Yee Shun guilty of second-degree murder, and Judge Axtell sentenced him to life in prison. Yee Shun was removed from the courtroom and transported to the Kansas State Penitentiary, where he awaited his appeal.[30]

Yee Shun's attorney filed an appeal with the New Mexico Territory Supreme Court upon conclusion of the trial. Green argued that oath taking in an American court required the belief in Judeo-Christian traditions or in a life hereafter. Because Chinaman admitted he was "of the Chinese religion," judicial error occurred when Judge Axtell allowed his testimony. The court, composed of Justices Axtell, Joseph Bell, and Warren Bristol, met, heard arguments, and in January 1884 decided against Yee Shun. Chief Justice Axtell did not participate in the opinion, which was authored by Bell, a former New York attorney who handled the judicial business of the Second District, headquartered in Albuquerque. Judge Bristol, originally from Minnesota, assigned to the Third District, centered in Taos, and who would die unexpectedly later that year in Deming, concurred. Knowledge of anti-Chinese activities in Silver City and Raton no doubt had reached both Bell and Bristol by the time they heard the *Yee Shun* case.[31]

The primary basis for appeal concerned the examination of Chinaman's fitness to take an oath. After reciting his testimony and the questions Green and Breeden had asked, Bell concluded that no reversible error had been committed in the trial and that the record did not show the witness to be incompetent.[32]

Bell went further, however. He noted that Chinaman had not been quizzed on his specific religious beliefs. Bell adopted the maxims found in *Greenleaf on Evidence* suggesting a twofold test: (1) if the witness is not a Christian, then the court can inquire into the custom used in oath taking in the witness's home country; and (2) if the witness takes an oath, then attorneys may ask if the witness believes the oath to be binding on his conscience. "The defect of religious belief is never presumed," Bell declared. "It is, therefore, incumbent on the party objecting to the competency of a witness on this ground *to show want of religious belief as to render him incompetent.*" Moreover, Bell ruled, such evidence must be evidence *aliunde*. In other words, outside sources must be used to impeach the witness.[33] It was not enough for Green to prove Chinaman did not believe in Judeo-Christian principles. Green should have called witnesses establishing Chinese oath-taking customs and Chinese religious beliefs. Not doing so allowed Chinaman's testimony to stand.

Twenty-two-year-old Yee Shun was in Leavenworth, Kansas, when he heard the results of his appeal. Life imprisonment awaited him without recourse. The prospect may have proved to be too much for him, for on September 11, 1884, sometime during the morning, Yee Shun committed suicide, hanging himself with a small cord taken from his bed.[34]

Territory of New Mexico v. Yee Shun proved to be an important legal hallmark in the relationship between the Chinese and American law and a significant social and political development among Chinese in the American West. These generalizations were as much a product of historical circumstance, however, as of substantive legal change.

The early 1880s were not easy times for Chinese living in the American West. Anti-Chinese violence and cultural attacks already had begun in the rural West and were spreading to the cities. Moreover, violence within Chinese communities was escalating. Early Chinese communities, especially in California, sought to maintain cultural identities and order from within. Based upon blood and region, social organizations such as the Six Companies evolved and sought to protect Chinese culture, religion, economic freedoms, and legal rights.[35] Three of the Six Companies—Kong Chow (through Sam Lee), Hip Wo (through Jo Chinaman), and Sam Yup (through Yee Shun) were represented at the trial.[36]

Chinese also were members of other social organizations, such as benevolent societies, trade groups, and lodges. Such groups concentrated in parlors or halls called "tongs." Much misunderstanding by nineteenth-century non-Chinese Americans occurred over the role of tongs. Writes Shih-Shan Henry Tsai, "It was difficult for outsiders to distinguish a militant tong from a pacific one. This difficulty was compounded by overlapping membership, since many people belonged to more than one tong. A respectable merchant, for instance, had automatic membership in one of the Six Companies; he probably held membership in one or two benevolent tongs. He might also join a secret society tong for protection against fighting tongs. Economic motives and the preservation of clan prestige were the most important causes of tong violence."[37]

Tong wars arose throughout the West in the 1880s. At first the Six Companies tried to prevent the violence. The trial record of the *Yee Shun* case suggests tong economic violence in Las Vegas over the control of the laundry business and an early attempt by the Six Companies to stop it. Most of the witnesses immediately left Las Vegas after the murder of Jim Lee, and yet they were encouraged to return for the trial. There is evidence of payments, free lodging, coercion, and influence from Denver and San Francisco Chinese. Even Jo Chinaman came forward to testify after refusing to participate initially.[38]

A fundamental question remains: Why would the Six Companies wish to have the John Lee laundry incident tried openly in court? Perhaps the situation was out of hand in New Mexico, and leaders could not control the violence through informal pressures. Perhaps no agreement could be reached among the three companies involved, and neutral parties forced a public hearing. Whatever the reason, the Yee Shun trial marked an early attempt by the Six Companies to quell intra-Chinese violence. This early example of Chinese cooperation to prevent further incidents proved futile as tong violence increased, eventually culminating in a major San Francisco feud in 1886 that caused heavy loss of property and lives.[39]

Although the Six Companies did not prevent future violence through the Yee Shun trial, the court action did result in a significant legal precedent. Prior to *Yee Shun*, the legal right of Chinese to testify in American courts was unclear. The stumbling block was the oath. After *Yee Shun*, Chinese clearly could testify in open court, but the cost was high. Chinese cultural and religious practices could be scrutinized by attorneys before non-Chinese juries, and racial and cultural discrimination was deemed appropriate. Non-Chinese did not have to submit to such treatment when they used American court systems.[40]

The *Yee Shun* precedent held sway throughout most of the trans-Mississippi West for Chinese litigants, and it was even used to apply to other Asian American minorities. In 1909 the Nebraska Supreme Court invoked *Territory of New Mexico v. Yee Shun* to determine if a Japanese witness, Jack Naoi, could be disqualified "for the alleged reason that Japan is a heathen country." Because counsel did not determine whether the witness practiced Buddhism or Shintoism or establish Japanese customs on oath taking, Justice Jesse L. Root ruled that Naoi was presumed competent to testify. The *Yee Shun* rule prevailed.[41]

Thus, when Yee Shun got off the train in Las Vegas that fateful night and walked to John Lee's laundry, he unknowingly became an important participant in developing Chinese legal relationships. Race and law collided in the courtroom, and the comprised outcome, although adopted as the law of the West, would prove unsettling, particularly to the Chinese. Western America's legal precedents were no more color blind than those made by other nineteenth- and early twentieth-century judiciaries and legislatures in the United States.

Notes

Originally published as John R. Wunder, "*Territory of New Mexico v. Yee Shun*: A Turning Point in Chinese Legal Relationships in the Trans-Mississippi West," *New Mexico Historical Review* 65 (July 1990): 305–18.

1. See Milton R. Konvitz, *The Alien and the Asiatic in American Law* (Ithaca, NY: Cornell University Press, 1946); and John R. Wunder, "The Chinese and the Courts in the Pacific Northwest: Justice Denied?," *Pacific Historical Review* 52 (May 1983): 191–211; John R. Wunder, "Law and Chinese in Frontier Montana," *Montana, the Magazine of Western History* 30 (Summer 1980): 18–30; and John R. Wunder, "The Courts and the Chinese in Frontier Idaho," *Idaho Yesterdays* 25 (Spring 1981): 23–32; 3 NM 100 (1884). See also 2 Pac Reports 80 (1884).
2. For an introduction to the *Yee Shun* case, see John R. Wunder, "Chinese in Trouble: Criminal Law and Race on the Trans-Mississippi West Frontier," *Western Historical Quarterly* 17 (January 1986): 25–41.
3. Colorado Constitution, art. II, sec. 4 (1876); Iowa Constitution, art. I, sec. 4 (1857); Nebraska Constitution, art. I, sec. IV (1875); Nevada Constitution, art. I, sec. 4 (1864); Oregon Constitution, art. I, sec. 67 (1859); Texas Constitution, art. I, sec. 5 (1876); *California Code of Civil Procedure*, sec. 2096 (1872); Arkansas Constitution, art. XIX, sec. 1 (1874).
4. See Arizona Revised Statutes, sec, 1866, 2037 (1887); Colorado Annotated Statutes, sec. 4821 (1891); Idaho Constitution, art. I, sec. 4 (1899); Montana Constitution, art. III, sec. 4 (1889); Nebraska Compiled Statutes, sec. 5939 (1899); New Mexico (Territory) Compiled Laws, sec. 3015 (1897); North Dakota Constitution, art. I, sec. 4 (1889); Oklahoma (Territorial) Statutes, sec. 4229 (1893); Texas Penal Code, sec. 776 (1895); Utah Constitution, art. I, sec. 4 (1895); Wyoming Constitution, art. I, sec. 18 (1889). States attempting to restrict the *Yee Shun* decision included Arkansas, Arkansas Statutes, sec. 2924 (1894); Kansas, Kansas General Statutes, chap. 95, sec. 351 (1897); Minnesota, Minnesota General Statutes, sec. 5665 (1894); Missouri, Missouri Revised Statutes, sec. 8842 (1899); and Washington, Washington Code and Statutes, sec. 6057 (1897). Only Louisiana continued to bar Chinese testimony if a Chinese witness refused to certify belief in God, Louisiana Criminal Proceedings, sec. 478 (1894).
5. This essay follows a legal biographical approach, tracing the "lifespan" of a legal dispute. For other models, see James R. McGovern, *Anatomy of a Lynching: The Killing of Claude Neal* (Baton Rouge: Louisiana State University Press, 1982); Marc A. Franklin, *The Biography of a Legal Dispute: An Introduction to American Civil Procedure* (Mineola, NY: Foundation Press, 1968); Anthony Lewis, *Gideon's Trumpet* (New York: Alfred A. Knopf, 1964); and John R. Wunder, "Constitutional Oversight: *Clark v. Bazadone* and the Territorial Court as the Court of Last Resort," *Old Northwest* 4 (September 1978): 259–84.
6. Warren Beck and Ynez D. Haase, *Historical Atlas of New Mexico* (Norman: University of Oklahoma Press, 1969), 45–46, 53, 58, 62.

7. F. Stanley, *The Las Vegas Story* (Denver: World Press, 1951), 179; *Sanborn Maps of New Mexico*, Las Vegas, San Miguel County, 1890, sec. 4. Laundries were located at 311, 411½, 419, 419½, and 421 Grand Avenue and 10 Lincoln Avenue. The laundry located at 411½ Grand was the site of the murder.
8. Francis A. Walker, ed., *Tenth Census of the United States, 1880: Population* (Washington, DC: 1880), 38–39; *Deming (NM Terr.) Headlight*, September 28, 1888.
9. *Silver City (NM Terr.) Enterprise*, November 27, 1885, December 11 and 25, 1885, January 1, 15, and 22, 1886. See also Roger Daniels, ed., *Anti-Chinese Violence in North America* (New York: Arno Press, 1978); and Elmer Clarence Sandmyer, *The Anti-Chinese Movement in California* (Urbana: University of Illinois Press, 1939).
10. Prisoner Ledgers A & E, number 2763, Kansas State Penitentiary Records, Kansas State Archives, Topeka.
11. *Territory of New Mexico v. Yee Shun* (1882), trial transcript, 49–55, 111–33, San Miguel County District Court Records, New Mexico State Archives, Santa Fe.
12. Ibid., 59–60, 113–36.
13. Ibid., 49–76, 86–111.
14. Ibid., 59–60, 107, 133–36.
15. Ibid., 1–14, 16–20, 77–80, 136–43.
16. Criminal Record Book A, US District Court of New Mexico Territory, San Miguel County, New Mexico State Archives, Santa Fe, 88, 90–91, 95, 99, 101, 115. See also Walter J. Donlon, "LeBaron Bradford Prince, Chief Justice and Governor of New Mexico Territory, 1879–1893" (PhD diss., University of New Mexico, 1967).
17. Criminal Record Book A, 115–16, 160–61.
18. *Yee Shun* trial transcript, 1–14.
19. Ibid., 14–24, 24–26.
20. Ibid., 26–48.
21. Ibid., 34–36, 38, 47.
22. Ibid., 49, 50–51.
23. Ibid., 54, 55–63, 75.
24. Ibid., 65–71, 80–81.
25. Ibid., 77, 85.
26. Ibid., 86–133.
27. Ibid., 109–10.
28. Ibid., 137.
29. Ibid., 168–75.
30. Prisoner Ledgers, Kansas State Penitentiary Records. New Mexico sent its felony prisoners to Kansas because New Mexico did not have a secure prison facility.
31. 3 NM 100 (1884); 2 Pac Reports iv (1884).

32. 3 NM 100 (1884).
33. 3 NM 100 at 103 (1884), italics added. See also Henry Campbell Black, *Black's Law Dictionary* (St. Paul: West Publishing, 1968), 97–98.
34. *Leavenworth (KS) Times*, September 12, 1884, 4.
35. Alexander Saxton, *The Indispensable Enemy: Labor and the Anti-Chinese Movement in California* (Berkeley: University of California Press, 1971), 7–9; Shih-Shan Henry Tsai, *The Chinese Experience in America* (Bloomington: Indiana University Press, 1986), 45–51; Shih-Shan Henry Tsai, *China and the Overseas Chinese in the United States, 1868–1911* (Fayetteville: University of Arkansas Press, 1983), 31–42. See also Sucheng Chan, "Chinese Livelihood in Rural California: The Impact of Economic Change, 1860–1880," *Pacific Historical Review* 53(August 1984): 273–307.
36. *Yee Shun* trial transcript, 49–76, 80–81, 86–136, 143–68.
37. Tsai, *Chinese Experience*, 51, 54.
38. *Yee Shun* trial transcript, 49–76.
39. Tsai, *Chinese Experience*, 54–55.
40. John Henry Wigmore, *A Treatise on the System of Evidence in Trials at Common Law*, 4 vols. (Boston: Little, Brown, 1904), 3:2365–71. See also Edward W. Cleary, ed., *McCormick on Evidence* (St. Paul: West Publishing, 1972), 141–42.
41. *Pumphrey v. State*, 122 Northwest Rep 19 at 20 (1909), 122 Northwest Rep 19 at 21 (1909). The former case also is found at 84 Nebr 36 (1909).

INDEX

Page numbers in italic text indicate illustrations.

Adams, G. W., 148
African Americans: Chinese immigrants and, 18, 74, 78, 80, 85, 99–100; legal precedent for, xv–xvi
"After the Gold Rush: Chinese Mining in the Far West" (Rohe), 25n3
Ah Fong v. McCalla et al., 151–52
Ainslie, George, 147
Alaska, 21
The Alien and the Asiatic in American Law (Konvitz), 123
America. *See* United States
American Society for Legal History (ASLH), xv
Angel, R. M., 149–51
anti-Chinese riots, 4, 8–9, 13, 17–18, 28n26
Arizona, 12, 16, 21. *See also* the Southwest; the West
Asian America: Chinese and Japanese in the United States since 1850 (Daniels), 13, 25n3
ASLH. *See* American Society for Legal History

Axtell, Samuel B., 39–40, 202–7

Bailey, Russell, 206
Baldwin, Edwin, 46–47
Baldwin, Joseph G., 37–38
Ballard, Tarbuck, 71
Barbour, William T., 59–60, 67–73, 76–77
Barnes, Sidney, 202
Bau, Ah, 187
Beatty, William H., 186
Beesley, David, 78–79
Bell, Joseph, 207–8
Bennett, J. W., 129–30
Bitter Melon: Stories from the Last Rural Chinese Town in America (Chan), 4
Black, James L., 180
Blake, Henry, 164–69
Bo On Tong Society, 46
Borden, D. B., 202–3
Borden, Jennie, 202, 207
Bow, Ah, 146, 155
Bow, Lee Ping, 128
Bowin, John, 68

Breeden, William, 40–41, 203, 205–8
Breen, Peter, 174
Bristol, Warren, 207–8
Brown, James H., 38
Brown, Moses, 70
Brown, N. J., 149
Brown, Richard Maxwell, 25n3
Brown v. Board of Education, 115
Buck, Norman, 148
Buckner, Stanton, 69
Burlington, William, 71

Cacotheism, 52n7
Cahalan, T. D., 148
Caldwell, A. B., 61
California: Chinese immigrants in, 143; Committee of Vigilance in, 10–11; criminal law in, 43–45, 95–96; culture of, 61–67, 93; *Days of Gold: The California Gold Rush and the American Nation* (Rohrbough), 66; economics in, 61–67; equal rights in, 97–106, 114; exclusionary rules in, 80; Hispanics in, 111–12; immigrants in, 9–10, 88n14, 94–95, 103, 108n13; law in, 109n34, 141n32; race relations in, 59–61, 95–96; *This Bitter Sweet Soil: The Chinese in California Agriculture* (Chan), 13, 26n6, 95; violence in, 3–5. *See also People v. Hall*; the West
Callaway, James E., 164–65
Carpenter, James S., 69
Carstensen, Vernon, xvi
Chabot, Anthony, 62
Chan, Sucheng, 4, 13, 19, 26n6, 95
Chase, M. S., 37
Chew, Ah, 185
Chin, Yee Ah, 44, 128–29
China, xii, 7, 65, 208–9; culture in, 70, 132–33; religion in, 38, 40–41

Chinatown. *See specific regions; specific states*
Chinese Exclusion Act (1882), xiii, 123, 148, 163; law after, 187–94, *193*; law before, 181–87
Chinese Gold: The Chinese in the Monterey Bay Region (Lydon), 95
Chinese immigrants, ix–xiii, xv–xviii, 28n34, 35–36; African Americans and, 18, 74, 78, 80, 85, 99–100; in Alaska, 21; in Arizona, 12, 21; in California, 143; *Chinese Gold: The Chinese in the Monterey Bay Region* (Lydon), 95; in Colorado, 23; companies by, 209–10; courts for, 135–38, *136–37*, 195n24, 197n66; criminal law for, 51n6, 53n31, 59–61, 100–103, *101–3*, 104–6, 133, 195n26; culture of, 50, 102–3, 113, 131–32, 147, 162–63, 187–89; economics for, 151–54; equal rights for, 78–86, 93–94, 159–60; exclusionary rules against, 47–50; Great Northern Railroad for, 10; in Hawaii, 23; Hispanics and, 16, 207; history of, 3–4, 65–66, 193–94; labor for, 124, 139n6, 173–74; laundromats for, 111–17, 160–62; law for, 154–55, 172–74; legal precedent for, 75, 87n6, 167–68; as miners, 6–7, 18–19, 25n3, 68, 200–201; in Montana, 23–24, 160–63; Native Americans and, 14, 77, 123–24, 140n9; in Nevada, 24; in New Mexico, 24; in Northwest Frontier, 21–24; in Pacific Northwest, 123–24; prejudice against, 162; prostitution and, 15–16; protests against, 10; race relations for, 20; as refugees, 7; religion for, 38–39; Rock Springs Massacre for, 6–7, 11, 14; in South Dakota, 24; in US,

121, *122*, 148; in Utah, 25; as victims, 15–19, 97–98, *98*, 108n25, 109n28, 122–23; violence and, 4–10, *6*, 19–20, 42–43, 65–67, 71–72, 80–81, 90n34, 95–100, *98*, *103*, 103–5, 108n18, 179–81; the West for, 144–45; in Wyoming, 25. *See also* California

Chinese litigations. *See* legal precedent

Ching Ling (court case), 42–43

Choi, Kuok Wah, 148–49

Chow, Ah, 145

Chow, Ho, 68

Choy, Ah, 145

Christianity. *See* religion

Chu, Hong, 147–48

Chuey, Ah, 186–87

Chung, Roe, 189

Chung, Yum, 130–31

Churchman, James, 68–69

citizenship, for immigrants, 86

Civil Rights Act (1875), 137

Clem, Ho, 70

Colorado, 17–18, 23, 28n26, 28n34. *See also* the Southwest; the West

Committee of Vigilance, 10–11

Conger, Everton J., 171–72

Cook, Jimmie Jean, xvi

Coons, Robert, 99

courts, 197n53; for Chinese immigrants, 135–38, *136–37*, 195n24, 197n66; ethnocentrism in, 135; in Idaho, 145–55; miners in, 187–89; in Montana, 163–65; in Nebraska, 210; in Pacific Northwest, 125–34; prejudice in, 172–73, 189, 192, 197n64; religion in, 128–29; violence in, 140n25; in the West, 153–55. *See also* criminal law; law; legal precedent

Cowan, John, 172

criminal law: in California, 43–45, 95–96;

for Chinese immigrants, 51n6, 53n31, 59–61, 100–106, *101–3*, 133, 195n26; discrimination in, 105–6; equal rights and, 109n34; legal precedent in, 39–41; Native Americans and, 50, 53n34, 109n35; in Oregon, 41–43; in Pacific Northwest, 124–25, 135–38, *136–37*; race relations and, 81–86; religion in, 45–46; in the Southwest, 183–87, 189–94, *193*; in trans-Mississippi West, 36–37, 43, 47–50, 192; in Washington (state), 46

Cruz, James, 37–38

culture: of California, 61–67, 93; in China, 70, 132–33; of Chinese immigrants, 50, 102–3, 113, 131–32, 147, 162–63, 187–89; of gold, 103; of immigrants, 66–67, 116; of labor, 102; law and, 69–70, 112–13; of miners, 71, 98–99; of opium, 15–16, 134–35, 183–85; of prejudice, 17–18, 25n2; of religion, 54n42; of US, ix–xiii, 88n14; of victims, 19–20; of violence, 14–15; of the West, 80–81; xenophobia in, 122

Cummings, C. O., 16–17

Curley, John, 71

Dake, B. Frank, 137–38

Dallen, Theodore, 44–45

Dan, Charley, 191–92

Dan, Yee, 192

Daniels, Roger, 13, 25n3

Davenport, W. H., 188

Davis, Mike, 99

Days of Gold: The California Gold Rush and the American Nation (Rohrbough), 66

Deer Lodge County v. At, 125–26

Denver riot (1880), 17–18, 28n26

deportation, 190

Dick, Fong Long, 42–43
Ding, Look, 189
Dixon, William, 66
Dixon, Willis, 66
Doe, Ah, 147–48
Dougherty, Andrew, 44–45
Dred Scott (1857), xi
Dysart, Frank, 191

Eagle, John, 66–67
economics: in California, 61–67; for Chinese immigrants, 151–54; in history, 139n4; of labor, 131–32; of law, 73; in US, 15; violence and, 209–10
education, for immigrants, 141n32
Endicott, W. H., 71
equal rights: in California, 97–106, 114; for Chinese immigrants, 78–86, 93–94, 159–60; Civil Rights Act (1875) for, 137; criminal law and, 109n34; history of, xv–xvi; in Idaho, 144–45; for immigrants, 176n36; Jim Crow (laws) and, xiii; in labor, 182–83; legal precedent for, 100–102, *101–2*; for miners, 151–54, 165–67, 170–72; *People v. Hall* (California) and, 59–61, 81–86; politics of, ix–xiii, 13–14; protests for, 111; race relations and, 73–78; in US, 12–13, 16–17, 47–50, 115–17, 135; US-China treaty for, xii; violence and, xi–xiii
ethnocentrism, 129–30, 135
Evans, J. M., 168
exclusionary rules, 47–50, 80

Farnsworth, George, 66
Farnsworth, William, 66
Fat, Ah, 96–97
Favorite, T. J., 160–61
Ferguson, W. C., 71
Field, Stephen J., 37–38, 48–49, 77, 79

Fing, Gum, 39
Fletcher, S. W., 76
Foe, Ah, 129–30
Fong, Ah, 151–52
Foon, Lim, 44
Frank, L. D., 124
Franklin, H. J., 202
Fuller (court case), 38
Fuller, Jane, 37
Fuller, Silas, 37
Fun, Wong, 190–91
Fung, Ah, 183–84

Gaffey, James P., 140n9
Galbraith, William J., 171–72
Gang, Ching, 185
Gardiner, H. C., 68–69
Gee, Ong, 190–91
Gee, Yee Ah, 97
George, Henry, 174
Georgia, 38
Gho, Jack, 123–24
gold, 61–67, 90n34, 103, 121. *See also* California; the West
Gong, Chee, 42–43
Gong, Lee, 95
Gong, Yee, 42–43
Goon, Ah, xvii
Goon, Lee Ching, 191
Great Northern Railroad, 10
Green, John, 99
Green, T. A., 40–41, 50, 202–5
Green, Tom, 38
Green v. State of Georgia (1883), 38
Gueng, Yee, 46

Hagerman, J. C., 181–82
Hagerman v. Tong Lee (Nevada), 181–82
Hah, Ung, 125–26, 163–64
Halfield, Michael A., 164
Hall, George W. See *People v. Hall* (California)

Hall, John Erastus Coble. See *People v. Hall* (California)
Hane, Chin, 107n8
Harris, Chance L., 11–12
Haskell, Henri J., 168–70, 172
Hawaii, 23
Hawley, Thomas P., 182, 184
Hays, Samuel H., 150–51
Heong, Ah, 97
Heong, Lee, 107n8
Hesser, R. P., 203–4, 207
Heydenfeldt, J., 81–86
highbinders, 95, 107nn7–8
Hing, Wing, 9–10
Hip Wo (company), 209–10
Hispanics, 16, 111–12, 207
Historians of the American West (Malone), 25n3
"Historiography of Violence in the American West" (Brown, R.), 25n3
history: of anti-Chinese violence, 10–15, 11–12, 21–25, 25nn2–3, 36; ASLH for, xv; of Chinese immigrants, 3–4, 65–66, 193–94; economics in, 139n4; of equal rights, xv–xvi; of Gilded Age, xiii; "Historiography of Violence in the American West" (Brown, R.), 25n3; of hueilum, 20; *Inferior Courts, Superior Justice: A History of the Justices of the Peace in the Northwest Frontier, 1853–1889* (Wunder), xvii; of labor, 6–10; of law, 43, 93; of legal precedent, 11–12, 19–20; of Montana, 159–60; Native Americans in, 83–84; in Northwest Frontier, ix–xii; of oath taking, 199; of Pacific Northwest, 121–23, 122; of *People v. Hall* (California), 61–67, 78–81; of prejudice, 20; of the Southwest, 179–81; of the West, 61–67, 73–74, 200–201

Ho, Ah, 147
Ho, Wong, 126–27
homicides. *See* violence
Hong, Chung, 192
hoodlums, 20, 29n39
Hop, Ah, 127–28, 147–48
How, Lee, 182–83
How, On Gee, 184–85
Hoy, Lee Tai, 46
hueilum, 20
Hung, Chang, 188
Huston, J. W., 146

Idaho, 10, 144–55, 158n57. *See also* Northwest Frontier; Pacific Northwest; the West
immigrants: in Black Hawk, 35–36; in California, 9–10, 88n14, 94–95, 103, 108n13; citizenship for, 86; culture of, 66–67, 116; deportation of, 190; dislocation of, 7–8; education for, 141n32; equal rights for, 176n36; gold for, 121; in Idaho, 10, 143–45, 158n57; Irish as, 107n7; Jews as, 64–65; law for, 113–14; legal precedent for, xvi–xviii; as politics, 12–13; Queue Ordinance (1876) and, 112; in US, 61, 108n13, 112, 139n6; violence and, ix–xi, 68, 154. *See also* Chinese immigrants
Inferior Courts, Superior Justice: A History of the Justices of the Peace in the Northwest Frontier, 1853–1889 (Wunder), xvii
In re Lee Sing, 104–5
In Search of Equality (McClain), 93–95, 104–6
Irish immigrants, 107n7
Irwin, G. W., 125–26, 163–64

Jack Gho v. Charley Julles, 123–24
Jews, 64–65

Jim, Ah, 168–69
Jim, Mah, 41–42, 132
Jim Crow (laws), xiii
Jo Chinaman, 39–41, 201–2, 204–6, 209
John, Lee, 45–46
Joy, Allan R., 173–74
Julles, Charley, 123–24

Kalloch, Isaac, 112
Kansas, 38, 50
Kay, Suey, 97
Kearney, Denis, 112
Kee, Ah, 190
Kent (Chancellor), 48
Kidder, E. A., 180, 200–201
Kie, Yee, 95
King, Ah, 97
King, Sam Ling. *See* Lee, Jim
Kingman, Samuel A., 38
Kle, Ah, 129, 152–54
Knowles, Ella K., 168–70
Knowles, Hiram, 127, 164–68
Kong Chow (company), 209–10
Konvitz, Milton, 123
Koo, Nau, 70
Kramer, Henry, 99–100

labor: in Arizona, 16; for Chinese immigrants, 124, 139n6, 173–74; culture of, 102; economics of, 131–32; equal rights in, 182–83; history of, 6–10; law for, 112–13; in Montana, 11–12; politics of, 16; in the West, 17–19, 104, 209–10
laundromats, 111–17, 134–35, 160–62, 169–70. *See also* labor
law, 140n9, *193*; *The Alien and the Asiatic in American Law* (Konvitz), 123; in California, 109n34, 141n32; in China, 208–9; before Chinese Exclusion Act (1882), 181–87; for Chinese immigrants, 154–55, 172–74; culture and, 69–70, 112–13; economics of, 73; ethnocentrism in, 129–30; history of, 43, 93; for immigrants, 113–14; for labor, 112–13; laundromats and, 134–35; for lotteries, 132–33; for miners, 127; in Montana, 165–74; for Native Americans, 47–48, 74–75, 80; in Northwest Frontier, 195n24, 195n26; for opium, 133–34; politics and, 73–78; prostitution in, 49; race relations and, 51n6; religion in, 37–38, 53n33, 64–65, 72; science in, 82–83; for segregation, 104–5; in the Southwest, 181–83, 187–89; in US, 53n34, 77–78, 175n14, 180–81; violence and, 15–18, 183–87; in the West, 50. *See also* criminal law
Leavenworth (KS) Times, 50
Lee, Ah, 45–46, 99, 128–29
Lee, Dorsey, 38
Lee, Fauk, 127, 165
Lee, Hing, 190–91
Lee, Jim, 39–41, 192, 201–3, 207
Lee, John, 35, 39–41, 200–202
Lee, Sam, 39–41, 201–2, 206
Lee, Sing, 15, 17–19, 28n26
Lee, Tong, 181–82
The Legacy of Conquest: The Unbroken Past of the American West (Limerick), 25n3
legal precedent, 47–50; for African Americans, xv–xvi; for Chinese immigrants, 75, 87n6, 167–68; in criminal law, 39–41; for equal rights, 100–102, *101–2*; history of, 11–12, 19–20; for immigrants, xvi–xviii; in Las Vegas, 50; for race relations, 36, 38–39; for segregation, 129–30; in Texas, 188–89; in trans-Mississippi West, 41–42, 45, 199–210; in US, 166–67, 210; in the West, 79. *See also* courts; criminal law; law; *and specific cases*
Lehow, 182–83
Leonard, Orville R., 186–87

Let, Chin, 132–33
Lim, Ah, 133
Limerick, Patricia Nelson, 25n3, 87n6
Ling, Ching, 42–43
Ling, Mok Che, 188
Littleton, Michael, 66
Locke, Ah, 39–41, 201–2, 206–7
Loi, Sam, 134–35
Long, Ah, 186
Long, Chong Bing, 15, 17–19, 180
Looke, Moy, 126–27
Loop, Ulysses, 46–47
Los Angeles. *See* California
lotteries, 132–33
Loveland, Cyrus, 66
Loy, Ah, xvi–xvii, 183–84
Lu, Ah, 97
Luck, Mon, 133–34
Lung, Charley, 191
Lydon, Sandy, 95

Malone, Michael P., 25n3
Marbury v. Madison, 146
Marker, P. N., 181–82
Matteson, Edward, 62
Matthews, Stanley, 115–16
McAllister, Hall, 114
McBride, John Rogers, 146
McClain, Charles, 93–95, 104–6
McConnell, John R., 69–73
McDonald, James, 170–72
McDonald, Platt, 201
McFarland, T. B., 80
McGarry, M., 187–88
McGraw, John, 8–9
McGuinness, John, 127–28, 147–48
McLean, A. C., 129, 152–54
McNeil, J. B., 192
Memphis race riots, 174
Mexican Americans, 39–40
miners: Chinese immigrants as, 6–7, 18–19, 25n3, 68, 200–201; in courts, 187–89; culture of, 71, 98–99; equal rights for, 151–54, 165–67, 170–72; gold for, 61–67; law for, 127; politics for, 35–36
Minner, J. C., 207
Minnesota, 50, 80
Mok, Ah, 183–84
Montana: Chinese immigrants in, 23–24, 160–63; courts in, 163–65; history of, 159–60; labor in, 11–12; law in, 165–74. *See also* Pacific Northwest; the West
Montana v. Lee, 127, 131–32
Moody, Isaiah, 70
Mook, Ah, 186–87
Morgan, John T., 148–49
Morrison, Robert E., 191
mulattoes. *See* African Americans; race relations
Murphey, Frank X., 187–88
Murray, Hugh C., 47–48, 74–77, 79, 81–86

Naoi, Jack, 210
Native Americans, 109n34; Chinese immigrants and, 14, 77, 123–24, 140n9; criminal law and, 50, 53n34, 109n35; in history, 83–84; in Kansas, 38; law for, 47–48, 74–75, 80; race relations for, 62–63; US and, 63–64; violence and, 35, 64
Nebraska, 50, 80, 210
Nelson, John, 168
Nelson, Kate, 203
Nevada. *See* the Southwest; the West
New Mexico, xvii–xviii, 24, 38–41. *See also* the Southwest; *Territory of New Mexico v. Yee Shun*; the West
Noggle, David, 145–46
Northwest Frontier: Chinese immigrants in, 21–24; history in, ix–xii; law in, 195n24, 195n26; race relations in, xvi–xviii; the Southwest compared to, 197n53. *See also* United States

oath taking, 36–39, 53n33, 81–86, 199, 208. *See also* courts; criminal law; law
Olcovich, Joseph, 191–92
On, Nu, 70
opium, 15–16, 133–35, 183–85
Oregon, 41–46, 125–27, 132. *See also* Northwest frontier; Pacific Northwest; the West
Oregon v. Charley Lee Quong, Lee Jaw, and Lee Jong, 125–26
Oregon v. Gitt Lee et al., 125
Oregon v. Mah Jim, 132
Oregon v. Moy Look, 126–27
Ow, Ah, 97
Owsley, William, 172

Pacific Northwest, 126–34; criminal law in, 124–25, 135–38, *136–37*; history of, 121–23, *122*
Palmer, A., 71
Palmer, John C., 69
Patterson, W. S., 72–73
peaceable expulsions, 8–9
People v. Ah Choy (Idaho Territory), 145
People v. Awa (California), 49
People v. Chin Mook Sow (California), 44
People v. Dallen (California), 44–45
People v. Hall (California), xi, 47–50, 68–77, 188; equal rights and, 59–61, 81–86; history of, 61–67, 78–81
People v. Howard (California), 48–49
People v. Jones (California), 49
People v. Kuok Wah Choi (Idaho Territory), 148–49
People v. Lim Foon (California), 44
People v. Lloyd (Idaho Territory), 145
People v. Sanchez (California), 43–44
People v. Washington (California), 49
Perkins, Elisha, 67

Perkins, Ozro, 46–47
Peterson, Charles, 168
Phifer, W. G., 182–83
Pierce, William H., 182–83
Ping, Ah, 183–84
Plessy v. Ferguson, xii
Po, Ah, 49
Poe, James W., 153–54
politics: of equal rights, ix–xiii, 13–14; of Gilded Age, 36–37; of hoodlums, 20, 29n39; immigrants as, 12–13; of labor, 16; of laundromats, 169–70; law and, 73–78; for miners, 35–36; of taxes, 147; of trans-Mississippi West, 36; in US, 143; of violence, 76
Pong, Ah, 147–48
Pong, Yee Ah, 97
population, of US, 122, 162–63, 179–80, 200
Powell, Thomas, 99–100
prejudice, 17–18, 20, 25n2, 105–6; in courts, 172–73, 189, 192, 197n64; stereotypes in, 162, 179
Price, Lyttleton, 149–51
Prickett, Henry E., 148
Prince, LeBaron Bradford, 39
property. *See* laundromats; miners
prostitution, 15–16, 49
protests, 10, 111
Pumphrey v. State (Nebraska), 50

Quang, Ching Bo, 46
Queue Ordinance (1876), 112
Quong, Ah, 96–97
Quong, Charley Lee, 126
Quong, Lee, 45–46

race relations: in California, 59–61, 95–96; for Chinese immigrants, 20; criminal law and, 81–86; equal rights and, 73–78; law and, 51n6; legal precedent for, 36, 38–39;

Memphis race riots, 174; in Minnesota, 50; for Native Americans, 62–63; in Nebraska, 50; in New Mexico, xvii–xviii; in Northwest Frontier, xvi–xviii; religion in, 130; in US, xiii, 15–19; violence and, 102–4; in Washington (state), 50; in the West, 43–44
racial stress, 19
Raten, Simon, 99–100
Reaves, W., 71
refugees, 7
Reid, James W., 153–54
religion, 140n9; Cacotheism, 52n7; in China, 38, 40–41; for Chinese immigrants, 38–39; in courts, 128–29; in criminal law, 45–46; culture of, 54n42; in law, 37–38, 53n33, 64–65, 72; in oath taking, 208; in race relations, 130
Ribble, H. H., 189
Robinson, Edward, 99
Rock Springs Massacre, 6–7, 11, 14
Rohe, Randall E., 25n3
Rohrbough, Malcolm, 66
Root, Jesse L., 210
rural violence, 26n6, 29n38

Sam, Ah, 185
Sam Yup (company), 209–10
Sandmeyer, Elmer, 53n31
San Francisco. *See* California
Sawyer, Lorenzo, 105
Scanniker, S. P., 146
Scott, Elmon, 133
Searls, Niles, 77
segregation, 104–5, 129–30
Servis, Francis G., 165–67
Sharon, William, 14
Shun, Yee, 38–41, 50, 192, 199–210
Shung, Charlie, 150
Simonton, Thomas H., 182–83

Sing, Camp, 169–70
Sing, Chung, 192
Sing, Ling. *See People v. Hall* (California)
Sing, Ye, 161–63
Sing, Yung, 147–48
Smith (court case), 38
Smith, Jacob, 38
Snake River Massacre, 7, 13
Son, Chee, 42–43
South Dakota, 24. *See also* the West
the Southwest, 179–80, 197n53; criminal law in, 183–87, 189–94, 193; law in, 181–83, 187–89
Speer, William, 70, 90n34
State of Nevada v. Ah Chew, 185
State of Nevada v. Ah Mook, 186–87
State of Nevada v. On Gee How, 184
State of Oregon v. Charley Lee Quong, Ah Lee and Lee John, 45–46
State v. Camp Sing (Montana), 169–70
State v. Foot You (Oregon), 46
State v. Lee (Montana), 168
State v. Mah Jim (New Mexico), 41–42
State v. Quong (Idaho), 148–49
State v. rel. Sam Toi v. French (Montana), 169–70
State v. Yee Gueng (Oregon), 46
State v. Yee Wee (Idaho), 148–51
Steele, William, 203
stereotypes, 162, 179
Stevens, S., 165
Stewart, William M., 62, 68–71, 77
Stockslager, Charles O., 149
Sue, Lee, 125–26, 163–64
Suey, Yip, 44
Sun, Chung, 15–17, 19
Swain, William, 67
Sweeney, A. W., 143
Sweet, Willis, 153

Tacoma Committee of Fifteen, 8–9

Tacoma riot, 8–9
Tai Ping Rebellion, 65
Talbott, James A., 172
taxes, 65–66, 111–12, 134, 145–47, 169–70
Territory of New Mexico v. Yee Shun, 38–41, 199–210
Territory v. Lee (Montana), 171–72
Texas, 188–89
Thayer, W. W., 143–44
This Bitter Sweet Soil: The Chinese in California Agriculture (Chan), 13, 26n6, 95
Tibbitts v. Ah Tong (Montana), 131–32, 153, 167, 170–72
Tie, Ah, 130–31
Ting, Gum, 201
Toi, Sam, 169–70
Tom, Ah, 183–84
Tompkins, Elijah, 71
Tone, Ah, 187–88
Tong, Ah, 131–32, 170–72
Too, Ah, 148
Torn, Ah, xvii
Townsend, L. T., 43
Toy, Ah, 97
Toy, See, 41–42
trans-Mississippi West, 36–37, 41–50, 53n33, 192, 199–210
trials. *See* criminal law; law; legal precedent
Tsai, Shih-Shan Henry, 4–5, 209
Tune, Ah, xvii

United States (US), 7, 26n6, 29n38; Chinese immigrants in, 121, *122*, 148; Civil Rights Act (1875), 137; culture of, ix–xiii, 88n14; *Days of Gold: The California Gold Rush and the American Nation* (Rohrbough), 66; equal rights in, 12–13, 16–17, 47–50, 115–17, 135; health in, 105; immigrants in, 61, 108n13, 112, 139n6; law in, 53n34, 77–78, 175n14, 180–81; legal precedent in, 166–67, 210; Mexican Americans in, 39–40; Native Americans and, 63–64; peaceable expulsions in, 8–9; politics in, 143; population of, 122, 162–63, 179–80, 200; race relations in, xiii, 15–19. *See also* Native Americans; Northwest Frontier; the West
United States v. Chung Sing, 192
US-China treaty, xii
Utah, 25. *See also* the Southwest; the West

victims: Chinese immigrants as, 15–19, 97–98, *98*, 108n25, 109n28, 122–23; culture of, 19–20
violence: anti-Chinese riots, 4; anti-Chinese violence, 5–7, *6*, 10–15, *11–12*, 21–25, 25nn2–3, 36, 104; in California, 3–5; Chinese immigrants and, 4–10, *6*, 19–20, 42–43, 65–67, 71–72, 80–81, 90n34, 95–100, *98*, *103*, 103–5, 108n18, 179–81; in courts, 140n25; culture of, 14–15; economics and, 209–10; equal rights and, xi–xiii; gold and, 90n34; health and, 114; immigrants and, ix–xi, 68, 154; law and, 15–18, 183–87; Native Americans and, 35, 64; politics of, 76; race relations and, 102–4; rural violence, 26n6, 29n38; in the West, 5–6, *6*, 10–15, *11–12*, 21–25, 25n3; in Wyoming, 112

Wade, Decius S., 127, 164–68, 171
Wah, Ah, 164–65
Wah, Sam, 149
Wah, Wee, 148–51
Wan, Ye, 128, 167–68

War of the Woods, 11
Washington (state), 8–9, 46, 50, 80. *See also* Northwest Frontier; Pacific Northwest
Washington, George, 49
Watsonville Pajaronian, 16–17
Way, Wong Chin, 130
Wee, Yee, 148–51
Weisbach, Jacob R., 8
Wells, Alexander, 74, 76, 86
the West: "After the Gold Rush: Chinese Mining in the Far West" (Rohe), 25n3; anti-Chinese violence in, 5–6, 6, 21–25; for Chinese immigrants, 144–45; courts in, 153–55; culture of, 80–81; *Historians of the American West* (Malone), 25n3; "Historiography of Violence in the American West" (Brown, R.), 25n3; history of, 61–67, 73–74, 200–201; labor in, 17–19, 104, 209–10; law in, 50; *The Legacy of Conquest: The Unbroken Past of the American West* (Limerick), 25n3; legal precedent in, 79; race relations in, 43–44; violence in, 10–15, 11–12. *See also* United States; *and specific states*
Wheeler, Alonzo, 46–47
White, Richard, xvi
Who, Yee Yot, 192
Wigmore, John Henry, 50, 80–81
Wing, Sam Ling, 201–2
Wing Hing v. Eureka, 9–10
Wiseman, Samuel. See *People v. Hall* (California)
Witt, James, 129, 152–54
Wo, Yick, 111–17
Won, Ah, 130–31
Wood, Fremont, 148
Wright, Thomas, 70
Wunder, John, xvii, 51n6

Wyoming, 25, 112. *See also* Pacific Northwest; the West

xenophobia, 122

Yan, Ah, 97
Yan, Don, 188–89
Yen, Ah, 164–65
Yick, Lee, 42–43
Yick Wo v. Hopkins (California and USA), xi–xii, 94, 104, 111–17, 134–35
Ying, Chin Sue, 45–46, 68, 70, 77, 126
Yo, Au, 68
You, Ah, 187–89
You, Foot, 46
Young, Look, 28n26
Yow, Chim, 99

www.ingramcontent.com/pod-product-compliance
Lightning Source LLC
Chambersburg PA
CBHW020945230426
43666CB00005B/179